Bloody HARLAN

THE UNITED MINE WORKERS OF AMERICA
IN HARLAN COUNTY, KENTUCKY
1931–1941

Paul F. Taylor

Bloody HARLAN

THE UNITED MINE WORKERS OF AMERICA IN HARLAN COUNTY, KENTUCKY
1931–1941

Commonwealth Book Company
St. Martin, Ohio

Copyright © 1990 by University Press of America
Copyright © 2017 by Paul F. Taylor
Copyright © 2017 by Commonwealth Book Company, Inc.
All rights reserved
Printed in the United States of America

ISBN: 978-0-9905351-9-5

In loving memory of my father, V. Floyd Taylor, native of Harlan County, and my mother, Clara Miller Taylor, to whom I shall always be grateful.

contents

PREFACE		IX
1	THE COLD CHILLS OF STEEL	1
2	A NEW DEAL FOR THE MINERS	35
3	OPEN SEASON FOR ORGANIZERS	49
4	A REIGN OF TERROR	69
5	STORM OVER HARLAN	81
6	HARLAN SHALL BE ORGANIZED	95
7	THE FEUDAL LORDS OF HARLAN	107
8	MURDER!	119
9	INQUIRY IN WASHINGTON	129
10	THE MARY HELEN CONSPIRACY TRIAL	147
11	THE TRIUMPH OF THE UNION	167
EPILOGUE		189
ACKNOWLEDGEMENTS		197
NOTES		200
BIBLIOIGRAPHY		237
INDEX		250

illustrations

COAL MINERS MARCHING IN PINEVILLE, KY	25
DORIS PARKS AND HAROLD HICKERSON	25
NEW YORK MINISTERS VISITNG PINEVILLE	29
PINEVILLE TRANSPORTATION COMPANY	29
HARLAN SHERIFF THEODORE R. MIDDLETON	41
UMWA ORGANIZER LAWRENCE "PEGGY" DWYER	51
LYNCH, KY	59
HARLAN FUEL COMPANY TIPPLE	109
UMWA ATTORNEY JOHN Y. BROWN	114
UMWA ORGANIZER L.T. "TICK" ARNETT	122
MONUMENT AT BENNETT MUSICK'S GRAVE	128
UMWA DISTRICT 19 PRESIDENT WILLIAM TURNBLAZER AND UMWA ATTORNEY T.C. TOWNSEND	125
HARLAN-WALLINS OPERATOR PEARL BASSHAM	138
MRS. MARTHA HOWARD	139
MARY HELEN COAL CORP. COMPANY HOUSES	165
MARY HELEN JUROR J.M. HIBBARD	163
NATIONAL GUARDSMEN AT CLOVER FORK COAL CO.	172
NATIONAL GUARDSMEN, 1939 STRIKE	179
HARLAN COUNTY COURTHOUSE AND JAIL	183
BROOKSIDE WOMEN WITH "SWITCHES"	192

preface

Harlan County is tucked away deep in the hills of southeastern Kentucky about fifty miles from Cumberland Gap and the historic Wilderness Road. Surrounded by Bell, Leslie and Letcher counties in Kentucky and by Lee County in Virginia, Harlan was long isolated from the mainstream of American history. In the eighteenth century, for example, Dr. Thomas Walker traveled through the Cumberland Gap and passed by Harlan as he followed the Cumberland River to present day Barbourville, Kentucky where three men in his party erected a log house, the first built by white men west of the Appalachian Mountains. A quarter of a century later Daniel Boone and thirty axemen avoided Harlan as they blazed the Wilderness Trail from Powell Valley in Tennessee to the banks of the Kentucky River where they built the fort called Boonesborough. For over a century, Harlan, its people and its coal deposits remained sequestered, untouched, and untapped as the winds of industrialism swept across the United States during the Gilded Age.

In the second decade of the twentieth century, the long arms of big business, reached into Harlan to uncover coal which had underlain its mountainous terrain for centuries. Overnight, the rapid and often rude, crude forces of the industrial age transformed a heretofore predominantly pastoral and peaceful scenario into a bustling industrial area. Capitalists from afar invaded Harlan and induced drawling, unknowing mountaineers to sign broadform deeds which transmitted mineral rights on lands which the same families had owned for generations. Subsequently coal companies entered the area, ripped down Harlan's virginal forests, bulldozed the land and erected company towns. Alas, the industrial revolution had come to sheltered Harlan County.

This is the story of Harlan's industrial revolution. It is also a classic saga of conflict between labor and management occasioned by the many attempts of the United Mine Workers of America to organize the miners of Harlan. For sheer drama, it is perhaps unequaled, throughout the Southern Appalachian coalfields and the history of the American labor movement. Central characters in the story are "gun thugs," union organizers, coal company executives, local sheriffs, and National Guardsmen. Discussed are pitched battles, beatings, shootings, kidnappings, and dynamitings. Happenings in "Bloody Harlan" became front page news in the *New York Times* as well as other distant newspapers.

Until recently, there were no complete studies of Harlan's industrial conflict. Tony Bubka and Lawrence Grauman, Jr. authored an article which dealt mainly with the events of the 1931-32 period. Harry Caudill's *Night Comes to the Cumberlands*, George Tindall's study of the New South and United States history survey text, and F. Ray Marshall's *Labor in the South* provide brief treatments of Harlan's labor struggle.

Later, George J. Titler, who helped organize Harlan in 1938-39 and then became international vice-president of the UMWA under the late Tony Boyle, published *Hell in Harlan*, his personal reminiscences of the events in Harlan. In 1978, John W. Hevener brought out the first scholarly, full-length book in *Which Side Are You On?*. While the Hevener study delves into the psychological, sociological and economic forces at work in Harlan, it falls short in recapturing the high drama of the Harlan controversy.

This book attempts to recreate some of the sensationalism of the Harlan struggle. For example, dramatic episodes introduce most chapters, setting the tone for what is to follow. By using this approach, much of the "color" of the Harlan story is emphasized. Oral history sources, which include interviews with many of the principals, have been utilized to add a personal touch and a human side to the book. It must also be pointed out that when more than one book on the same subject is written, differences of emphasis and interpretation occur. As the succeeding pages justifiably demonstrate, this book contains both with respect to earlier published works on Harlan. Having once resided in the area, and having lived with the Harlan conflict since the mid-1950's, it is my hope that this book adds a new dimension to one of the most significant chapters in American Labor History.

As the pages of this story unfold, the reader will see that songwriter Florence Reece was correct when she intoned that there were no neutrals in Harlan during the labor warfare of the New Deal era. After four junkets into Harlan with his Labor History classes in the 1980's, the writer has learned that even now when the subject of the union is brought up, there still are no neutrals in "Bloody Harlan."

THE COLD CHILLS OF STEEL

On February 10, 1932 the Waldo Frank "sweet milk brigade," which included Quincy Howe, editor and newsman, Edmund Wilson, novelist, poet, and playwright, Malcolm Cowley, editor of *New Republic*, and Allan Taub, a New York attorney, went to the Bell-Harlan coalfield. Ostensibly they were on a mission of mercy to distribute old clothing and milk to the embattled families of local coal miners. Because of the recent unpleasantness associated with the visit of the Dreiser Committee,[1] Pineville Mayor Dr. J.M. Brooks, Bell County Attorney Walter B. Smith, Harlan Sheriff John Henry Blair, and Circuit Judge Davy Crockett (Baby) Jones warned that speeches, meetings, parades and demonstrations would not be tolerated. However, Doris Parks and Harold Hickerson, two organizers representing the National Miners Union, used the occasion to challenge the miners to join that organization.

A short time later Waldo Frank and his associates were hauled into Pineville's Police court on charges of disorderly conduct. To their surprise, the local prosecutor motioned to drop the charges. Returning to Pineville's Continental Hotel, local officials and citizens warned the group to get out of town and the county. As night fell, they were thrust into cars with Frank and Taub occupying the same vehicle. In a motorcade numbering fifteen automobiles, they were driven to the Kentucky-Tennessee state line at historic Cumberland Gap. As the caravan stopped on top of Cumberland Mountain, a voice boomed out of the darkness, "Put out the lights." In the dim light, Taub and Frank saw several men getting out of the cars. For a moment the two were alone, but then, a stern voice demanded, "Get out." Obeying, the two men left the car and in the next moments, the sounds of blows, scuffles, and the cries of anguish filled the frosty night air. Left alone in a bloody, beaten condition, the two men finally secured a ride to Knoxville, Tennessee from a passing motorist. There they laid their beating on Bell-Harlan "vigilantes" and called for a Senate probe of terrorism in the two coal counties.[2]

In Washington, in the spring of 1932, a Senate subcommittee looked into those charges as well as similar complaints lodged by other delegations who visited Bell and Harlan Counties during that same period. Before the Senate investigation took place, as John Fox, Jr. dramatically has pointed out in *The Trail of the Lonesome Pine*,[3] the Bell-Harlan area was mightily, and in some respects uglily, transformed from a rural, farming region into a teeming industrial area by "King Coal."

I

The terrain of Harlan, the southeast Kentucky county that became equally famous for its high quality coal and mine warfare, is dominated by majestic mountains and sprawling valleys. To enter the county it is necessary to follow two-laned roads built atop precipitous cliffs that follow watercourses. Before modernization, for example, the "Rhododendron Trail," or U.S. 119, which links Harlan and Pineville, the county seat of Bell County, zigzagged along the Cumberland River. Steep embankments lined one side of the road, while the peaks of Pine Mountain soared grandly up the other side. Harlan's roads in spring offered colorful vistas of redbuds, pink and white dogwoods, mountain laurel and rhododendron. In October, red, gold and orange autumn leaves splashed abundant color across the landscape. Across Cumberland River the tracks of the Louisville and Nashville railroad conveyed slow-moving coal trains, transporting Harlan's most important product to the nation's industrial centers. At the bottom of Harlan's numerous mountains and ridges nestled hazy valleys, jammed with company towns, filled with miners' houses, their ever-present chimneys spiraling forth black coal smoke from fireplaces and cookstoves.[4]

Mountains surround the county seat, Harlan Town,[5] on all sides. Narrow streets radiate from the county courthouse located near the central business district. Stretching out from the town are the secondary state roads leading into the coal mining "hollows." In the 1930's, on Clover Fork and Poor Fork, which merge about a mile from the county seat to form the Cumberland River, and on Martin's Fork, Puckett's Creek, and Wallins Creek, coal camps were everywhere.[6] In fact, Clover Fork, the heart of Harlan's coal field, was a continuous chain of coal camps from the county seat to the Virginia state line.

Before the mining of coal, Harlan County was a backwoods farming region. Farmers mined a few "country banks," to obtain coal for cooking and heating. Otherwise, they cultivated hard scrabble farms, or the more fertile river "bottoms," and lived simply on subsistence agriculture. Nearly every farmer owned a mule for spring plowing and hauling coal and wood. When they needed to go into Harlan, they rode their mules. When several farmers congregated in town, "mule swapping," and the swapping of knives, watches, and guns became a pastime. Most of them owned a dependable milch cow and several hogs which roamed at large in the woods. Water came from sparkling mountain streams.

Harlan's farmers lived in log cabins or frame houses perched on the hillsides. They ate bread made from a coarse corn meal, potatoes, shuck beans, "bulldog" gravy, fresh garden vegetables in the summer, and in the winter fresh hog meat.[7]

During its backwoods era, Harlan County was virtually a roadless region. Narrow lanes often followed the beds of creeks, and in times of drought creek beds served as roads. To travel from place to place, mountain people often used winding trails through the woods or across the mountains. Since most Harlan farmers enjoyed hunting, they possessed an intimate knowledge of these early roads and trails.[8] Still it was the discovery of "black diamond," or coal which lifted Harlan out of its primitive environment and spread its fame throughout the United States.

In 1750, after Dr. Thomas Walker of Virginia and his surveying party had made their way through the Cumberland Gap into present day Bell County, Kentucky, he noted the existence of coal:

> At the foot of the hill on the North West side we came to a Branch, that made a great deal of flat land. We kept down it 2 miles, several other branches coming in to make it a large creek, and we called it Flat Creek. We camped on the Bank where we found very good coal.

Subsequent surveys made toward the end of the eighteenth century covered much of what later became Harlan County and revealed the presence of coal on Martin's Fork, Puckett's Creek, and Crummies Creek.[9] Lying in the Cumberland coalfield, a subdivision of the Jellico district, in the southern Appalachian field, Harlan County contains as many as fifty specimens of coal valuable for both industrial purposes and home use.[10] Alas, Harlan County was the last of the southeastern Kentucky counties to experience the invasion of its peaceful hollows by the mining industry. Although the Louisville and Nashville Railroad reached Pineville in adjoining Bell County in 1888, it did not penetrate Harlan until 1911. A short time later the first rail shipment of Harlan coal left the Wallins Creek section, about a dozen miles southwest of Harlan.[11]

Absentee capital was largely responsible for the development of Harlan's coal industry.[12] Henry Ford owned Fordson on Wallins Creek, which produced coal for Ford Motor Company. The Insull interests had mines on Puckett's Creek and Black Mountain, located a few miles from Evarts, while Detroit Edison opened up operations on Clover Fork. On Poor Fork Wisconsin Steel Company of Benham, a subsidiary of International Harvester, and United States Coal and Coke Company of Lynch, owned by the United States Steel Corporation, operated the county's major captive mines. While distant owners monopolized most Harlan mines, local residents owned mines on Wallins Creek and on Martin's Fork.[13]

By the 1930s Harlan County contained five major coal-producing areas: (1) the Puckett's Creek sector, site of the Insull coal camp and mines of the Black Star Coal Corporation; (2) Wallins Creek, locale of mines of the Kentenia Corporation, in which former President Franklin D. Roosevelt once had an interest,[14] and those of the locally-owned Creech Coal Company; (3) Poor Fork, which, in addition to the Wisconsin Steel Company and United States Coal and Coke mines, supported Harlan Central Coal Company's resident-owned mine at Totz, near Cumberland; (4) Clover Fork, the county's richest producing section, had eleven operations, including Harlan-Wallins Coal Corporation and Harlan Collieries; and (5) Martin's Fork, along which stretched ten companies, including Harlan Fuel Company at Yancey, R.C. Tway Coal Company at Tway, and Mary Helen Coal Corporation at Coalgood.[15] Into these five areas, Harlan's coal operators built coal camps.[16]

Just beyond the city limits of Harlan Town, the first coal camp burst into view. Each camp was a self-contained village consisting of company houses, a large company store[17] which stocked every conceivable item from bubble gum to appliances, a school, and a community church. Some of the larger camps, such as the one located at Lynch, which employed about 3,000 miners, included a "hotel containing 133 spacious, carpeted, steam-heated rooms," a sixty-room hospital, a company service station, a railroad station, a fire station, and a water system which matched modern systems.[18]

In most company towns, the houses were all alike: small, wooden, unpainted and unpretentious "shot-gun" houses built extremely close together. Each one had a porch, and was lighted by a single bulb dangling from a drop cord in the ceiling. Since few houses had indoor plumbing, an outdoor privy out back furnished unsanitary toilet facilities. Water for the family's cooking, drinking, and bathing needs came from a nearby spring, creek or river. Miners rented the houses for $1.00 to $2.00 per month. Narrow dirt roads, dusty in dry times, muddy during rainy seasons, separated the houses and afforded transit for miners, their families and their livestock. Into these roads, the yards of their houses, and into creeks and streams miners and their families threw garbage.[19] When the family car no longer ran, they dumped it over the bank into the creek or let it rust in the yard.

Most companies required miners to shop at company stores, where credit could be obtained and where scrip, or company money, could be redeemed. The company store, or commissary, also contained the local post office, where miners, their wives, and children congregated to exchange pleasantries, discuss working conditions, and gossip. Young people often converged at the company store to engage in a bit of "sparkin."[20]

Blacks comprised only a small percentage of the mining population in Harlan County at this time. Scattered through the entire county, mining operations which employed blacks separated them from whites. They shopped at the company store with whites but attended segregated camp theaters, schools and churches. (On a visit to Lynch in the spring of 1982 the author and his Labor History class viewed the Lynch Colored Public School located on a principal street in that town.) In the 1930s, as today, it was common to see both white and black miners sitting on their haunches, engrossed in a card game at some secluded spot in the camp. Although blacks and whites worked separately or on different shifts in most mines, the Evarts local UMW union installed a black miner as an officer prior to the first "Battle of Evarts." Several blacks also were in the group that "bushwhacked" deputy sheriffs at Evarts and at least two were convicted and sentenced to prison. During a visit to Clover Fork during the summer of 1954, the writer noticed the segregated camp at Black Mountain, an all-black baseball team preparing for a game in the same camp, and signs on the bus station wall at Evarts telling blacks to sit on rear benches. Blacks also sat in the back of buses which served the Clover Fork area at that time.

Nearly every mining camp had one or more churches. Several camps had community churches with various denominations alternating services. While most miners believed in God, they were not regular church attenders. The most common denominations were Baptists and Holiness, or "Holy Rollers." A demonstrative sect, these "Holy Rollers" spoke in tongues, rolled on the floor or ground, jumped over benches, exerted their bodies in all sorts of contortions and convulsions, and handled poisonous snakes. The Baptists, or Primitive Baptists, had foot-washing rituals and used nearby creeks or rivers as baptismal pools. Some coal companies donated a plot of ground for the building of a church and paid the construction costs. Self-styled preachers, exhorters, or perhaps a miner who had felt the call, pastored these churches. They delivered impassioned and emotional exhortations on the evils of this world, called sinners to repentance, and promised eternal life for those who trod the straight and narrow path.[21]

In addition to fulfilling the religious needs of the people, community churches were social centers. On "meeting" nights, most of the people went to church. While some of the adults busied themselves with reverential matters and lent their undivided attention to the exhorter, many of the miners stood outside, talking, smoking, and chewing tobacco. Meanwhile, young folks, inside and outside, often became involved in each other. At the conclusion of the service many of the young fellows escorted some winsome lass back to her household. Inevitably many a coal camp romance bloomed and blossomed in this way, followed by the usual wedding and shivaree. As a result, the young men settled down in coal camps and followed their fathers into the mines. The children of these camp liaisons grew up as either coal miners' daughters or coal miners' sons, perpetuating this livelihood in the hills of Harlan for generations to come.

The children of coal miners attended school in unadorned frame or concrete block school houses which the company often built and rented to the county. The county school board appointed and paid teachers' salaries which the companies supplemented, permitting a longer school term. In one camp, employees contributed $.25 per month to a school fund, which the company matched with deductions from miners' pay. (In the late 1940s I taught in a one-room graded school at the head of Martin's Fork. Most of the students were children of coal miners, who after finishing the eighth grade, either married or went into the mines. Most decided not to go on to high school.)

The coal companies built roads and streets which led to the mines, the company store, and throughout the camp. Privately owned and constructed on company property, these roads were under complete company authority. Some of them were interspersed with gates that could be opened and closed, especially when labor difficulties arose. A few companies kept their streets chained in order to control workers. The county or state financed the highways which connected one camp with another. Since these roads were publicly owned, no barricades blocked them. Although coal corporations built roads to be used in connection with business, the growth of Harlan's coal industry accelerated road-building by the county and state. The graded passageways of the 1930s were an obvious improvement over the narrow trails travelled by the public before the coming of the coal boom.

Of all innovations brought by Harlan's industrialization, roads caused the most controversy. While many people were enthusiastic about the new "hard roads," there were old-timers who regarded the coal corporations as trespassers. As one old white-haired mountaineer put it, "For years I've lived in my peaceful hollow, unmolested, and now they've built a highway into my hollow and I must live to see my grandchildren running up and down the highway in automobiles."[22]

The establishment of the coal camps introduced the people of Harlan to a paternalistic way of life. One author has described this arrangement as an industrial phenomenon because "it is forced on the operator largely through the isolation of mining camps."[23] With the newness of the coal industry and its rapid expansion in the area, the mine owners had to provide living quarters for their workers as well as stores where they could buy life's necessities. Once the operators began to provide every service, the miners depended on them to supply every need. These circumstances enabled the coal men, whether they intended to or not, to assume almost complete control over the lives and actions of their employees. In this same manner an unscrupulous boss could take advantage of his hirelings. The system of "paternalism" which made much headway during the first few years of Harlan's coal industry, became entrenched with the passage of time. Philip Murray, vice-president of the United Mine Workers of America, sketched conditions in 1922 that have "never been approached since the time of the feudal baron."[24] Many owners became obsessed with their private fiefdoms so that they strongly resisted all efforts of miners to join the unon. As long as conditions were prosperous, the paternalistic society remained intact. With the coming of hard times—in the 1930s—many miners turned away from their bosses and to the union for help.

2

Although commercial mining began in Harlan County in 1911, the first serious attempt by the United Mine Workers of America to organize Harlan's miners took place in 1917 when organizers William Turnblazer and George Edmunds entered Harlan. Like international United Mine Workers president John L. Lewis, the two-hundred twenty pound Turnblazer had started out in the pits as a coal digger. He first worked in the western Pennsylvania coal fields, and after the World War he was an organizer in the Southern Appalachian area. In the 1930s he was president of District 19, UMWA which included east Tennessee and southeast Kentucky. A fiery, emotional type, in the mold of AF of L leader Samuel Gompers, Turnblazer more than once stirred the miners to action and to the union with rousing speeches.[25]

On June 10th of that year 2,500 miners jammed Harlan's courthouse square, the site of many similar future meetings, where Turnblazer urged them to take the union obligation. Enthusiastically, many workers answered the call so that the UMWA was able to establish three local unions with a membership of about 1,500. The UMWA had secured a foothold in Harlan County.

From the outset, the operators declined to meet with union officials. On August 11, 1917 a general strike marked by violence occurred, setting the pattern for Harlan's violent and turbulent labor history for the next twenty-two years. At Benham, Wisconsin Steel used armed guards, or "thugs," and imported "scabs" to break the strike. Shooting broke out and when it ended, Luther Shipman, one of the strike's leaders, was dead from a bullet which caught him in the back of the head. The miners stood their ground, however, and since the country was at war the Federal government intervened. Summoning both representatives of the operators and the union to Washington, Fuel Administrator Harry A. Garfield, after several days of negotiations, announced a five-part settlement: (1) a general wage increase; (2) shorter work day; (3) checkweighmen on all coal tipples; (4) recognition of the UMWA; (5) establishment of a mine committee to handle grievances. After fifty-seven days on strike, Harlan's miners returned to work on October 8, and a final agreement, good for the duration of the war, was signed on November 1, 1917.

After the war the UMWA assigned organizer Thomas N. Gann to the Harlan field. Concentrating on building up union membership, Gann unionized the entire county except for the Benham and Lynch mines. The next year District 19 achieved autonomy but because of inexperienced leadership, the district treasury was depleted in less than a year. By 1920 the district organization was deeply in debt and ineffective.

Following these initial successes, union membership and activity foundered in Harlan. Despite the signing of a national two-year contract on March 31, 1920, Harlan's mines, for the most part, remained non-union. Unyielding operators, using methods which became standard in Harlan—employment of gun "thugs," house evictions of union miners, refusal of jobs to union miners, discharge of miners who joined the union or attended union meetings—made Harlan an open shop territory for most of the decade.

One notable exception to the county-wide open shop policy was Black Mountain. At that mine, in 1922, a two-year closed shop contract was signed. With its expiration in 1924, a strike ensued. The company used guards armed with machine guns and high-powered rifles, and house evictions to break the union and the strike. On September 23, 1924, the local union at Black Mountain disbanded. (The Black Mountain Mine became the center of the trouble in 1931 which culminated in the famous "Battle of Evarts.")

In the mid-1920s a brief flurry of renewed union activity developed. Companies, using the same methods that had earlier curbed the union, aborted the campaign.

On May 1, 1924, the UMWA rallied at Harlan's courthouse square. Addressing this gathering were International Secretary-Treasurer Thomas Kennedy, Turnblazer, and Lawrence (Peggy) Dwyer, field representative from Illinois. Dwyer, who had been an UMWA international representative for thirteen years, was nicknamed "Peggy" because he had lost a leg at the knee in a mining accident.

Thereafter he wore a hollow wooden leg. An Irishman and the father of eleven children, he was an aggressive organizer who "would fight anything that walked or crawled if he felt the cause was just." A good union man and a great organizer all his life, Dwyer earlier had actively organized miners in the Cabin Creek-Paint Creek, West Virginia coal fields. Neither house evictions, threats, nor attempts on his life could stop the dogged Dwyer from organizing the UMWA in "Bloody Harlan."

Local officials and the operators attempted to thwart the May rally by cutting off the water supply. Although, according to one observer, "obtaining a drink of water was more difficult than getting a 'shot of corn,'" more than 1,000 members joined the national organization and re-established local unons throughout the county. For a brief instant the flame of unionism flickered, then died. Operator resistance and apathy among miners brought union organization to a virtual standstill by the end of the decade.

Thus Harlan's miners faced the grim days of the depression earning wages ranging from $2.00 to $3.50 for a twelve- to sixteen-hour work day. Coal loaders reportedly drew as low as twenty cents per ton.[26] Women and children had little to eat because the miner-husband-father did not earn enough to feed them. Resolute in their opposition to the union, operators used "thugs," evictions, and "yellow dog" contracts to keep the union out of Harlan County. But sometimes in the course of history, desperate men commit desperate acts. As the funereal days of the depression hung over the valleys of Harlan, hungry, forlorn and destitute coal miners turned to the UMWA as a possible source for relief.

While Harlan's miners were hurting, the country's coal industry suffered in the economic collapse which had engulfed the nation. Operators were confronted with two alternatives; bankruptcy or reduction of operational costs. Most chose the latter course which resulted in fewer working days and reduced wages. National labor leaders, citing President Herbert Hoover's request that wage standards must be maintained, supported workers who protested.[27] But in early 1931 another wage cut took place. The wages of a Harlan miner employed at a Clover Fork mine fell from $3.90 to $1.65 per day.[28] In March 1931 the UMWA moved back into Harlan to try to correct the miners' plight.

On March 1, nearly 2,000 Bell and Harlan miners crammed into Pineville's Gaines Theater. Desolate but not dispirited the workers heard UMWA District 5 President Patrick Fagan and UMWA International Vice President Philip Murray challenge them to support the organizational campaign headed by Lawrence (Peggy) Dwyer.[29] According to Bell County miner-organizer Jim Garland, the miners heard many speeches on that occasion. Later, Garland remembered that the financially-strapped UMWA could not make a contract and that many of the miners went home disgruntled because the union had asked them for ten dollars to join the union.[30]

The union meeting did not catch Harlan operators off guard. As miners gathered at the theater, informers stood outside taking the names of those who entered. Jim Garland recalled Petrie, (probably Roscoe Petrie) a foreman for the Whitfield operation at Kitts, standing at the door and checking out men who attended the rally. Within a matter of days, many workers, including Garland, received discharge slips. Several operators charged reduced demand for coal as reason for the dismissals, while others cited laxity in work or infractions of mining regulations.[31] The "blacklist" came to Harlan County, as operators shunned miners demonstrating pro-union views. One miner who took part in the campaign of 1931 later remarked that "blacklisted" men could not get jobs anywhere in the county.[32]

Most discharges were from Black Mountain Corporation, which operated two mines at Kenvir, about twelve miles from Harlan. E.B. Childers, superintendent, regarded by the miners as rugged and cruel, was deeply hostile toward the union. After firing his workers, company guards boldly marched into the company houses, and before the helpless eyes of the miners, their weeping wives and children, threw their meager possessions out into the yard or beside the road.[33] Homeless, with no place to go, the families wandered about four miles down the road to Evarts where a pro-union property owner made temporary quarters available. Thus, Evarts became a rendezvous for evicted miners as well as an operations center for union activities.

At Evarts, miners convened with little interference in the town theater, owned by Dr. P.O. Lewis, company doctor at Black Mountain. On other occasions they found it safer to meet in the hills to plan strategy and to appoint relief committees who purchased food with funds sent in by the national UMWA headquarters for distribution to the miners' needy families. Local merchants, moved by compassion more than sympathy for the union, also helped out by supplying food and clothing. Few needy families were turned away.[34]

On several occasions idled miners met in Harlan, paraded through the business section, then rallied at the courthouse square. UMWA circulars, urging affiliation with the union, criticized wage reductions, the "yellow dog" contract, the ten-hour work day, the "clean-up" system, the lack of checkweighmen at coal tipples, and miserable working and living conditions.

Both local and national union officials urged the miners to proceed peacefully. W.B. Jones, secretary of the Evarts local union, told a group of about 400 men at the county courthouse to work for the union "in a peaceful way, without the use of arms." Turnblazer cautioned them to act in an intelligent, respectful manner, and Phil Murray early on emphasized that the campaign must not assume a revolutionary or radical character.[35]

As the new crusade commenced, Harlan County officials almost to a man opposed the union. Sheriff John Henry Blair, a husky two-hundred pound ex-soldier, who drew support from the miners when he ran for office, later turned against them by appointing over two hundred deputy sheriffs employed by coal companies as mine guards.[36] Howard N. Eavenson, a Harlan coal operator, admitted that the deputies were armed, usually with a shoulder holster. In describing their general character, he declared, "Of course, they are not Sunday School superintendents. That is not the type of man you want."[37]

Called "gun thugs" by the union, the deputies, armed with sawed-off shotguns, pistols and tommy guns, stayed in Harlan hotels where they could be dispatched immediately to any area of the county. Often they rode up and down the roads with gun barrels protruding from the windows of their cars.[38]

As efforts to re-implant the union in Harlan proceeded, operators presented nearly a solid wall of opposition in the form of the Harlan County Coal Operators' Association.[39] Most of the leading coal corporations belonged to this powerful body which dominated local politics, evidenced by the fact that its secretary, George S. Ward, headed the county's Republican organization and Silas J. Dickenson, president of the Mary Helen Coal Corporation, chaired the local Democratic party. This coalition controlled the county courthouse. For example, Sheriff Blair secured the signatures of leading operators on his official performance bonds upon taking office. Later, in 1932, Blair opposed Ward for the county Republican chairmanship. Supported by Circuit Judge Jones, Ward defeated the sheriff who angrily retorted that since the operators had "slapped him in the face," eighty-six deputized mine guards would have to turn in their badges.

Judge Jones and Commonwealth's Attorney W.A. (Will) Brock also were strongly anti-union. Jones, who presided over the Bell-Harlan judicial circuit, married into the W.F. Hall family who operated mines in Harlan which belonged to the HCCOA. A leading Harlan attorney and several Evarts town officials later remembered that Jones was pro-operator, but an HCCOA spokesman calculated that the courts were impartial. Brock favored the operators. In August, 1931 in announcing that he would seek the death penalty for those charged with murder in connection with labor disorders. Brock declared, "We've got to put the cold chills of steel down the backs of the criminal element in the county."[40]

Despite the powerful alliance which defied the union, coal miners stood fast during the labor disorders of March and April, 1931. At Evarts, where the only local union functioned, union meetings, followed by evictions and the blacklist, continued. There was also a great deal of looting of Evarts food stores and Clover Fork commissaries. A Harlan physician practicing in Evarts later recalled that he was in an office above the A&P one night when he heard a great commotion outside in the street. Going over to an upstairs window, he peeped out just in time to see people running up the streets with loaded sacks. Most of the looting was blamed on miners who had done some "after-hours shopping" to feed their hungry families.[41]

Violence, of course, was inevitable. It first occurred on April 16 in the Evarts school yard, where W.B. Jones was admonishing the men to obey the law. As he spoke, a scuffle broke out in the rear of the crowd. Several union men grabbed Charles Carpenter, a black miner on his way home from work at Black Mountain, called him a "scab" and severely beat him with sticks. A few days later a special grand jury indicted nine miners on charges of banding and confederating to "intimidate, alarm, disturb, and injure the said Charles Carpenter by seizing him with force and violence and whipping him with a stick."[42]

On April 18 another clash occurred when thirteen deputy sheriffs went to Evarts to arrest Carpenter's assailants. When the lawmen drove up, a group of miners was sitting and standing on the railroad tracks. Deputy Jim Daniels, Black Mountain's most feared mine guard, reportedly jerked a Negro miner to his feet and pushed him toward one of the cars. While the rest of the miners scattered, Bill Burnett opened fire on the officers. The deputies returned the shots, and when the gun battle ended, Deputy Sheriff Jesse Pace was dead and Deputy Sheriff Frank White and Burnett nursed wounds.[43]

The April 18 Shootout at Evarts was just the beginning. That same day miners patrolling railroad tracks at Yancey shot at Deputy Sheriff Bob Blair. The next day dynamite ripped the drift mouth, or mine entrance, of Berger Coal Mining Company. Ten days later a battle erupted at Black Mountain where snipers opened fire on guards who accompanied miners to work at 5:00 a.m. In the ensuing affray, which lasted for more than an hour, two thousand shots flew through the pre-dawn air. No one was injured. On May 1, sixteen vacant camp houses at Ellis Knob Coal Company mysteriously burned to the ground. Authorities believed the fire to be of incendiary origin because six men ran from the scene afterward. These violent events set the stage for the most serious altercation, the "Battle of Evarts."[44]

3

The morning of May 5, 1931 dawned warm and sunny. There was no hint of violence in the small mountain community of Evarts which, spread out between two ridges along Clover Fork nine miles east of Harlan, presented the appearance of a boom town.[45] Groups of men walked the streets or congregated at convenient spots, such as the L&N depot. Hogs, cattle and other animals roamed the dirt streets. Directly below the railroad station, the highway to Harlan crossed the railroad and passed through a cut, bounded on the upper side by a wooded area and on the lower by a high embankment strewn with railroad ties. Connecting the depot with the business section of Evarts was a narrow bridge over Clover Fork. On the morning of May 5 a highway maintenance crew was making repairs on this bridge.

Around 9:00 or 9:30, a company truck driven by John Hickey made its way from Kenvir to Verda, about three miles below Evarts, to transport the household possessions of Roy Hughes, a "scab" hired on at Black Mountain to replace a miner fired because of union activity.[46] At about the same time, three carloads of deputy sheriffs departed Kenvir to escort the truck on its return trip. In charge of this group of ten deputies was Jim Daniels.

Before the loaded truck reached the western outskirts of Evarts the three carloads of deputies crossed the bridge and traveled toward the railroad crossing below the depot. As the cars crossed the tracks, a Negro stationed on the embankment reportedly gave a hand signal.[47] The next instant a rapid barrage of gunfire rained down upon the three cars from the wooded hillside, the embankment, and from two buildings in Evarts several hundred yards away. When the shooting broke out, Daniels, armed with a submachine gun, leaped from his car and started up the embankment. Suddenly, a well-aimed shotgun blast nearly took off his head and he died instantly. George Dawn, another deputy, grabbed Daniels' weapon and apparently shot and killed Carl Richmond, the only miner slain in the battle.

Pinned down, the other deputies managed to get their submachine guns operating. So rapid and intense was the fire from ambush, however, the lawmen retreated with their wounded. Estes Cox, a Black Mountain mine guard, whose arm dangled from the shoulder, jumped into a car and raced into Harlan to ask Sheriff Blair for reinforcements.[48] Shepherd Purcifull, another mine guard was shot at least seven times, only to be saved by the Black Mountain company physician who dragged his bleeding body into his office.[49] Besides Daniels, Otto Lee, a deputy sheriff and the son of Deputy George Lee, and Howard Jones, member of a prominent Harlan County family and commissary clerk at Black Mountain, were killed before they could get out of their cars.[50] The only known casualty suffered by the miners was the previously mentioned Carl Richmond, a Negro.

Following the "Battle of Evarts" the entire county seethed. Since Sheriff Blair and his deputies seemed incapable of handling the situation, the sheriff, County Judge H.H. Howard, William Turnblazer, and Kentucky Federation of Labor Secretary Peter Campbell requested that Governor Sampson send enough soldiers to restore order and to protect the citizens of Harlan and Bell Counties.

Acting upon this request, Governor Sampson on May 6 declared a state of terror and lawlessness in and around Evarts and ordered 300 troops, under the command of Colonel Daniel M. Carrell, into Harlan.[51] The soldiers remained in the county until July 19. With troops on hand, Judge Jones empaneled a special grand jury to probe every act of lawnessness caused by the labor disorders. He declared:

> We have got to respect organized law and order, or else we haven't any county. The only things that will follow conditions like this are grief and sorrow, widows and orphans and bloodshed, and everything that is disagreeable and disturbing to the citizens of this county.

On May 9 the grand jury indicted Evarts Police Chief Asa Cusick, Evarts City Clerk Joe Cawood, W.B. Jones and Evarts policeman Al Benson for the murder of Daniels, Lee and Jones at Evarts. None of the four was allowed bond. Before recessing on May 23, it charged thirty-seven additional persons, including Evarts union leader W.M. Hightower in the slaying of Daniels, Lee, and Jones, and Bill Burnett for killing Deputy Sheriff Jesse Pace. Numerous other indictments named coal miners for landing and confederating and store-house breaking.[52] No one was indicted in connection with the death of Negro miner Carl Richmond.

Preliminary hearings for many of these defendants got underway in Harlan Circuit Court on May 20. At that time legal maneuverings began to prevent Judge Jones from hearing the cases against defendants Cawood, Cusick, Benson and Jones. The grounds: Jones had opposed Cawood's candidacy for sheriff; was related by marriage to the coal mining Hall family; had appeared before the grand jury seeking these indictments. Judge Jones, however, refused to vacate the bench.

These four defendants and three others, W.M. Hightower, Jim Reynolds, and Floyd Murphy, then applied for a writ of habeas corpus. During a hearing patrolled by state troops who searched all who entered the courtroom, the court denied the defense petition and all seven were returned to jail.[53]

The defendants languished in jail until the August term of Harlan Circuit Court. In an unprecedented move, which surprised the defense, Commonwealth's Attorney Brock abruptly called for a change of venue for fifteen defendants, including Hightower, Jones, Cusick, and Benson, because conditions in Harlan were too tense to permit impartial trials. Defense counsel John M. Robsion, former United Stated Senator and later congressman from Kentucky's ninth district, in a table-pounding scene, strongly protested the transferrals: "It is a denial of justice to send these murder cases so far away from home."[54] To no avail Judge Jones ordered fifty-one cases transferred to Clark and Montgomery counties, more than one hundred fifty miles from Harlan. In Mt. Sterling, county seat of Montgomery County, beginning in November, 1931 and continuing into January, 1932 juries from Kentucky's farmer-dominated Blue Grass region held in their hands the fate of Harlan union leaders and coal miners.

4

Presiding over the November term of Montgomery Circuit Court was Judge Henry R. Prewitt, a Blue Grass tobacco and stock farm owner, who ruled his court with an iron hand. In an apparent move to head off possible trouble during the tense proceedings, the judge fined spectators $5.00 who left the courtroom while a witness testified; fined lawyers $10.00 who repeated a question already answered by a witness; threatened the local sheriff with a $25.00 fine for delaying attorneys leaving the courtroom; and fined an Associated Press photographer $10.00 for contempt of court. In addition, Judge Prewitt, during the lengthy trial, admonished a lawyer for calling a black man "mister."[55]

Appearing for the state and the defense were some of the state's most notable and competent lawyers. The battery of attorneys for the prosecution included R.L. Pope, known throughout the mountains for his oratory and for his abilities as a criminal prosecutor, assisted by Harlan lawyers, Brock's assistant, J.B. Snyder, retained by the Black Mountain Coal Corporation, and local Commonwealth Attorney W.C. Hamilton. On the defense side of the courtroom sat former governor James D. Black, of Barbourville, Ben B. Golden, distinguished union lawyer of Pineville, W. Bridges White, brilliant Mt. Sterling attorney, and John M. Robsion.

The first Harlan defendant to go on trial at Mt. Sterling was thirty-three-year-old Bill Burnett, father of two children. Prosecution witnesses, mostly deputy sheriffs, claimed that Burnett fired first at Deputy Pace when he tried to arrest a Negro miner in connection with the beating of Charles Carpenter. In rebuttal, several defense witnesses testified that the defendant first had raised his hand in a token gesture of surrender. Then when the deputies opened fire he drew his gun and answered shot for shot. Burnett answered that he shot only after he was cursed and fired at twice.

The Blue Grass jury evidently believed Burnett. After listening to four days of testimony, the jurors on November 20 returned a verdict of acquittal. On hearing the decision, the defendant smiled blandly, then said that he planned to go back to Harlan County.

The prosecution was caught off guard by the surprise verdict in the Burnett case. Two days later, Judge Prewitt suddenly quashed the Harlan indictments and hurriedly empaneled a new grand jury which reindicted ten Harlan defendants for "conspiracy to murder.[56] This move stunned the defense since early on the judge had overruled a motion to dismiss the charges against the defendants.

The slightly built W.B. Jones was the first defendant to go to trial. Jones, 48, father of seven children, belonged to the UMWA during his entire twenty-nine years as a miner. Following a shutdown in the Ohio mines, he had moved to Black Mountain where company officials discharged him after he attended the March 1 union meeting at Pineville.

The prosecution based its case against Jones on evidence that Evarts union leaders had planned the attack on Harlan deputies at a union rally the night before the ambush. Several Commonwealth witnesses testified that Jones, at this meeting, selected twenty-five men, called them to one side and said, "we have got to get rid of Jim Daniels and Mr. Childers, and there is only one thing to do and that is to kill them...to shoot at their heads." He allegedly told the miners to "get your guns and get on the highway, not one day, but stay there until this thing is over...(and) when you shoot, shoot at their heads, shoot to get meat, shoot their god-damned heads off." Another witness stated that Jones boasted that "the happiest day of his life would be the day he could wade through Jim Daniels' and Childers' blood and that he did not think but damned little of Sheriff Blair." Indicted as a participant in the battle, Fred Lester turned state's evidence and swore that Jones told the men, "All that has not got high powered rifles take shotguns, and them that has not got shotguns take pistols, and anybody that has not got a pistol, get a red handkerchief, anybody that hain't got any gun at all, get some rocks, and said, if there is any of you not able to throw rocks get a red handkerchief, you can wave it."

The state also presented testimony which portrayed Jones as a fiery union organizer. Fred Lester and his brothers Hugh and John charged the union secretary with making inflammatory speeches in which he urged the men to prevent the "law" from coming to Evarts. Further testimony showed that Jones required union members to take a "black oath" signed in blood which bound the men to secrecy about union activities, to do away with the American flag, to reject the Bible and to harbor no prejudices should someone kill your close relatives.[57] Although several men allegedly took such an oath at Evarts, Al Benson, Evarts policemen and one of the union's chief supporters, recalled that he knew nothing about a "black oath," and that no one took such a pledge at any Evarts union meeting.[58]

The prosecution also introduced a letter from District 19 President Turnblazer to Jones a month before the battle of Evarts. In this letter, Turnblazer encouraged the Harlan union miners to continue the "fighting spirit," that it is "just such a fight that gave birth to our union," and that men "may as well die fighting against starvation and inhuman treatment and bad working conditions as to work and starve at the same time and receive nothing for there (their) labor."[59] The state attempted to show that the language of that letter premeditated the ambush of May 5 because Jones and the men had taken the words "fight" and "fighting spirit" literally. Thus they armed themselves and ambushed three carloads of deputies.

Jones was on the witness stand for four hours and forty-five minutes on November 30 and December 1. Describing his role in Harlan as that of a "Good Samaritan," he revealed using his home as a relief depot to feed and clothe women and children. In regard to the meeting on the eve of the battle, Jones testified that its main purpose was to discuss the mistreatment of people by Black Mountain guards and to consult Sheriff Blair about the matter. "There was no trouble talked at that meeting that night by anybody," Jones said. Confessing to having made speeches for the union at Evarts and from the courthouse steps in Harlan and to having participated in several union demonstrations, the union leader avowed he had always advised the men to conduct themselves in an orderly and lawful manner. Adamantly denying that he had conspired to kill the deputies at Evarts on May 5, Jones told the court that he supported the union in Harlan because of his desire to improve working conditions in the mines and lifestyles of the miners in the coal camps.

Defense counsel successfully refuted and impeached the testimony of the Lester brothers by producing witnesses who testified that Jones had not told the men to get on the road and attack the deputies. Those witnesses also noted that the credibility of the three brothers was "bad" and that generally they had sordid reputations.

In short, Jones' testimony and that of the defense witnesses directly conflicted with that of the prosecution.[60]

Near the end of Jones' lengthy interrogation, prosecution counsel R.L. Pope jumped to his feet and shouted in a voice which echoed throughout the building, "Who killed Jim Daniels?" Jones paused, reddened, then responded, "I don't know."[61]

In closing arguments to the jury, Pope charged that the murders at Evarts were a "bloody conspiracy," and called Jones the "arch conspirator." Defense counsel claimed Jones wanted only to establish the union in Harlan County. John M. Robsion blasted the efforts of Harlan gunmen to keep the union out. "You'll never run the railroads of this country, you'll never run the mines of this country, and you'll never run the farms of this country at the point of a bayonet."[62]

Finally, on December 9, the court gave the case to the jury. After deliberating for six hours and ten minutes, the jury found Jones guilty and recommended a sentence of life imprisonment. Turnblazer and other union officials expressed shock at the verdict, but Jones showed little emotion. The defendant afterward announced intentions to seek a new trial "on grounds of incomplete evidence and improper arguments by the Commonwealth."[63] Montgomery Commonwealth Attorney Hamilton remarked that "the law had been vindicated."

Nearly three weeks later, Judge Prewitt ordered W.M. Hightower, the 77-year-old union president at Evarts, to trial. Married to a 27-year-old woman and the father of two children, Hightower was in Harlan on the day of the Evarts shoot-out but nevertheless was named a party to the conspiracy. An illiterate and veteran miner, the local union president was fired because he joined the union in March 1931. Hightower testified that he supported the union in the interest of better conditions for the miners, including checkweighmen, the right to trade at retail stores instead of company stores where prices were about doubled, and the right of the men to select their own doctors. He stated that the men were upset over the Black Mountain officers "punching them in the ribs with their guns," and that he had gone to Harlan on May 5 to confer with Blair about the situation. When asked about the general feeling of the union miners toward the officers, Hightower declared, "Oh, of course it was not kind."

The most damaging evidence against Hightower may have been a cartoon that Deputy Sheriff R.G. Blair had confiscated following the arrest of the union president. The crude drawing depicted three cars, two people in the first, two in the second, and three in the third, and three men on the ground, with captions reading "Blair's Gun Thugs," "O, boys, it's Evarts, you can't whip 'em," "We better run it's Evarts," "How do you like Buck shot?" and 'Let's clean ''em up." Alongside the cars, the cartoon pictured men wearing UMWA shirts, armed with rifles, a sling shot, a bowie knife, and a hand grenade. One man was bare-headed, two had on ordinary caps, and two wore miners' caps. Words directly in front of the figure with the sling shot read, "I blacked his eye" and over the one with the hand grenade a caption read, "Let me have him."[64]

A flow of oratory characterized the final arguments in the Hightower case. Ben B. Golden called Hightower a "lamb upon the sacrificial altar of the Harlan County Operators' Association." Robsion proclaimed that "the HCCOA wanted to make an example of this old man for all time for those who dare to unionize their mines." Pointing a finger at the union president, Pope declared him to be the "crowned head of assassins, ambushmen, and bushwhackers."[65]

Hightower received the same penalty as Jones, a verdict which he received with no outward sign of emotion. On January 18 Judge Prewitt formally denied the defendants' petition for a new trial, sentenced the two labor leaders, and remanded seven remaining cases back to Harlan County. There, in trials that extended into 1933, special judges and imported juries heard evidence which resulted in convictions and life terms for UMWA activists Al Benson, Chester Poore, Elzie Phillips, Bill Hudson, and Jim Reynolds.[66] Bill Burnett, acquitted in Montgomery County, was tried in Harlan on charges of shooting at Deputy Frank White. Found guilty, he received a five year sentence. Joe Cawood never went to trial, and Asa Cusick was cleared of the conspiracy charges.

With convictions of its chief leaders, the UMWA temporarily withdrew from the Harlan coalfield. The violence which marked that period, combined with the appearance of the communistic National Miners Union, the discovery of "red" literature in the county, and the invasion of the area by several teams of self-styled investigators, ended the UMWA's unionization efforts in 1931-32. From here on, Harlan operators prepared to fight the United Mine Workers with every resource at their command.

The issue of communism was injected into the W.B. Jones trial in Mt. Sterling. Commonwealth's Attorney Hamilton, in a four-and-one-half-hour tirade, told the jury that if Jones was freed there would be "bonfires of rejoicing" in Moscow. The three Lesters, as described earlier, characterized the union leader as "radical" and mentioned the waving of a "red handkerchief" or "red flag" at the Evarts ambush. Other witnesses had Jones delivering "fiery" speeches and insisting that the men take a "black oath." Prosecution counsel attempted to link the union secretary with the Industrial Workers of the World because at least one miner, identified as a member of that leftist organization, called for miners to take a "black oath" at a union meeting. In May, 1931 Sheriff Blair's deputies raided a house in Evarts, uncovering communistic and I.W.W. literature. In September, 1931 a search of the home of J.I. "Ike" Layne, an I.W.W. organizer in Evarts, turned up a charter issued to the "Evarts, Ky. branch of the I.W.W. Union No. 220, May 18, 1931."[67]

The National Miners Union, a Pittsburgh-based organization formed in 1928, replaced the UMWA in Harlan County during the summer of 1931. NMU organizers went into the coal counties, convened mass rallies, made speeches, and converted a handful of miners, including Straight Creek's Jim Garland who became an organizer. It set up soup kitchens, dispensed pinto beans and corn bread to hungry miners and their families, and distributed clothing. It also rallied local women to the cause including the legendary "Aunt Molly" Jackson and Florence Reece, who became union balladeers.[68]

Coal miners marching past Bell County jail in Pineville, Ky. in response to strike call of National Miners Union, January, 1932.
(University of Kentucky Photo Archives)

Miss Doris Parks, secretary of National Miners Union, and Harold Hickerson, New York playwright spoke to coal miners in Pineville.
(University of Kentucky Photo Archives)

Local authorities resisted this movement by seizing radical literature, jailing several organizers, breaking up rallies, and raiding the homes of the union's leaders. In one instance, a soup kitchen at Evarts was dynamited.[69] Interestingly enough, despite substantial efforts by the NMU to unionize the coal mines in Harlan, when a call went out for a county-wide strike to take place on January 1, 1932, only eighty-three of over 4,000 miners responded. Most Harlan miners were conservative in politics and fundamentalist in religion. When they began to understand that the NMU was an atheistic, communistic organization, their enthusiasm for that union declined. In the beginning the food, clothing, milk and potatoes were attractions but in the end, the majority simply would not support the NMU.[70] It might well be said that the miners were "grabbing at straws" when they turned to the NMU, an organization which of course utterly failed to organize the miners of Harlan County.[71]

Methods used by local officials against the NMU attracted national attention in late 1931 and early 1932. As a result, several teams of self-styled investigators decided to go to Harlan.

The first of these groups, a committee headed by American novelists Theodore Dreiser and John Dos Passos, entered the region on November 5, 1931. Dreiser and associates spent less than a week interviewing miners and their wives, several prominent citizens, including Herndon J. Evans, then editor of the Pineville Sun, Harlan County Sheriff John Henry Blair, and Bell-Harlan Commonwealth's Attorney W.A. (Will) Brock. They departed unceremoniously after practical jokers victimized Dreiser at the Continental Hotel in Pineville. While stopping there overnight, a comely young secretary, Marie Pergain, a member of the author's troupe, entered Dreiser's room late in the evening. Several onlookers, probably some Pineville natives, crept up to the door and placed a row of toothpicks along the bottom. The toothpicks were still intact the next morning. Dreiser immediately left the area as Circuit Judge Jones called for an investigation and issued a warrant for adultery. At Bristol, Tennessee, Dreiser stopped long enough to repudiate charges of misconduct. "You may say it is useless for Bell County (Kentucky) to spend much-needed money investigating me, " he said, while admitting that he did "enjoy the companionship of ladies" and was "fond of their conversation." But Dreiser maintained he could not have committed adultery because, according to *Time*, November 23, 1931, "I am completely and finally impotent." Nevertheless, the Pineville Sun advised the author to "reach for a toothpick instead of a sweetie" next time.

After the departure of the Dreiser committee, Waldo Frank's entourage, as previously described, visited the Bell-Harlan area. Following their exclusion, Frank and Taub continued to work through student groups on the campus of Columbia University and in other eastern and midwestern colleges and universities. As a result they successfully organized a student delegation to investigate conditions in the southeastern Kentucky coalfield. Sponsored by the National Student League, a group of 200 students, representing largely New York and Ivy League schools, traveled to Kentucky during Easter vacation in March, 1932, although Sheriff Blair and Bell County officials emphasized they were personae non grata. Met at Cumberland Gap and told to turn back, the students, through their spokesman Rob Hall, demanded a hearing. Bell County officials then chaperoned them to Middlesboro's City Hall where Bell County Attorney Smith informed them that the area resisted outsiders because additional unrest among the miners followed each investigation. Local officials thereupon accompanied the students to the state line and sent them on their way back to Knoxville where they had assembled prior to their trip to Middlesboro. Later they appealed to Governor Ruby Laffoon of Kentucky and to the governor of Tennessee, but both declined to offer assistance to their proposed investigation.

Following the expulsion of the eastern students, the president and three students of tiny Commonwealth College, located in Mena, Arkansas, attempted to use the Bell-Harlan area as a testing ground for constitutional rights. According to reports, they traveled in a battered old jalopy in which they carried a bag of potatoes, a sack of flour, and a few other articles of food; in other words, provisions for one family, for distribution to the miners. To the sheriff and other local officials they handed copies of the Bill of Rights printed on the school press. The Arkansas travellers did not remain in the area long, for Bell officials conducted them into Harlan where deputies picked them up and chased them into Virginia. Later the Arkansans reported that Harlan County "vigilantes," including Deputy Sheriff Lee Fleenor, had assaulted and beaten them.

The last of the "outlanders" attempted to enter Bell County during May, 1932 and it was this group that landed in federal court at London. Sponsored by the American Civil Liberties Union, the delegation included Arthur Garfield Hays, a New York attorney, Dudley Field Malone, a Cleveland barrister, Professor Broadus Mitchell of Johns Hopkins University, the Reverend C.C. Webber of Union Theological Seminary in New York, Jesse C. Duke, a Washington lawyer, and Dr. Ernest Sutherland Bates, a well-known author, editor, and former college professor of New York City. After notifying Bell County officials in advance of their intentions to go into the area for the purpose of making a constitutional and civil rights test, they proceeded to the Bell-Knox line. There a motorcade led by Pineville Mayor J.M. Brooks and Bell County Attorney Smith blocked the highway. Prepared for this rebuff, they retraced their way to London and requested Federal Judge A.M.J. Cochran enjoin these officials from interfering with their mission.

In the lengthy and heated court hearing that followed, Hays argued that he did not advocate violence, but believed that a man had a right to make a speech advocating it. "Language should not be punished but the acts should," he asserted. Hays was then invited to inspect the coalfields by Harry Bullock, who had toured Harlan County as Governor Sampson's personal representative during the summer of 1931. He declined, emphasizing that while he did not wish the protection of any individual or group, he only desired to test the right of any person to go anywhere in the United States to speak. County Attorney Smith severely reprimanded Hays:

> We dare you to come under the veiled camouflage of your pretense of constitutional rights. You are a godless, non-descript, iconoclastic minority of grandiloquent egotists who arrogate to yourselves the right to meddle in other people's business. It is now time for you to put up or shut up... If a mad dog has a constitutional right to run rampant in Bell County, biting people and spreading hydrophobia, then the American Civil Liberties Union has the same

Pineville and Bell County pastors meeting with New York and eastern clergymen who visited coalfield in 1931-32. L-R, Revs. G.M. Haggard, Pineville M.E. Church; E.L. McClurkan, Pineville Presbyterian Church; E.P. Hall, New York; R.P. Mahon, Pineville Baptist Church; Reinhold Niebuhr, N.Y.; W.B. Spofford, N.Y.; L.C. Kelly, Pineville Baptist Church; L.W. Buckley, Pineville Christian Church; S.E. lull, Middlesboro Baptist Church; W.F. Pettus, Pineville M.E. Church; and C.R. Barnes, N.Y.
(University of Kentucky Photo Archives)

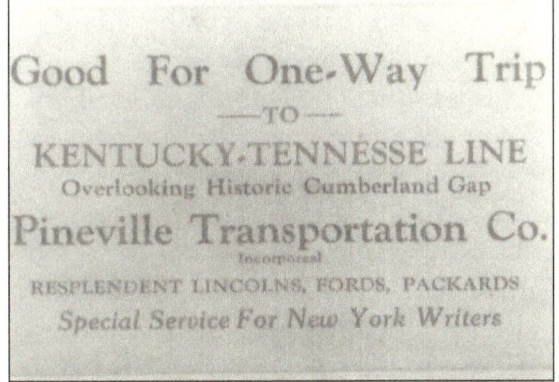

Calling card in possession of the late Herndon J. Evans, Pineville, Ky., advertising quick, one-way transportation out of Bell-Harlan area for outside writers and investigators. (University of Kentucky Photo Archives).

right. But, just as we would suppress the mad dog, we will also suppress this un-American organization in spite of its deathbed call for protection of a document which it despises and traduces. This document will not serve you in Bell County as a cloak for the iniquities of your organization.

After hearing the antithetical arguments, Judge Cochran condemned the ACLU and other self-appointed investigating teams for invading the southeastern Kentucky coalfields. He declared "there is such a thing as 'freedom of' and 'freedom to,'" while pointing out that there is the "right of freedom from annoying, uninvited, pestering investigations." Cochran continued, "What right has one person to investigate another? The only constitutional provision I know of investigations is against it—the Fourth Amendment. The whole country would be in a turmoil if investigations of behavior of others could be made by just anybody. No individual has any such1 right."

This federal court ruling ended the proposed Hays-Malone civil rights test. Hays' final remark on the unsuccessful venture was that "civil liberties do not exist in the southeastern Kentucky coal region."[72]

In addition to the "unofficial" investigations of conditions in Harlan by teams of outsiders, two official inquiries took place. First, on November 8, 1931, Governor Sampson appointed two attorneys, A.A. Bablitz of Lexington and Judge Smith Hays of Winchester to conduct a state-level probe. Both visited Harlan where they took testimony from many witnesses who accused Harlan officials of lawless acts in attempting to break the rebellion of the miners against starvation wages and deplorable working conditions. Miners reported being whipped, beaten, tortured, arrested without warrants, jailed, and given the "third degree." In some instances, after being hustled to nearby hills, they received a special brand of "Harlan justice." Personal liberties were ignored, freedom of speech and assembly suppressed. Local courts had used Kentucky's criminal syndicalism statute as a convenient tool for intimidating unionists. The Hays-Bablitz report blamed the National Miners Union for causing labor trouble after the UMWA withdrew following the battle of Evarts. It also observed a "lawlessness of the law," initiated by the coal operators and carried out by mine guards in Harlan County. Hays and Bablitz summarized conditions as benevolent feudalism at best. They submitted their nine-volume report to Governor Sampson in December, 1931, but the governor left office without giving it any consideration.[73]

In May, 1932 a subcommittee of the Committee on Manufacturers chaired by Senator Bronson Cutting (N.M.), heard all about the "lawlessness of the law" and a "reign of terror" in Harlan County.[74] For example, Jim Garland, a National Miners Union organizer from Bell County's Straight Creek section, said that the coal miners did not have the right to join a labor union. Mrs. Elizabeth Baldwin, widowed when Harlan Deputy Sheriff Lee Fleenor allegedly gunned down her husband at a NMU-sponsored soup kitchen in Harlan County, told all about the miserableness of life in Harlan's coal camps.[75] Rob Hall, a fiery Columbia University student representing the National Student League, vividly described the strong-arm tactics of local lawmen. Arnold Johnson, a Union Theological Seminary student, charged that Harlan Circuit Judge Jones, Sheriff Blair, and George S. Ward, secretary of the Harlan County Coal Operators' Association, had warned him to leave the area and that free speech, free press, and free assembly did not exist in the two coal counties. The Rev. Reinhold Niebuhr, one of the country's eminent theologians, called the miners' lifestyle "essentially peonage," while Major George M. Chescheir, a Kentucky National Guard official dispatched to Harlan during the turbulent summer of 1931, blamed Harlan's difficulties on Communist and radical infiltration of the area, and the resentment all that caused among the people.[76]

As the Senate hearings neared a climax on May 13, Senator M.M. Logan, like Chescheir, fervently accused Communists of financing visits by eastern delegations to the coalfield. The treatment various persons had received in Bell and Harlan, he concluded, was a local matter, beyond the scrutiny of the United States Senate.[77]

The Senate subcommittee, at the urging of Senator H. D. Hatfield, agreed with the Kentucky Senator and decided against a full-scale investigation into the coalfield conflict. Although conditions in "Bloody Harlan" had received national exposure, the United States Senate did not launch a full-scale inquiry into the "reign of terror" until the 1937 La Follette investigation.

6

The initial attempt to unionize the coal mines of Harlan County failed in the decade of the 1930s. Hostility from coal operators, mine guards, and local authorities foiled the efforts of miners to join the UMWA in order to improve wages and working conditions. The preservers of peace, notably Sheriff Blair, and the dispensers of justice were arrayed squarely against the union. Acting under orders from the HCCOA, Blair appointed a veritable army of deputy sheriffs, including deputies imported from outside the area. Armed with the law as well as guns, deputized officers roamed the county dispersing union rallies and intimidating miners and organizers. Judge Jones and Commonwealth's Attorney Brock displayed little sympathy for the union. Special grand juries returned wholesale indictments against miners and their sympathizers. Wholesale arrests and incarcerations of union stalwarts in the unsanitary Harlan County jail followed. These tactics effectively suppressed the union in 1931-32.

Protected by the law, Harlan operators unflinchingly refused all efforts by their workers the right to join the union. They used blacklists, "yellow dog" contracts, and house evictions to prevent the miners from organizing the mines.

The influx of the National Miners Union and other communist-affiliated organizations came after the demise of the UMWA. These groups, who came cloaked with the veil of benevolence, displayed a wanton disregard for constituted law and order. When local officials curbed their activities, they waxed indignant. A region taut with tension certainly should not be used as proving ground for constitutional rights regardless of their importance. As Judge Cochran pointed out, citizens in the southeastern Kentucky coalfield had "freedom from" the annoyance of self-styled investigators.

The efforts of tne NMU misfired. Harlan's conservative officials and citizenry almost to a man rigidly opposed unionization and staunchly resisted leftist and liberal-oriented establishments. Subsequently the local folks became more intolerant of future efforts to organize the miners by any agency. While the UMWA was not connected to any of these radical groups and, in fact, repudiated them, local authorities because of the violence and bloodshed emanating from the organizing campaign of March-May 1931, subscribed to the William J. Cash equation that "labor unions + strikers = Communists + atheism + social equality with the Negro." As a result, coal operators from 1932 unrelentingly repulsed all efforts by their workers to join the UMWA. Harlan became a closed society which outsiders found nearly impenetrable or penetrable only at the risk of personal injury, harassment, and intimidation.

Lack of proper leadership in the Harlan County local unions of the UMWA proved detrimental. Local leaders, over protests of the national organization, called a strike during one of the most critical periods in labor history. With industry suffering from the effects of the Great Depression, the time was not ripe for a strike on any front. Harlan miners, however, believed that they had nothing to lose, since wages were approaching a starvation level. Division within the local ranks and nominal support from the national organization assured the defeat of the Harlan campaign in 1931.

Having won the first round, Harlan County continued to be dominated by its coal barons. As A.A. Bablitz put it, the system was "benevolent feudalism" at best. With operators, law-enforcement agencies, and the courts aligned against them, the miners nurtured little hope for the future. But then in 1933, the enactment of the N.I.R.A. came to renew their hopes as the UMWA launched a brand new organizational campaign in "Bloody Harlan."

A NEW DEAL FOR THE MINERS

On August 3, 1933, two days before the primary to nominate candidates for local offices in Harlan County, Theodore Middleton, a "new deal" candidate for sheriff, accompanied by his brother Clarence, a county patrolman, knocked on the front door of Bill Farley's house in the Black Mountain precinct. Receiving no answer and finding the door locked, the brothers Middleton slipped around to one side of the house, looked through a window, and saw a group of men seated around the kitchen table stuffing ballots into a ballot box. In the group were Fred M. Jones, a Harlan attorney who was a candidate for county attorney; Jim Forester, whose son Edgar was running for county court clerk; Robert Roark, an election official; Bill Farley, another election officer; and Arthur Roark. The Middletons demanded admittance and when they entered the room, a gunfight broke out. In the wild melee, Robert Roark was fatally shot, Jones suffered a slight neck wound, and Arthur Roark was slightly injured. Jim Forester slipped out of the house and disappeared.

The Middletons confiscated the ballot box and took it to Harlan's City Hall. Upon opening the container they discovered that of 811 ballots delivered to the Black Mountain precinct, 432 had been "voted" for most of the incumbents, members of the courthouse gang: D.C. Jones, Circuit Judge; Fred M. Jones, County Attorney; W.J.R. (Willie Bob) Howard, sheriff; John Henry Blair, County Judge; W.A. (Will) Brock, Commonwealth's Attorney; L.M. Davisworth, Circuit Court Clerk; Hiram Hensley, Tax Commissioner; and Edgar Forester, County Court Clerk.

Civil war seemed imminent. The entire county was in an uproar, as several hundred people carrying high-powered rifles and pistols converged on the narrow streets of the county seat. Fortunately, quick thinking by Major L.O. Smith averted further strife and bloodshed that day. After conferring with Governor Ruby Laffoon, the mayor called out the local National Guard unit, the 149th Infantry under Captain Diamond E. Perkins to patrol the town and to supervise the upcoming primary election.[1]

I

As Harlan Countians prepared to nominate candidates for county offices, a new effort to organize Harlan County miners followed the passage of the National Industrial Recovery Act. President Franklin D. Roosevelt called the measure the most important legislation ever enacted by Congress while the *United Mine Workers Journal* hailed it as one of the greatest victories ever achieved by the workers of any country.

Before the president signed the law, UMWA District 19 President William Turnblazer announced plans to enter Harlan at once under the protection of the government. Calling the proposed Industrial Recovery Act labor's Declaration of Independence, he revealed UMWA strategy to organize miners at Pineville, Harlan, Lynch, Middlesboro, and Benham in Kentucky and various places in eastern Tennessee.

To acquaint Bell-Harlan miners with both the provisions of the NIRA and organizational plans, Turnblazer ordered the distribution of 20,000 circulars. Captioned, "A New Deal for the Miner," these brochures challenged workers to join the UMWA now that the miners had the right to organize and bargain collectively through representatives of their choice.[2]

Assigned to direct the new campaign was union veteran Lawrence (Peggy) Dwyer, who in the early 1920s moved to Pineville, the county seat of Bell County. Since Dwyer's plans included holding mass rallies and establishing local unions at every mine, it was almost inevitable that he would clash with Sheriff Blair and his legion of mine guards. Of Blair, Dwyer recalled: "He, like every other sheriff that was down there, worked in conjunction with the operators, and at the instruction of the coal operators, to prevent the union from organizing."[3]

The new union campaign kicked off in Pineville on a warm Sunday afternoon in June. As 2,500 shirt-sleeved, overalled miners stood on the shaded green lawn of the Bell County courthouse, Turnblazer discussed the new Industrial Recovery Act, plans for organizing the union, and pledged cooperation with the operators as long as they followed the law.

This initial rally met in Pineville because the union was afraid that a Harlan meeting would incur reprisals from Sheriff Blair and his army of deputy sheriffs. The union's fears seemed well-founded because Bell County officials stopped two or three cars containing several Harlan gunmen apparently on their way to disrupt the Pineville assembly. Dwyer also remembered two deputies who were present to report miners who attended to their employers.[4]

About ten days later, a second Pineville rally took place in the Bell County circuit courtroom. Assembled miners crowded the main floor, the balcony, and sat in windows as Turnblazer exclaimed, "Every mine in this field will have a union, and that includes the powerful United States Coal and Coke mines at Lynch." The district president then challenged the men to join the union as he announced a scheduled Harlan meeting for the following Sunday.[5]

Prior to that meeting, however, Harlan County Judge H.H. Howard, in a talk to the Harlan Kiwanis Club, revealed that he had refused use of the county courthouse to "Peggy McGuire" (sic) of Bell County. Despite this rebuff, Dwyer urged the men to attend the Harlan rally. The *Knoxville News-Sentinel* was critical of Judge Howard's action:

Even the constitutional right of a peaceful Sunday meeting in Harlan is refused miners, it seems...Refusals and repressions only antagonize and cause trouble. No harm could come from an orderly meeting, held in accordance with provisions of the Industrial Recovery Act sponsored by President Roosevelt and approved by Congress.[6]

Although the county courthouse was off limits, the men met in front of Harlan's City Hall. James S. Golden, a Pineville attorney who was chief UMWA counsel in the Bell-Harlan area, introduced Dwyer who delivered the principal address from the steps of Harlan's First Christian Church, across the street from City Hall. Speaking to a large throng, estimated at between five hundred and four thousand, the union organizer announced that all but two mines in Bell County and all but six in Harlan County had local unions, but that Harlan Fuel Company had attempted to intimidate men who joined the union and United States Coal and Coke had violated the NIRA by forming a company union. Attended mostly by Bell County miners, the meeting was orderly throughout.[7]

Dwyer later recalled that the union had decided to proceed with the rally because Harlan Police Chief Theodore R. Middleton promised protection. Attending the meeting, as well as several other union gatherings in 1933, Middleton flanked Dwyer as he spoke.

As a result of the Pineville and Harlan meetings, according to Dwyer, more than sixty local unions were established in the two-county area. Comprising between six thousand and seven thousand members, nearly twenty locals were organized in Bell County and more than forty in Harlan County. From his Pineville headquarters, Dwyer directed the entire operation, making numerous trips to Harlan.[8]

Turnblazer was ecstatic over the success of the new organizational campaign. In a statement released from Knoxville, he indicated that eighty-five percent of the miners in southeast Kentucky and east Tennessee had enrolled in the union during a two-week period, and forty-nine local unions in Bell and Harlan counties had requested union charters. "It is marvelous," he observed, "the way the coal miners have responded to the call to 'organize' into the union."

With "gun thugs" on the prowl throughout the county, organizers were frequently under surveillance and attack. In July, Dwyer notified Governor Ruby Laffoon that organizer Frank Elliott was "shot from ambush" and that another organizer named Williams was spirited from his home by men claiming to be mine guards. In response, the governor, in a telegram, reminded Sheriff Blair of his duty to protect citizens who exercised their rights under the laws of our country and that the state of Kentucky expected such treatment for all its citizens.

Despite the governor's admonition to Blair, Harlan gunmen continued their onslaught against UMWA organizers. In one incident four officers of the Closplint local, located on Clover Fork, were "rough-shadowed" by a dozen gunmen who, at gunpoint, seized a box containing their union charter and other supplies. On another occasion a car occupied by Dwyer and three other organizers was shot at as it passed beneath a cliff near Harlan. No injuries were reported. Several months later organizers were victims of a second assault on returning from a meeting at Liggett, a mining camp on Catron's Creek. On that occasion Gloster Reed, the driver, lost control of the car which careened down an embankment, Robert Childers was hit in the back, James Bates was shot in the hip, and Dwyer was showered with glass as bullets shattered the windshield. The organizers recalled seeing Harlan deputies Marion "Two-Gun" Allen, Ben Unthank, and Frank White at the ambush scene.

Preacher-organizer B.H. Moses, of Closplint, remembered two additional terroristic incidents: the discovery of an explosive device beneath the church building into which he and his family moved following his discharge from the mines and "a warning from Deputy Sheriff Allen Bowlin that he leave or be killed.[10]

2

In the interim, the all-important primary election took place. The Republican primary was especially significant because three incumbents, who were unsympathetic to the union during the coal mine war of 1931-32, entered as candidates. Judge Jones, who was six feet, six inches tall, decided to stand for re-election. The *Harlan Daily Enterprise*, called for his renomination by acclamation on the ground that he had fearlessly done his duty and deserved to be re-elected. Likewise Commonwealth's Attorney Brock, who, as noted above, had promised "cold chills of steel" to the "criminal element," declared for another term. Sheriff Blair, prohibited by state law from succeeding himself, announced that he would seek the county judgeship. Thirty-eight-year-old Morris Saylor, a political newcomer and a Molus merchant, divulged his intention to oppose Blair.

Brock and Jones faced formidable challengers. Daniel Boone Smith, a dapper, young, aggressive Harlan attorney who enjoyed playing practical jokes on his peers and who had served as defense counsel in some of the Evarts labor cases, made public his desire to unseat Brock. At the eleventh hour, James M. Gilbert, a Pineville lawyer, jumped into the contest against Jones. The *Knoxville News-Sentinel* called Gilbert's announcement a ray of hope because it gave citizens of the strife-torn area a chance to redeem two counties from the blazing guns of law violators and quick-triggered deputy sheriffs.

Two strong candidates vied to succeed Blair as sheriff. W.J.R. (Willie Bob) Howard, a former county judge and member of a politically prominent family, was first to announce his candidacy. Toward the end of the qualifying period, Theodore R. Middleton decided to oppose Howard. According to the local press, Middleton had made one of the most efficient police chiefs in Harlan's history and promised "NOTHING BUT SOBER AND DISCREET DEPUTIES." Proclaiming that "Harlan County needs cleaning up," Middleton called for a "new deal in law and order," and promised to crack down on "the gun thugs, the highwaymen and the lawless who have been permitted to thrive here."

Promise of a "square deal" and "an honest administration" also came from Gilbert. He invited all law-abiding citizens, both men and women, to join in an effort "to wipe from the good name of this Judicial District the stigma that has attached to it during the last six years." As part of his "square deal," Gilbert pledged fair

Sheriff T.R. Middleton, Harlan sheriff, 1933-1937: anti-union coal operator. (Courtesy: Knoxville News-Sentinel).

elections to an area long noted for its election irregularities, and a reduction in the incidence of murder in "Bloody Harlan."

During the campaign, Judge Jones accused his opponent of favoring the miners and then switching to accommodate the coal operators. On the other hand, the incumbent claimed that his administration, which sided with the operators, had always delivered a "square deal" to the miners.[11]

According to Lawrence Dwyer, the miners supported "new deal" candidates in the primary election. Dwyer later remembered an interesting conversation with Theodore Middleton during the campaign:

> He swore to his God Almighty, in my presence and in the presence of others, if we would endorse and support him he would be elected, he would give us, the miners, the same protection as the other citizens of Harlan County.

Dwyer emphasized that Middleton had given assurances that none of Blair's deputies, specifically Ben Unthank, Frank White, and George Lee, would be reappointed. The miners, he noted, had endorsed Daniel Boone Smith for Commonwealth's Attorney, Morris Saylor for County Judge, Elmon Middleton, a youthful Harlan lawyer, for County Attorney, and John B. Gross, Evarts union leader, for jailer, because they sympathized with the union.[12]

Despite Dwyer's contention, other UMWA organizers did not recall formal endorsements of any candidate in the primary election. Both William (Bill) Clontz, a preacher-organizer at Wallins Creek, and Marshall A. Musick, another preacher-organizer on Clover Fork, while remembering that the union had supported Middleton and had allowed him to speak at union meetings, could not recall whether the union had formally endorsed the Harlan police chief.[13] Likewise, another local labor leader preferred anyone who could defeat John Henry Blair. Contending that Morris Saylor had promised not to approve the reappointment of any of Blair's deputies, B.H. Moses said that he had supported him (Saylor) and allowed him to speak at his (Moses) home.[14] While the union may or may not have endorsed any of the "new deal" candidates in 1933, the miners, desiring deliverance from the Jones-Brock-Blair regime, were nevertheless willing to risk a "new deal" with Gilbert, Smith and Middleton.

Under the watchful eyes of the local National Guard unit, the primary election took place on August 5. As a precautionary measure, following the attempted Black Mountain election "steal" the governor ordered an additional one hundred National Guardsmen, under the command of Adjutant-General Henry H. Denhardt, to Harlan. Governor Laffoon dispatched the troops following an agreement between Dr. E.M. Howard, a Harlan physician and brother of W.J.R. Howard, and Theodore Middleton. The document called for representatives of both factions to inspect ballot boxes and other election paraphernalia before voting commenced at each precinct. Both sides also requested special vigilance at Tway, Yancey (two), Loyall (two), Benham and Verda (three) precincts. Arriving at 4:00 a.m. on election day, the guardsmen established headquarters at the city hall.

Despite the presence of troops in the county, violence exploded at Tway at dawn on August 5. A group of men headed by Theodore Middleton entered that camp to inspect election materials under the terms of Friday's truce. Another group supervised by

T.M. Gibson, the mine's general superintendent, was inside the company commissary. Suddenly, shooting broke out. Middleton and his men took refuge behind a concrete abutment near the commissary. For more than two hours the "Battle of Tway" raged. Five hundred shots from rifles, shotguns, and pistols filled the air. Finally, at about 6:00 a.m., National Guardsmen arrived, disarmed the combatants, and arrested Middleton and Gibson. Both were later released after agreeing not to participate in further violence.

Fortunately no one was killed although three men in Middleton's group were wounded. Theodore Middleton sustained a leg injury; Jim Cawood lost a finger when a pistol was shot from his hand; and Bob Gilbert was seriously injured when a stick of dynamite, tied to a lump of coal, exploded.[15]

One fatality marred the primary election. On Main Street in Wallins, nine miles from Harlan, Deputy Sheriff Joe Lee was gunned down after he allegedly ripped down a poster which described Harlan's big election "steal." When a bystander protested Lee's action, a quarrel and the fatal shooting ensued.

With National Guardsmen on patrol in downtown Harlan and throughout the county, election day passed without further incident. After the polls had closed, no one was allowed to enter Harlan's City Hall without a pass and no one was permitted to enter the county courthouse without first being searched for weapons. Troops patrolled the streets around the courthouse during the vote tabulation and soldiers remained in the city until all votes were counted, a full week after the election.

The "new deal" candidates swept all county offices. Daniel Boone Smith, Elmon Middleton and Theodore Middleton registered overwhelming victories. Morris Saylor defeated retiring Sheriff Blair for the county judgeship. James M. Gilbert won the circuit judge's contest outright by impressively taking the Republican and Democratic primaries in the two-county judicial circuit.

The full-fledged turn-out of the courthouse clique received favorable comment in the *Knoxville News-Sentinel*. Reflecting on the defeat of the Jones-Brock-Blair administration, it stated:

The pleasing thing about their defeat is that their winning opponents are men identified as at least sympathetic toward labor. James Gilbert...is a legal associate of attorneys who defended miners in murder trials and on charges of criminal syndicalism.

Daniel Boone Smith...was also a member of defense counsel for miners in trials at Harlan and Mt. Sterling.

Harlan County citizens have created their own New Deal.

The *Louisville Courier-Journal* criticized Harlan's electoral process after the primary election. Describing the county as "a political plague spot," it blamed Harlan's current controversy on the control of its politics by the coal interests. "Such political plague spots are exceedingly dangerous," the *Courier-Journal* concluded.[16]

The cause of the wholesale turnover in the Harlan County courthouse is not entirely clear. The vote of the miners was a factor. The repression and harassment they had suffered under the Jones-Brock-Blair combine caused them to support the "new deal" ticket. The miners apparently believed that a new coalition, which seemed sympathetic to the union, offered hope for future union campaigns. Of larger importance, probably, was the "Black Mountain Steal." A deputy tax commissioner under the "new deal" later posited that protests over the attempted vote fraud caused the overthrow of the incumbents. This attempted election thievery threw the county into turmoil, brought in the guardsmen, and apparently was the chief factor in the downfall of the courthouse gang.[17]

The November general election was anti-climactic. Harlan County Democrats, for the first time, entered a slate of candidates chosen at a county-wide convention. In the election of November 7, however, a Republican flood engulfed the virginal Democratic venture. Successfully elected were Theodore Middleton, sheriff; Morris Saylor, county judge; Elmon Middleton, county attorney; and Daniel Boone Smith, Commonwealth's Attorney. The lone Democrat to survive the Republican avalanche was Clinton C. Ball, who was elected jailer over John B. Gross by a 209-vote margin.[18] Now that the county courthouse was safely in the hands of the "new deal" officeholders, the union concentrated on the drafting of an NIRA-sponsored bituminous coal code.

3

While the Harlan political tempest was raging, efforts were under way in Washington to establish a NIRA code of fair competition for the bituminous coal industry. NIRA Administrator Hugh S. Johnson, who headed the negotiations, urged the operators to adopt a code immediately. A National Coal Association committee, directed by Charles O'Neill, came up with a "Model Code" which Johnson rejected because it lacked any provision for the actual organization of the industry.

At the outset operators generally were not receptive to a national code. Instead, they wanted local codes under their control while Johnson and the UMWA urged a single industry-wide agreement. The UMWA meanwhile staged widespread organizing campaigns that were generally successful throughout the coalfields. The lone exception was Harlan County where organizers, as discussed earlier, faced repression and violence. It was the hope of UMWA leadership that union operators, principally from the Midwest and West, would negotiate a code in conjunction with the union. The main goals were a nationwide wage scale and, of course, acceptance of the union by bituminous coal operators.[19]

Code hearings began in Washington on August 9. Representing District 19 was William Turnblazer who joined discussions with other district union chiefs, the union hierarchy, and operator representatives from around the country.[20] The talks produced more than thirty codes, most of which paralleled the "Model Code." While most of the discussions involved wage scales, the chief area of debate had to do with unfair "labor practices."[21]

A month later General Johnson, after President Roosevelt had warned that the government would intervene unless both sides reached agreement on a national code, presented his own bituminous coal code. The government's code called for a maximum work week of thirty-six hours, the abolition of child labor, the cessation of compulsory company store purchases, and the discontinuance of the use of scrip. The code also guaranteed the miners' right to a checkweighman[22] and to payment on a net-ton basis.

Despite general condemnation by the operators, the code served as a basis for a final version formulated in mid-September following a Roosevelt ultimatum to representatives of both the miners and operators. Within twenty-four hours, an agreement calling for a forty-hour week and a minimum age of 17 was reached. The President signed the code on September 18 and it went into effect on October 2.[23]

The final code, a disappointment to the miners, contained several notable provisions. It awarded employees the right to organize and to bargain collectively, stated that employees should not be compelled to trade at company stores, and except for maintenance and supervisory personnel, miners should not be forced to live in company houses. The code abolished payment in scrip, established an eight-hour day, and included the check-off of union dues. Finally, the code recognized the right of the miners to elect a checkweighman and set up a minimum wage scale.[24]

Charged with implementing the code in the southern Appalachian region, including Harlan County, was Charles B. Barnes of Cincinnati. Assisting Barnes were Van A. Bittner, Charleston, West Virginia, the UMWA delegate; and E.G. Mahan, of Knoxville, the operators' representative. But it was Barnes who faced the herculean task of enforcing the code in the tough anti-union Harlan County coalfield.[25]

The scene now shifted to Knoxville's Market Hall. There, 250 District 19 UMWA delegates, convening for the first time in ten years, unanimously ratified the code. Approval came only after Turnblazer and Dwyer had overcome objections raised by coal loaders who claimed the wage scale favored machinists and drillers.

With union acceptance assured, Turnblazer next turned to the task of dealing with Harlan's operators. In late October, fifteen coal men, led by W. Arthur Ellison, who owned extensive coal properties in the county, met with union leaders at the Farragut Hotel in Knoxville. After two days of talks, the two sides agreed on working conditions, hours, and wages. In accord with the NIRA code, a five-day week and a daily wage scale of $4.20, retroactive to October 2, went into effect. It was the first time Harlan operators and miners had been in "friendly" agreement since 1919.[26]

The historic code covered the period from October 2, 1933 to April 1, 1934. The collaboration of both the union and the operators was invaluable in the code's preparation as well as in its final acceptance by both parties. The real test was to come with its operation in Harlan County.

4

As the year 1933 drew to a close, the UMWA had experienced only limited successes in Harlan County. The reorganizational campaign under the NIRA had resulted in the establishment of local unions throughout the county. UMWA organizers nonetheless faced intimidation and harassment at the hands of Sheriff Blair's "gun thugs." They could not travel the state roads of Harlan without fear of attack and injury. The union continued to receive stiff opposition from the operators and local officials.

A county-wide election in 1933 placed officials in county offices who seemed supportive of the union. As Theodore Middleton, Daniel Boone Smith, and James M. Gilbert replaced Blair, Brock and Jones, coal miners believed that they had friends instead of foes in the county courthouse. Apparently their votes had aided in the election of the "new deal" candidates. Now they expected a "new deal" with regard to implanting the UMWA in Harlan County.

Under the NIRA, an unprecedented county-wide agreement between the union and the operators went into operation. On the surface this meant improved wages and working conditions. It did not include recognition of the union. While the operators agreed to the code, it must be emphasized that they only did so after the federal government had demanded compliance with federal law. Meanwhile, Harlan's operators continued to flout the reorganizational efforts of the UMWA. As the year 1933 ended, Harlan's coal miners wondered if, in fact, a "new deal" had actually come to the coal field.

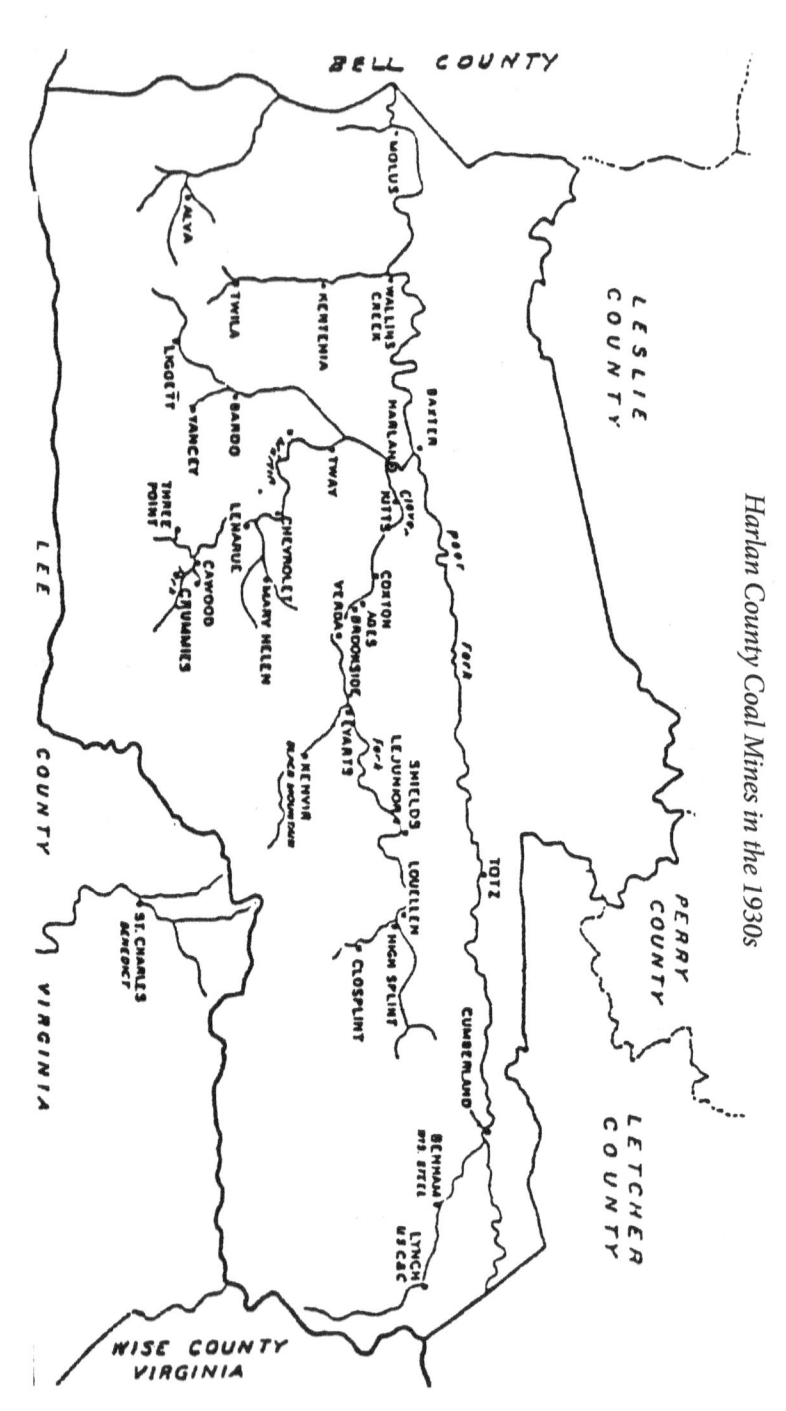

OPEN SEASON ON ORGANIZERS

Harlan miners expected a "new deal" from both the new county administration and from the coal code which went into effect in September, 1933. However, terrorists shadowed almost every step of UMWA organizers in the area. The prime target was Lawrence (Peggy) Dwyer, who narrowly escaped two assassination attempts in autumn 1933, when dynamite charges exploded at his apartment in Pineville. In the first attack, which came at 2:30 a.m. on Sunday, September 10, Dwyer miraculously escaped serious injury when an explosion went off under a stairway adjoining a nearby garage instead of under a similar stairway next to his room.

The second attempt on Dwyer's life occurred at midnight, November 25. Although cut by flying glass and bruised by falling plaster, the UMWA organizer suffered only severe shock because a heavy mattress on which he was sleeping absorbed most of the impact from that blast.[1]

Following the second assault, Kentucky Adjutant-General Henry H. Denhardt called for an end to the dynamitings and warned Bell County Sheriff James W. Ridings that if local authorities did not protect Dwyer state militia would intervene. At the same time, a Kentucky Federation of Labor official requested an investigation by Governor Laffoon into the attempted murder of the UMWA stalwart.

The first break in the case came on New Year's night in Pineville. Based on allegations made by Mrs. Mary Thomas of Harlan County, Bell County authorities arrested Larkin Baker, a union organizer and a vice president of the KF of L, Chris Patterson, a crippled coal miner from Bell County's Straight Creek section, and Richard C. Tackett, a Harlan mine guard during the administration of Sheriff John Henry Blair. Mrs. Thomas swore that the three men had received $100 for the two dynamitings and that she had observed Baker unloading a case of explosives at his home in Pineville just before the second attack on Dwyer.

I

On the morning of January 10, 1934, the examining trial for the three defendants took place before an overflow crowd which jammed the main floor and the balcony of the circuit courtroom. Steam radiators sputtered and hissed and the bluish haze of tobacco smoke hung over the room as Defense Attorney Jay H. Taylor[2] relentlessly grilled Mrs. Thomas. Unruffled, the star prosecution witness testified that the defendants had visited her house on various occasions, that Patterson once brought a bag of dynamite, some fuses, and caps which she concealed in a trunk, and that she once overheard the three men complain that although they were promised $400 for the two jobs they had only received $100. Implicating Harlan deputy and HCCOA "field man" Ben Unthank, Mrs. Thomas declared that he and the defendants always had plenty of money which she believed they had received for various bombing and burning operations. She also stated that on one occasion Patterson had remarked that "they" were going to overthrow the government, that airplanes of "theirs" would land on the White House, and that Ben Unthank had paid one of the three men $60 a month to blow up various places. Finally, Mrs. Thomas testified that she once watched while Tackett burned four camp houses at Cawood.

UMWA organizer Lawrence (Peggy) Dwyer whose Pineville apartment was dynamited twice in 1933, while he was leading the organizing campaign. (Reprinted by permission—Knoxville News-Sentinel).

When defense counsel introduced several witnesses in an effort to impeach the character of Mrs. Thomas, the prosecution's chief witness snapped: "Air ye a-tryin' these men for dynamitin' er air ye tryin' to prove my character?"

Four other witnesses testified in the examining trial. Two of them told the court that Patterson had offered $150, transportation, and explosives if they would dynamite Turnblazer's home. Both men stated that they declined the proposal. A Harlan taxi driver reported that on one occasion, as he drove Baker to Pineville, they stopped at a small Harlan store to pick up groceries and a small box. The taxi driver later peeked into the box and discovered several sticks of dynamite which Baker took when he got out of the cab in Pineville. John A. Surgener, owner of the store where Baker allegedly obtained the dynamite, denied selling the explosives.[3]

At the conclusion of the hearing, the court placed the three defendants under a $5,000 peace bond as well as a $5,000 bond for the dynamiting charges.[4] In March a thorough probe into the attacks on Dwyer led to grand jury indictments against Baker and

Patterson, ordered held without bond. Also indicted were Tackett, Unthank, John Surgener, and Chester Surgener.[5]

With the second floor courtroom of the Bell County courthouse again providing the setting, the sensational trial of Chris Patterson began on Saturday, March 10. Tall, thin, stern-visaged Circuit Judge Gilbert presided while some of the southeastern Kentucky's best legal minds participated in the case. Commonwealth counsel included: Daniel Boone Smith, newly elected Commonwealth's Attorney; fiery Bell County attorney Walter B. Smith, assisted by Pineville's James S. Golden, Ben B. Golden, and D.M. Bingham, and W.R. Lee and W.R. Lay of Barbourville. The defense was represented by N.R. Patterson and Jay H. Taylor of Pineville, Hiram H. Owens of Barbourville, J. S. Forester of Harlan, and R. L. Pope.

The courtroom was filled to capacity throughout the four-day trial. More than forty witnesses appeared for the Commonwealth while the defense produced over twenty witnesses. For the prosecution Mrs. Thomas basically stuck to the story she had given three months earlier during the examining trial. She also testified that Tackett and Patterson had explosives several days before the second attack on Dwyer and that Patterson had remarked that the explosion had "just addled" the organizer. Another witness, Babe Hensley, testified that Patterson had offered him and a companion $150 to "blow up Bill Turnblazer." Defense witnesses countered that both Mrs. Thomas and Patterson had dubious reputations. Patterson completely refuted all the state's evidence when he told the jury that he was sick in bed at the time of the attack, a contention supported by a Harlan physician. Both Baker and Tackett denied involvement in the two dynamitings of Dwyer's apartment.

In closing arguments, defense attorneys R.L. Pope and Hiram H. Owens called for a verdict of acquittal. They contended that the prosecution had failed to prove the "actual guilt" of any of the defendants. Commonwealth's Attorney Smith, in making an impassioned plea for the restoration of law and order to the area, likened the present case to a war between civilization and barbarism.

With the completion of final arguments, the Knox County jury received the case at 11:10 a.m. on Tuesday, March 13. After deliberating throughout the night, they found Patterson guilty. The defendant sat silently throughout the reading of the verdict. Then he rose, faced the judge, and received a ten-year prison sentence.[6] None of the remaining cases went to trial. In separate motions filed in May, 1935 by Commonwealth's Attorney Smith, and in November, 1936 by .Commonwealth's Attorney Pro-Tern Cleon K. Calvert. the court dropped all charges against the defendants.[7]

Subsequent information linked Harlan's chief thug, Ben Unthank, to the two Dwyer dynamitings. Recalling that Ben Unthank had hired him for $75 a month to keep Dwyer and other organizers under surveillance, Baker made a sketch of Dwyer's apartment and its environs a few days before the second bombing and while he was in jail, Harvey H. Fuson, a Harlan attorney, confided that Harlan coal operators would protect him and obtain his release. After Baker got out of jail, Unthank suggested that Dwyer be "done away with." When he reneged, Unthank enlisted a Middlesboro man for the assignment, but the plan aborted when the unidentified person demanded payment in advance. At that point, Baker attempted to sever his relationship with Unthank, only to be reminded that "it would be a very easy matter for him (Unthank) to lay the dynamiting on to me if he seen fit to." So " I could not get away from him."

Patterson recollected that Unthank had hired him for $75 a month during the summer and autumn of 1933 and that he had received an additional $100 following the November dynamiting. On the attempted murder of Dwyer, Patterson recalled sending Tackett down there (to Pineville) to blow up Dwyer's house on an order from Ben Unthank who furnished the explosives.

Tackett remembered that Ben Unthank had employed him for about $100 a month in 1933 and 1934. On the night of the November attack on Dwyer, Baker, Tackett, Patterson and Unthank had traveled to Pineville together. After they had "floated around beer rooms" until nearly midnight, the men, accompanied by county attorney Smith, attended a mysterious midnight parley at an unidentified Pineville residence. Told to remain outside, Tackett did not know what was discussed and left after learning that Unthank was "sore" at him. While neither admitting nor denying participation in the scheme, Tackett received $30 from Unthank "to shut up and not talk."[8]

From the evidence, the chief planner of the assaults on Dwyer was Ben Unthank. He singled out Baker, Tackett and Patterson to carry out the plot. All three men took part in the attacks. One, Chris Patterson, became the scapegoat.

While Bell County authorities were attempting to bring Dwyer's assailants to justice, Harlan's "new deal" administration prepared to take control of the county courthouse. Before assuming his duties. Circuit Judge Gilbert told a large crowd of union miners at Cumberland that "life is too cheap in Harlan and Bell Counties," that he would not tolerate outlawry and "pistol-toting," and only "sober, discreet, sensible law-abiding citizens" should be appointed peace officers. The *Harlan Daily Enterprise* commended the new judge, urged the cooperation of the people, and challenged law-abiding citizens to support Gilbert in his efforts to make the area a "safer and better place in which to live."

In late November Judge Gilbert took office. Putting his preachments into practice, he charged the November grand jury to investigate lawlessness, "pistol-toting," officers who carried pistols while off-duty, roadhouses, and lie swearers. Declaring that too many Harlan County men wanted to be officers so that they could carry guns, he promised to stop the wholesale murder in his district.[9]

Supportive of the new judge was Commonwealth's Attorney Smith who disclaimed political debts and political ties with any person or organization. He pledged to prosecute aggressively "gun toters," murderers, and lie swearers in an all-out effort to clean up Harlan County. Less than a month after entering office, Smith sent a letter to hundreds of persons and to coal companies throughout the county. Dealing principally with "pistol-toting," the letter suggested that (1) companies or corporations discharge immediately any employee who illegally carried pistols; (2) companies or corporations agree not to employ persons discharged for violation of the pistol law; and (3) companies or corporations acquiesce in the prosecution and conviction of persons illegally carrying pistols.[10]

At least three Harlan coal operators reacted favorably. J.C. Stras, president of the Kentucky Cardinal Coal Corporation, offered his cooperation and commended Harlan officials for their stand against lawlessness. Denver B. Cornett, president of the Cornett-Lewis Coal Company, called Smith's proposal exceptional and urged Bob Lawson, his local mine manager, to cooperate. Pearl Bassham, vice president of Harlan-Wallins Coal Corporation, one of the county's largest, wrote that Smith's idea was "an excellent suggestion" which would receive his full support.[11]

The election of Theodore R. Middleton as sheriff gave hope to the miners that the reign of Blair's "gun thugs had passed." The new sheriff's first days in office nonetheless precipitated mixed emotions. First, Middleton demanded bonds of $5,000 from every deputy sheriff he appointed and warned each one that the law must be enforced. "I'll have no deputy of mine wearing two guns, " he ordered. "If an officer can't keep order with one gun, he isn't much of an officer."[12]

Still, within forty-eight hours after taking office Middleton had appointed more than seventy deputies, including Merle Middleton, a cousin, Clarence Middleton, a brother, and several other kinsmen. Reappointed were several deputies who had served under Sheriff Blair, notably Lee Fleenor, Frank White, and George Lee. Both William Turnblazer and Lawrence (Peggy) Dwyer expressed dissatisfaction with the number and character of Middleton's deputy sheriff appointments. Turnblazer noted that on March 6, 1935, there were 244 deputy sheriffs, deputy constables, and county patrolmen in the county, while Dwyer charged that Middleton violated a campaign promise by reappointing Lee, White and Unthank. Reminded of his pledge, Middleton told Dwyer that he had renominated some of Blair's lawmen because of certain campaign obligations.[13]

That the union was not apt to receive support from Sheriff Middleton is revealed by information excerpted from the Sheriff's Bond Book No. 4 for the years 1934-1937. Kentucky sheriffs had to fulfill two performance bonds of $70,000 each; one to insure collection of state revenues, the other to guarantee collection of county taxes. During the period from 1934 to 1937, these leading operators signed one or more of the sheriff's official bonds: Pearl Bassham, Harlan-Wallins Coal Corporation; A.F. Whitfield, Jr., Clover Fork Coal Corporation; S.J. Dickenson, Mary Helen Coal Corporation; Bryan W. Whitfield, Harlan Collieries Company;

R.C. Tway, R.C. Tway Coal Company; and Elmer D. Hall, Three Point Coal Corporation. Many of the foregoing also had signed Blair's bonds. Alas, from the beginning Sheriff Middleton, like Sheriff Blair, had established close ties with Harlan's coal operators.

Several leading Harlan physicians and businessmen also signed the sheriff's bonds. The physicians included W.E. Riley and W.P. Cawood as well as E.M. Howard who opposed Middleton's nomination in 1933. Prominent businessmen included: James S. Greene, coal operator and businessman; W.W. Lewis, county treasurer and banker; J. Ray Rice, realtor; Andy Saylor, father of the new county judge; Grant Saylor, the judge's brother; C.B. Cawood, banker; J.B. Carter, attorney; and J.M. Alverson, editor of the *Harlan Daily Enterprise*.[14]

County Judge Morris Saylor followed the leadership of the circuit court in declaring war on the county's criminals. Saylor's warning to "gun toters" that once apprehended they could expect little mercy in his court complemented the efforts of other county officials in "breaking up this wave of crime."[15] Despite this forceful declaration, the new county judge, during his first year in office, gave 244 residents a license to carry guns by approving their appointments as peace officers. The bright hope that the union and its organizers nourished for the termination of "gun thug" rule quickly dimmed as an army of "thugs" swarmed over the county during the years 1934 to 1937. One veteran miner of more than forty years experience in the pits of Harlan later recalled that it was not safe to speak for the union nor admit to union membership during that era.[16]

The new county attorney was young Elmon Middleton, a cousin of the sheriff. From the outset, he exhibited courage by launching an all-out war on crime. Middleton first issued an edict that slot machines would have to go. Then he initiated legal actions against moonshiners and bootleggers, operators of bawdy houses, prostitutes, and vagrants.[17] Throughout his shortened term of office, Elmon Middleton also championed the causes of the miners. One of the most harassed union organizers in the county later reflected that Middleton was the union's friend.[18]

The new county administration responded to the war on crime in several ways. The sheriff's office raided "jenny barns"[19] and arrested men and women on charges of prostitution, "moonshining," and dope-peddling. Commenting on this activity near the end of January, Sheriff Middleton vowed the continuation of the "clean-up campaign" until it reached a successful conclusion. The *Harlan Daily Enterprise* commended the new sheriff for "waging a relentless war against law violators."[20]

When the first term of criminal court opened on Monday, March 19, Judge Gilbert delivered a sweeping charge to the grand jury. Demanding a thorough investigation of lawlessness, the judge called for indictments of "gun-toters," murderers, drunk drivers, operators of bawdy houses, rapists, and false swearers.

The grand jury responded to its charge with vigor. In a nine-day session ending on March 28, it returned 230 indictments, about thirty of which were for murder. In the term that followed, the court tried seven murder cases resulting in three life sentences, two twenty-one year terms, one acquittal, and one mistrial.[21] Judge Gilbert termed the session a successful beginning toward reducing crime in "Bloody Harlan."

Following additional bloodletting in the spring. and summer of 1934, Judge Gilbert called several special sessions of court. One session considered the case of Deputy Sheriff Lee Fleenor who had gunned down Deputy Sheriff Bige Gross in the courthouse hallway outside the county judge's office. According to reports, bad feelings existed between the two lawmen because Gross earlier had killed Fleenor's half-brother. Eyewitnesses reported that Fleenor opened fire as Gross entered the courthouse. He shot five times; three bullets found their mark in Gross's body. As onlookers fled outside, Sheriff Middleton ran from his office, grabbed Fleenor, and placed him under arrest. Judge Gilbert ordered a special grand jury to investigate the slaying of Gross. The grand jury indicted Fleenor, the alleged killer in the "soup kitchen murders," and one of Harlan's most feared lawmen. Charged with willful murder, Gilbert denied the deputy bond.

The trial of Fleenor got underway on Wednesday, May 2, before a Madison County jury. Representing the Harlan lawman were several leading Harlan attorneys, notably Fred M. Jones, W.A. (Will) Brock and J.S. Forester. W.R. Lay of Barbourville and R.L.

Pope were chief prosecutors. The Commonwealth called more than thirty witnesses in an effort to prove that Fleenor killed Gross before the latter had a chance to remove his revolver from its holster. Testimony showed that Fleenor was "laying" for Gross because of past troubles between the two men. Fleenor's defense, on the other hand, rested on two points: (1) that he shot the deceased only after Gross went for his gun; (2) that Gross had threatened him repeatedly.

Following two days of testimony, the Madison County jury found Fleenor guilty of manslaughter. Judge Gilbert sentenced the Harlan deputy to fifteen years in the Kentucky state penitentiary. For the first time under Harlan's "new deal" a deputy had gone to prison for a crime. The *Knoxville News-Sentinel* reflected that Fleenor had received a "light sentence" but that "Harlan County has begun to know and respect the majesty and power of law and order."[22]

2

Meanwhile, strong anti-union opposition from Harlan law enforcement officials stymied reorganizational efforts. In May 1934, Sheriff Middleton warned that interference with industrial operations would not be tolerated. Declaring that men had the right to work with the protection of the law, the sheriff forewarned that his office would not allow banding and confederating, coercion, intimidation by mob assembly, or mass demonstrations at mine operations. Middleton cautioned that persons engaging in such activities would be arrested.

To back up his admonition, Middleton ordered the arrest of UMWA organizer Marshall A. Musick on a charge of disturbing the peace by uttering threatening statements. Lean and of small stature, Musick was the father of several children. A devout union man who kept a framed picture of John L. Lewis hanging on his bedroom wall, Musick was one of the most harassed organizers in Harlan County.

Musick described his arrest to a reporter: As he was preparing to attend a funeral, armed gunmen came to his home, called him "a felonious character," arrested him, and lodged him in the county

OPEN SEASON ON ORGANIZERS

The Lynch Company town of anti-union United States Coal and Coke Company in the 1930's. (University of Kentucky Photo Archives).

jail. The gunmen did not produce a warrant, the court never called the case, and a few hours later Musick was a free man.[23]

An apparent hotbed of resistance to union organizers during 1934 was the unincorporated town of Lynch which had a population of about 10,000. There in March, the UMWA established a local union. At one union meeting members charged that the company had forcibly ejected union members from the bathhouse, that company agents had "rough shadowed" union members, and that the local union could not post notices of its meetings. Manhandled while distributing union literature was James Westmoreland, president of the local union.

The Lynch local union also accused the company of intimidation, diffidence over loss of jobs, and with threats of evictions without due process of the law. It blamed the company for endeavoring to convince black miners that they would lose their jobs to white men if Lynch miners joined the union.[24]

The United Coal and Coke Company which operated the mines at Lynch was staunchly anti-union. To enforce its policy, the company named Captain Joseph R. Menefee, formerly an industrial policeman at the H.C. Frick Company in Pittsburgh, to head its private police force.[25] So that the Lynch officers, as well as industrial policemen from other United States Steel subsidiaries, would receive expert training, the company ran a school for its policemen near Washington. Conducted by a H.C. Frick official, the officers received instruction in every phase of policemanship, including the handling of workers in labor disturbances. The school's main purpose was to prevent the unionization of Lynch and all other United States Steel employees during the 1930's.

The size of the company police force at Lynch remained constant at nine to ten officers, except at times of increased UMWA activity. In 1934 the company added three officers and during the first quarter of 1935 the force ballooned to twenty. Of the seven additions, six were Kentucky residents and one was a former Frick guard from Pennsylvanis. It was Captain Menefee's view that there would have been no trouble at Lynch had the UMWA not entered the camp. When union activity diminished, the company cut back its police force.

To equip its policemen, United States Coal and Coke retained a sizeable arsenal which included the following weapons and ammunition:

Weapons:	Shotguns	4
	Revolvers	25
	Winchester rifles, 30-30's	42
	Gas guns	8
Ammunition:	Tear gas shells	120
	Special cartridges, 38's, rds	150
	30-30 Calibre cartridges, rds	400
	12-guage shotgun shells, rds	125
	Jumbo tear gas grenades	48
	Tear gas masks	8[26]

Lynch, then, was off limits to the union until the late 1930's.

In various ways gun thugs harassed miners and organizers throughout 1934. One Sunday in May, the Reverend Carl E. Vogel, pastor of the Cornett Memorial Methodist Church in Harlan, saw several heavily armed deputies turn back a crowd of miners who were on their way to a union meeting at Shields. That evening Vogel, from his pulpit, lashed out at the deputies. The next day he reminded Sheriff Middleton about his campaign pledges of free speech and peaceable assembly, and criticized the type of deputies he had appointed. Middleton rejoined that Vogel did not understand the entire situation.

The Harlan clergyman also confronted Judge Saylor, George S. Ward, Judge Gilbert, and Commonwealth's Attorney Smith about the Shields incident. Gilbert restated his determination to use the full power of his office to halt such incidents while Smith indicated that he was waiting for more information about the episode. The truth is that the chief prosecutor was accepting retainers from several coal companies and Harlan grand juries were staffed by persons favorable to coal operators. Indictments against deputy sheriffs, or "thugs," were highly unlikely.

Vogel also discussed the Shields incident with county attorney Elmon Middleton. Deploring the affair, Middleton said that he was a "marked" man who probably would not live to see conditions cleaned up. As the only county official who consistently opposed crime and anti-union activities, the county attorney roundly criticized the lack of indictments against Harlan deputy sheriffs. Middleton claimed that although the grand jury heard evidence from dozens of miners, it failed to charge a single lawman in connection with the Shields affair.[27]

Among UMWA organizers allegedly terrorized by Harlan deputies were William (Bill) Clontz, Marshall A. Musick, and James Westmoreland. Clontz, a former employee of Creech Coal Company who lived at Wallins Creek, was a union field representative who had established four local unions. Of average height and stature, Clontz was an emotional union stalwart. Like Musick, he was constantly hounded by Harlan deputies.

One of Clontz's functions consisted of handling mine grievances with the mine manager. If he could not resolve the dispute, Clontz consulted Turnblazer who appealed to the district arbitration board. It seems that Clontz had the Creech operators before the board frequently for some mining infraction. One night while attending an arbitration session in Knoxville, night-riders shot into his home with high-powered rifles. One bullet passed through the headboard of the bed where his son was sleeping. Upon arriving home and learning of the assault, Clontz called Sheriff Middleton. The sheriff advised him to leave the county. Clontz then contacted Judge Gilbert. Gilbert confessed, "My hands are tied, and yours is, too. I cannot get my court waited on." Recalling these events thirty years later Clontz remarked, "it makes chills go all over me sometimes when I get to thinking about it." [29]

Harlan's gun "thugs" repeatedly harassed Musick and Westmoreland. Corroborating Vogel's testimony regarding the highway episode at Shields, Musick counted seventeen deputies who took part in the attack. George Lee, he said, jabbed him in the hip with either a submachine gun or an automatic rifle while Deputy Sheriff Merle Middleton kicked him so hard that walking without assistance was difficult. Because deputies constantly "shadowed" him, Musick often resorted to a disguise of artificial teeth and a blackened face. In 1934 he successfully established a local union at the Cornett-Lewis mine. When that company grew hostile and began to discriminate against the union and its officials, the local ceased to function.[30]

James Westmoreland was most active at the Lynch camp where he worked as a coal loader. In July, 1933 he set up a local union which the company refused to recognize. Like Musick, Westmoreland was constantly watched by Ben Unthank, George Lee, and Frank White. On one occasion, at the request of Turnblazer, he went to the Cornett-Lewis Camp to arbitrate three cases. While there, general manager R.E. Lawson, who earlier had refused to appear before the arbitration board, agreed to the check-off[31] if the men asked for it individually. On another occasion, Lawson called out his office window and told Westmoreland to get off company property before deputies threw him off.[32]

During the final, two months of 1934, several events set the stage for the first investigation into Harlan County industrial strife since the Hays-Bablitz inquiry of 1931. The first happening was an Armistice Day rally scheduled for Harlan on Sunday, November 11. After receiving reports that an attempt would be made to disrupt the meeting, Governor Laffoon authorized Adjutant-General Henry H. Denhardt to send Brigadier-General Ellerbee W. Carter and three aides to Harlan as observers. While the National Guard officials watched, approximately four thousand unionists, in an atmosphere marked by tension and punctuated by snow flurries, paraded through downtown Harlan in commemoration of those miners who had died in the World War. After winding through Harlan's narrow streets, the miners gathered at the southern edge of town to hear addresses by Turnblazer, Van A. Bittner, a personal representative of John L. Lewis, John Saxton, District 28 president, and Sam Caddy, District 30 president. Each urged organization of the Harlan field and affiliation with the UMWA. The speakers also called upon the miners to support a seven hour day and a five day week, and inferred that several Harlan operators were not abiding by the NRA code.[33] Following the speaking, the chilled miners quickly withdrew from the town and the day passed without incident.

Following the rally, Dwyer and Bell County Sheriff James W. Ridings consulted with Sheriff Middleton about the union's planned organizational campaign. Dwyer told the sheriff that fifteen UMWA organizers would register at Harlan hotels to organize the county. Sheriff Middleton replied that this would cause bloodshed. Dwyer then offered to send only three "unknown" organizers who would not hold mass rallies if the sheriff offered protection and severed his ties with the coal operators. The sheriff considered this proposition for several days, then placed himself more squarely on the side of the operators by rejecting it.

With efforts toward a truce at an impasse, the UMWA proceeded with its plans. In November International Representative A.T. Pace of Middlesboro and Carl Williams, a field representative of Pineville, entered Harlan County to head up the campaign. About six miles inside the county line, they noticed that Ben Unthank was trailing their car, but they continued to Harlan and registered at the New Harlan Hotel. Following them into the lobby, Unthank checked their names on the hotel register. Ben Lewallen, proprietor, upon learning the nature of their business, told the men that he could not furnish rooms because of fear that the hotel might be blown up. Meanwhile, Pace observed that gun "thugs" swarmed the lobby and the street outside. While standing in the hotel lobby, Williams was knocked down, pummeled with a pistol, and escorted to the county jail by Deputy George Lee. Present and probably watching the assault were Deputies Frank White, Ben Unthank, and Bill Brock, each armed with two pistols. Williams remained in jail until Monday morning, while Pace, assisted by the hotel elevator operator fled Harlan during the night. Williams later obtained a warrant for Lee and attempted to have him indicted, as Judge Gilbert had suggested, only to have the grand jury foreman slam the door in his face.[34]

The attack on Carl Williams prompted the national UMWA headquarters to request protection for its organizers from Governor Laffoon. Since the organizers were guests at the hotel and "without provocation were attacked by a number of alleged deputy sheriffs and mine guards,"[35] the union urged the governor to take steps to halt such assaults. That union plea did not receive any response from Governor Laffoon.

Later, on December 8, Harlan faced a graver crisis. Accompanied by about ten organizers in a three-car caravan, Turnblazer headed to Harlan to initiate the organizational drive. As the union delegation entered the county, they saw a car parked directly on the highway with Ben Unthank and others standing beside it. When the deputies attempted to intercept them, the unionists increased their speed and raced into Harlan, where they signed in at the Lewallen Hotel. Soon fifty armed deputies infested the hotel. An explosion seemed imminent. Turnblazer, Mayor Smith, and County Attorney Middleton went into a hurried conference and, while eavesdroppers stood at the door and firecrackers exploded in the hallways, decided to ask for state protection. From the time of their arrival, Turnblazer and his lieutenants were confined to their quarters by the surly attitude of deputy sheriffs.[36]

With civil disturbance a real threat, Adjutant-General Denhardt, after conferring with Governor Laffoon, called out the local National Guard Unit, under the command of Captain Perkins, to protect the organizers. Called to duty at 8:30 p.m. by the city fire alarm, the presence of the guard threw the town into an uproar.

Following a visit to Turnblazer's quarters, Captain Perkins stationed a patrol in the fourth floor hallway of the hotel. At 10:00 a.m. the next morning, the organizers left Harlan under military escort. Deputies followed one group to the Letcher County line and pursued another group to the Bell County line. Organizer Jim Bates escaped in a coffin transported by a hearse.[37]

The "hemming in" of the Turnblazer delegation brought General Denhardt and General Carter to Harlan to investigate. A conference of county officials and coal operators met at the Lewallen Hotel where General Denhardt chided the Harlan group to maintain law and order, or else face military rule. He criticized Sheriff Middleton's deputies who included "too many killers." The sheriff responded that "some of them have gotten into trouble," but most were high class men who had reduced the crime rate of Harlan County almost fifty percent. Strangely, it was Middleton's view that Harlan would be "much more peaceful if we can keep radical organizers, agitators, and 'Reds' out of the county."

The operators backed the sheriff by calling for the barring of outside organizers. R.W. Creech, president of Creech Coal Company, told Denhardt that the miners simply did not want to organize and that harassment by radicals had caused many to desert the UMWA. Denhardt, on the other hand, responded that the right of free speech, free press, and free assembly must be upheld.

Circuit Judge Gilbert and county attorney Middleton conferred privately with state officials. The county attorney, whose life had been threatened, expressed the opinion that it was better for radical agitators to stay out of Harlan. Gilbert, who likewise reported threats on his life, reiterated that seventy-five percent of the deputies were causing all the trouble, and that he would clean up the district if his health remained good.[38]

The Harlan conference ended in a deadlock because the operators contended that the source of the trouble was outside agitators while the union blamed the deputies. It must be noted that in southeastern Kentucky any person who came into the area from afar was an "outside agitator." Bearing this stigma were Turnblazer, from Tennessee, and other organizers from more distant states such as Iowa and Illinois. It needs to be emphasized, moreover, that eighteen of the sheriff's "high class men" had been charged recently with the following crimes: false swearing, detaining a female, gaming, manslaughter, malicious striking and wounding, mayhem, illegal possession of liquor, and assault and battery.[39] While eighteen represented only a fraction of the 191 deputies in Harlan, it was apparent that some housecleaning was in order.

Earlier in the year a special Harlan grand jury had recommended dismissal of several deputy sheriffs, including Henry C. Stepp, Milt Middleton, Charlie Middleton, Logan Middleton, Merle Middleton, Bill Lewis, Tom Trent, and Palmer Cox. The grand jury reasoned that since each of these men was under one or more indictments for felonies, they were no longer fit law enforcement officers.

Of the eight deputies mentioned above, four were relatives of the sheriff. Merle Middleton had been indicted six times, from March 22, 1934 to May 5, 1934 for various crimes, including false swearing, malicious striking and wounding, banding and confederating, assault and battery, and murder.[40] While his record was typical of the others cited, Sheriff Middleton, despite the recommendation of the grand jury, refused to dismiss any of the men

In a report to Governor Laffoon on the Harlan situation. General Denhardt blamed Harlan deputies for all the trouble and recommended that Middleton either be ordered to "clean up" his staff or be removed from office. Laffoon, however, was reluctant to intervene until local authorities had reasonable time to remedy conditions.[41]

Although forced to abandon Harlan County at the end of 1934, UMWA officials were determined to organize its mines. For example, Lawrence Dwyer told an audience of miners in Pineville: "Harlan County will be organized. It may not be by me or by Bill Turnblazer" but we intend "to take the union to Harlan County and we are going to do it."

Turnblazer echoed Dwyer's proclamation: "We are not quitting," he said, as he announced that the union would continue to seek state and federal aid in its attempts to organize the coal miners.[42]

In Frankfort on December 11, Congressman A.J. May of Kentucky's Seventh District, union leaders and state officials conferred with Governor Laffoon about Harlan conditions. Turnblazer, reiterating his intention to organize the county, stated the union's desire to meet without interference, let both sides present their cases, and permit the miners to make their own decisions. Laffoon, restating his belief that local authorities should maintain law and order, vowed to do all in his power to see that order was preserved and the rights of everyone protected. Congressman May, re-elected in November, 1933 on a "support Roosevelt" platform, recommended a congressional probe of strife-torn Harlan unless violence ceased.[43]

In support of this strong determination of UMWA leaders, a convention of miners gathered at the Fayette County courthouse in Lexington. In calling this assembly, Sam Caddy said, "the purpose...is not incendiary. it is simply being called to insure the right of mine organizers to work in Harlan County." Attended by 534 registered delegates of Districts 19 and 30 and by about one hundred visitors, the convention featured addresses by Caddy, Turnblazer, and Congressman May. Described as a champion of labor. May restated his intentions to call for a congressional investigation of Harlan conditions.[44]

Although Caddy had called the meeting non-incendiary, he and Turnblazer delivered incendiary speeches. Offering to supply the governor with a division of coal miners with military training that would march into Harlan County and place the American flag over the sheriff's office, Caddy shouted, "The governor says we have a right to go in there and, by Heaven, we're going." Harlan operators, said he, established their own private fiefdom and elections there are a farce because the sheriff and certain operators had entered into a conspiracy for mutual gain. "Something is going to be done," Caddy boomed, for "we are going into Harlan County and remove T.R. Middleton and his cut-throats and organize the miners 100 percent. We'll show them a battle." Turnblazer said that while he had recently stopped a mass march of miners to rescue "hemmed-in" organizers, "I will not stop them any more. If I had not prevented them when I did, the Cumberland River would have run red with blood. I wash my hands of anything that may happen if another outbreak occurs." Several other speakers charged that Sheriff Middleton had "decorated criminals with badges."[45]

In other actions, the convention called for a congressional inquiry in Harlan and for continuance of NRA. It voted $25,000 to support the Harlan campaign, and commended Laffoon on his stand for law and order in the county. The union mapped organizational plans, challenged the miners to support pro-labor candidates, and urged a boycott of industries which bought coal from anti-union Harlan operators. "We must hit the operators where it hurts most—in the pocketbook," exclaimed Turnblazer as he revealed that the union had succeeded in getting several large businesses to cancel coal orders with anti-union operators.[46]

A banquet at Lexington's Phoenix Hotel climaxed the day-long activities. In attendance were A.T. Pace, toast-master, Congressman May, KF of L Secretary Campbell, and several county officials from eastern Kentucky. Conspicuous by their absence were officials from Harlan who, only a year earlier, had pledged friendship to labor and the union.[47]

Thus, the stage was set for all-out warfare in Harlan. The union had expressed determination to organize the county while Harlan operators and officials had resolved to bar organizers and hold the miners in check through the use of gunmen masquerading as deputy sheriffs. But if the union countered with its own gunmen, it could not expect to match the power of the coal barons.[48]

A REIGN OF TERROR

On Saturday, February 9, 1935, Harlan Sheriff Theodore Middleton and about ten of his deputies, later called the "Modern Nabobs of Kentucky,[1]" burst into the union hall at Cumberland, Kentucky. Brandishing revolvers, Middleton and Deputies George Lee, Frank White, and John P. Mickey ordered twenty-five union organizers to raise their hands. After searching the union men, the lawmen told Tom White, an International UMWA board member from Colfax, Iowa, to "get the hell out of here." Securing a taxi, White started for Whitesburg, only to be chased by deputies who seized and returned him to Cumberland where he was thrust into an undersized "sardine" jail cell with his fellow organizers. The arresting officers did not show warrants and did not formally charge the union men.[2]

Detained for approximately three hours in the Cumberland jail later referred to as the "Black Hole of Calcutta," officers escorted the organizers to the Harlan County jail. After spending a weekend in jail for creating a "public nuisance," the organizers had their day in court before Judge Saylor. In an uneventful hearing, County Attorney Elmon Middleton motioned to dismiss the case and release the defendants.³

The "public nuisance" arrests were an outgrowth of efforts to organize the "captive mines" of International Harvester at Benham and United States Coal and Coke at Lynch. According to Cumberland Police Chief Talton Hall, local businessmen had complained that the organizers were ruining business by annoying Benham and Lynch miners who came to town to shop. On the other hand, since the Benham and Lynch camps were off-limits to organizers, workers were afraid of reprisals from the company if observed talking to UMWA leaders in Cumberland. Despite this diversity of opinion, the wholesale arrests at Cumberland was the catalyst which finally moved Governor Laffoon to intervene in the Harlan conflict.

I

Earlier, as a new year began, the Bituminous Coal Labor Board began an inquest into Harlan conditions at Pineville. Charles B. Barnes chaired the session, assisted by Van A. Bittner, for the union, and E.G. Mahan, for the operators. The hearing was a result of UMWA allegations that several coal companies had refused to comply with the decisions of the Harlan County arbitration board by violating the hours provision of the NRA code and intimidating and discharging miners. While the board summoned officials from eleven Harlan coal corporations, only representatives from Creech Coal Company showed up.

The board heard charges against the following coal concerns: Kentucky King, Harlan-Wallins, Green-Silvers, and Creech. Kentucky King and Creech had reportedly discharged and then refused to reinstate men for union activities. One miner accused Harlan-Wallins of working its employees twelve hours a day at its Verda operation. Two Green-Silvers employees charged that they worked more than the maximum hours, without overtime pay, that the company paid only forty-six cents a ton for mined coal instead of the prescribed forty-nine cents a ton, and that the company had refused a checkweighman.⁴

The highlight of the Pineville sessions, however, was a continuous recital of charges against Sheriff Theodore R. Middleton and his alleged gang of "thugs." William Clontz, Marshall A. Musick, and A.T. Pace reconstructed the terrorism of the summer and autumn of 1934.[5] Following this testimony, Chairman Barnes rose majestically from his chair, surveyed his audience, and announced dramatically, "If I know there is a man in this house with a gun I am going to take it off of him." After sitting mutely for a moment, the stunned gathering broke into spontaneous cheering.[6]

Following the Barnes' ultimatum, Van A. Bittner told the gathering: "If the Governor of Kentucky fails to remove Theodore Middleton as Sheriff of Harlan County then the matter will be placed before the President of the United States." If conditions such as those found in Harlan County existed on a large scale, he said, "the United States would be destroyed in twenty-four hours." Bittner ended by calling Harlan County "a greater menace to the United States than was Germany during the World War," and by describing Middleton as a "greater enemy of the United States than was the Kaiser of Germany."[7]

When the Pineville hearing ended, the union pressed Laffoon for immediate action on the charges against Middleton. Once again, the governor demurred while the local press audaciously called Middleton "one of the best sheriffs Harlan County ever had" and "one of the outstanding high peace officers in Kentucky."[8]

2

Although Governor Laffoon momentarily dragged his feet over intervention into Harlan's labor troubles, he dramatically altered his course following the fiasco at Cumberland on February 9. Three days later he appointed a special commission chaired by General Denhardt to investigate the underlying causes of Harlan's industrial turbulence. Laffoon pointed out that the bitter controversy between the UMWA and the coal operators had caused a long period of unrest and if it was not settled, additional loss of life and destruction of property would occur. He instructed the commission to conduct a thorough investigation and write a report with recommendations to resolve the conflict.[9]

The UMWA submitted to the Denhardt Commission a list of fifteen grievances against Harlan coal operators and peace officers: denial of free speech and assembly, the right to elect a checkweighman, assaults upon UMWA organizers, dynamiting the houses of UMWA miners and representatives, shooting into the houses of UMWA miners and organizers, kidnapping and assaulting miners, discharging and evicting miners for exercising their rights under the coal code, "hemming-in" organizers at hotels, threatening UMWA counsel on several occasions, barring organizers at the county line, commissioning more than three hundred men to carry arms in Harlan County, and failing to bring alleged killers to justice. In addition to these grievances, the UMWA asked the committee to investigate the business connections the sheriff and the county judge had with the Harlan-Wallins Coal Corporation; dishonest elections; arsenals kept by several coal companies; the refusal of the county administration to protect UMWA personnel; and the failure of certain coal operators to comply with decisions of the BCLB."[10]

The *Harlan Daily Enterprise* denounced Laffoon's appointment of the Denhardt Commission:

> Like a clap of thunder over a peaceful valley comes the announcement that the Governor foresees dire results in Harlan County. His foresight is likened unit (sic) the vision of a clairvoyant, seeing more than the average person can imagine, but exercising the same judgment that had made him a dreamer of imaginary things.

An investigation was not needed, the paper chided, since the miners were content, and Harlan County was a land of serenity and peace. Harlan's troubles, the Daily Enterprise concluded, were the result of a "group of leeches" who "would set up another reign of terror," and who "would crawl through the mining camps of Harlan County like a slimy snake, spitting venom of hate between employer and employee..."[11]

The Denhardt Commission opened its deliberations in the Senate chamber of the state capitol on Thursday, March 7. The union, first to present its side of the controversy, produced thirty-eight witnesses who dramatically recounted Harlan's "reign of terror."

One of the first to testify was William Turnblazer, who recreated the "hemming-in" of his party at the Lewallen Hotel in December 1934, and then said, "I do not go into Harlan County because I am afraid for my life." J.B. Snyder, counsel for the operators, asked if there were other reasons why he (Turnblazer) did not go into Harlan. Turnblazer replied negatively, but Snyder, obviously referring to the "Battle of Evarts," asked if he (Turnblazer) was not president of the union when three officers were shot and killed in 1931? Turnblazer nodded affirmatively and stared stolidly as Snyder produced the "fighting letter" which Turnblazer allegedly had written to W.B. Jones in 1931. Afterwards, the district president responded that he had used the term "fight it out" in the "American spirit," had never advocated violence, and had warned his men to refrain from carrying weapons. Snyder pressed Turnblazer: "Don't you know that the relatives of those men who were slain (at Evarts) are bitter to you and that is why you don't go into Harlan?" Unmoved, Turnblazer answered that he had avoided Harlan because he feared for his life.[12]

Several organizers relived days and nights of terror at the hands of Harlan deputy sheriffs. James Westmoreland described his arrest at Cumberland on February 9 and remarked that he never saw a warrant. Marshall A. Musick, recalling the incident at Shields, said he was kicked so hard by a deputy that it was necessary to have a pillow to sit on for five weeks. Dwyer, reconstructing the two dynamitings of his Pineville residence as well as several assaults upon his fellow organizers, said that Harlan conditions were horrible and that only County Attorney Middleton and Judge Gilbert had attempted to do their duty. On the December 1934 "hemming-in" incident, Jim Bates remarked: "I said my prayers more that night than I ever did before." He, A.T. Pace and Frank Hall remembered the dynamiting of a house, the stoning of a car, and that the Harlan post office refused to rent the union a box. Tom White said that in forty years of union experiences all over the United States, he never realized there were such conditions. Mine guards, said he, constantly shadowed organizers and at times "rough shadowed" them so closely that they (organizers) received "skinned heels."

Several UMWA witnesses described physical abuse by Harlan mine guards. John C. Smith, a black miner, told of a harrowing mountain ride with Deputies George Lee and Frank White, who beat him severely and threatened to kill him if he ever returned to Harlan. Two little girls of the Lynch area, ages fifteen and nine, sobbed as they spoke of a brutal assault by a mine guard at Cumberland. The older girl testified that while distributing union circulars the officer asked her to hand them over, and when she refused he struck her and knocked the younger girl to the ground. "He hit me in the stomach and I almost fainted," fifteen-year-old Geneva Timmins said.[13]

During the UMWA presentation, Turnblazer charged that Harlan operators brought organizers of the Progressive Miners' Union, an AFL affiliate, into the county in an attempt to discredit the UMWA, divide the miners, and prevent either from unionizing the county. In support of Turnblazer's charge, James Westmoreland testified that he had been offered both a position as a PMU organizer and protection by the sheriff's office.[14]

Several statements in the *United Mine Workers Journal* substantiated Turnblazer's accusations. In one affidavit, Larkin Baker said that three PMU organizers had requested a meeting with Ben Unthank. Later at the conference in Harlan, Unthank inquired: "Are you in any way connected with the United Mine Workers of America, for if so, we don't want you in Harlan County?" After the PMU organizers had assured Unthank that they were not connected with the UMWA, Unthank said, "There are 30 miles of mines and the field is yours, providing you will wage a fight to exterminate the United Mine Workers of America." The PMU accepted the offer and Unthank placed about forty-five PMU members from Illinois in various mines and on several camp baseball teams.

Two local PMU officials corrroborated Baker's affidavit. Both PMU organizer J.W. Brooks of Middlesboro, and H.C. Johnson, a PMU officer from Briceville, Tennessee, described a similar conference with Unthank in the Lewallen Hotel basement and verified the testomony of Baker and Brooks.[15]

The UMWA called the plan a "scab deal." Despite alleged attempts by Unthank, Ward, Sheriff Middleton, and the HCCOA, to turn the county over to PMU organizers, AFL-affiliates unionized only Wisconsin Steel during 1935. At the conclusion of UMWA testimony, union attorney A. Floyd Byrd of Lexington, summarized the Harlan conflict as a fight in which capital has attempted to oppress labor. Harlan authorities, he said, were a law unto themselves.[16]

3

During the latter part of March the Harlan operators presented their side of the conflict. In stark contrast to the "reign of terror" alleged by the UMWA, several of Harlan's business and professional leaders blamed union organizers and agitators for all the trouble. J. Ray Rice, realtor, said that there had been no objections to union members in Harlan but "usually it's these organizers who come in and raise hell." Dr. E. Murphy Howard, whose nephew had died in the Evarts shoot-out, charged the union with concocting the ambush at a UMWA meeting. Julian Erwin, hardware dealer, attributed the strife to outside agitators and organizers; both he and E.V. Albert, automobile dealer, claimed that the miners did not want to join the union. "If they organize peacefully," Albert asserted, "they should be allowed to go ahead, but I've never seen one like that yet." Coal operator R.E. Lawson accused the UMWA of having violated a contract with his company by calling a strike. For that reason, he said that he would never deal with the union again.

Mayor L.O. Smith told the commission that the people are satisfied. Outside agitators, he said, were responsible for all the trouble. In response to a Denhardt question regarding the number of Harlan deputies with police records, Mayor Smith retorted: "You can't get preachers and Sunday School teachers to keep order in mining camps." Echoing the mayor's sentiments were Dr. W.M. Martin; the Rev. J.G. Root, a Methodist minister; the Rev. W.L. Clark, Danville, presiding elder of the Methodist Church; Ben Middleton, realtor; R.E. McNew, grocer; A.C. Jones, banker; J.C. Acuff, Boy Scout executive; and C.L. Smith, merchant.

Deputy Sheriff L.E. Ball, and several non-union miners, charged the UMWA with intimidation and violence. Non-union miners spoke of threats made by union miners because they had refused to join the union. Ball, who was on the payroll of two coal companies, and Deputy Jim Black Howard told of being kidnapped and threatened by three men who boasted that "they were going to organize if they hid to kill every damned deputy sheriff in the county."[17]

On the final day of the Frankfort hearings Colonel Daniel M. Carrell, formerly of the Kentucky National Guard, and Harry M. Moses, general manager of the United States Coal and Coke Company, testified Carrell, who commanded troops in the county during the coal mine war of 1931, said that most miners wanted to work if they could do so without being intimidated. The best way to prevent trouble in Harlan County, according to Carrell, was to keep outsiders out unless they acted peaceably and to limit demonstrations during troubled times like the outbreak at Evarts in 1931. Moses categorically denied charges made by UMWA witnesses. Lawmen, he said, had followed organizers around Lynch because UMWA members had threatened miners who would not join the union. Nearly 2,000 Lynch residents, said Moses, had signed a petition requesting that the governor rid the town of certain undesirable non-residents who were stirring up trouble.[18]

To climax the hearings, Charles B. Barnes singled out Harlan as the "sore spot" of his district. Said he, "You'll have to have a new sheriff" in Harlan if present labor conditions are to be remedied. Pending before his board, said Barnes, were these grievances against Harlan coal companies: intimidation of miners, discrimination against union members, lack of checkweighmen, unreasonable discharges of miners, and violations of code hours and wages. "During the last six weeks," he mused, "almost every mine up there had violated the code."[19]

Upon completion of the Frankfort hearings, the Denhardt Commission took off on a 600-mile jaunt into eastern Kentucky coal country. At Whitesburg, (UMWA organizers Frank Hall and John Stines displayed scars on their heads and showed pictures of their heads and faces wrapped in bandages) as they described an assault by two Harlan deputies who had trailed them from the Lynch camp. At Jenkins, the Denhardt troupe heard unionized miners express satisfaction with working conditions.

Following those two stops, the commission entered Harlan County. At Lynch, Captain Menefee and County Court Clerk H.C. Howard emphatically denied Lynch officials had attacked Hall and Stines. Also visited were mines at Three Point, Blue Diamond, Tway, and Evarts. At Tway Denhardt and his associates talked to several taciturn miners while the operator emphasized that the real problem in Harlan was the lack of trust and good will between the miners and the mine owners.

By the end of May the Denhardt Commission had completed its investigation into Harlan's labor controversy. In Frankfort, they settled in to prepare a final report for Governor Laffoon.[20]

4

In summary, the Denhardt report unanimously supported the following charges raised earlier by Turnblazer and Caddy: A group of coal operators in collusion with certain public officials had imposed a virtual reign of terror in Harlan County; although Sheriff Middleton had made a good record as police chief and organized labor had supported his election as sheriff, he had connived with the operators to keep the union out of the county; the extensive influence of the operators "reached into the very foundation of the social structure and even into the church of God" where ministers who complained about intolerable conditions became victims of reprisals by bankers and coal operators; the only weekly newspaper in the county was owned by a gentleman who was an enthusiastic ally of the operators; while the Constitution afforded the UMWA the rights of free speech and assembly, miners and their families hesitated to criticize conditions because those First Amendment freedoms were scarcely tolerated. The principal cause of the labor unrest, the report emphasized, was the employment of "flying squadrons" of mine guards to terrorize and intimidate persons throughout the county.[21]

To solve the Harlan conflict, the Denhardt Commission offered five recommendations:

(1) The abolition of the mine guard system to create better understanding and promote trust between the miners and the operators;

(2) A clean-up of local elections to eliminate ballot-box stuffing and illegal voting;

(3) The ouster of Sheriff T.R. Middleton;

(4) The appointment by the Governor of a similar commission to investigate further outrages committed by sheriffs or deputies;

(5) The use of state police officers to enforce the law "in the event that local officials do not see fit to 'clean house' themselves.[22]

Local newspapers strongly condemned the report. Seeing Denhardt's "blunt handwriting" in the document, the *Harlan Daily Enterprise* charged that the commission had vilified a sheriff whose law enforcement policies had kept the peace by protecting the people from the hatred, confusion, and lawlessness of radicals. Further, it observed that the report's reference to the use of state police "conforms to the militaristic view of the militaristic chairman" of the commission and urged a "house cleaning under the Capitol Dome" in Frankfort. Finally, without reservation, the Daily Enterprise blasted the attempt of the Laffoon administration to crucify "the sheriff of Harlan County upon the altar of duty well-performed," and declared that "this paper will stand by him till Hades freezes over."[23]

Admittedly unfamiliar with conditions in Harlan, the *Middlesboro Daily News* felt that the report had maligned the coal operators. Instead of accumulating wealth, the operators had actually struggled to break even in the worst of times. It was a "serious thing," the *Daily News* admonished, to accuse the sheriff of being in league with the operators when in a large county it was often necessary to keep a large force of deputies to preserve law and order. In conclusion, the *Daily News* recognized that while some of Harlan's lawmen might be unfit for the task, it was unreasonable and unfair to give the sheriff a blanket indictment for acts punishable in the courts.

After commending Harlan operators for presenting their side of the controversy, the *Pineville Sun* ranked the Denhardt account with other resumes of self-styled investigators of 1931-32. "Any one of the previous reports... could have been used merely by changing the names of the original members to those of the latest Commission," it charged.[25]

Only the *Knoxville News-Sentinel* defended the report. While the investigators of 1931-32 had been branded troublemaking Communists, and while labor leaders had been called "union agitators," the Denhardt Commission spoke in an official capacity:

> These...words evidently are the considered opinions of Kentuckians.
>
> They only add to the proof that there must be a clean-up in Harlan County...
>
> The "reign of terror" must be obliterated. It has no place in a free country.[26]

Following the release of the Denhardt report, Sheriff T.R. Middleton was unavailable for comment. George S. Ward stated tersely, "I haven't had time to analyze the report." Expressing little interest in the controversy between the operators and miners, Governor Laffoon said he planned no immediate action on the ouster of Sheriff Middleton nor the use of state police in Harlan. His chief interest in the conflict, he contended, was to uphold the law for the benefit of both miners and operators.[27]

Whether or not it was intentionally prepared as a political document, the Denhardt account had one large effect on the Harlan conflict; it created an ever-widening chasm between the state administration and local officials. The year 1935 was an election year in Kentucky. Voters would choose a new governor and state officials. In the August gubernatorial primary the bitter feelings between the Laffoon administration and Harlan County officials came to a head.

5

In the aftermath of the coal mine war of 1931-32, several teams of outside investigators, as noted, probed conditions in the Harlan coalfield. Although most of the groups were denounced as Communists, or libertarians, the conclusions of the Denhardt Commission, interestingly enough, paralleled those of Rob Hall, the Dreiser Committee, Arthur Garfield Hays, and others. When these outsiders visited the Bell-Harlan area in 1931-32, they also found a "reign of terror" in the coalfield. The opinions of those groups were cast aside because they were the judgments of "Reds" or "Roosian Reds." As mentioned above, most were abused, mistreated and harassed by the local authorities. Civil liberties and human rights were practically non-existent in Harlan.

Now, a group of Kentuckians, including a distinguished clergyman, had rendered the same verdict about conditions in Harlan. Indeed, there was a reign of terror just as in Paint Creek-Cabin Creek, West 'Virginia (1912-13), "Bloody Mingo," West Virginia (1920-22), Ludlow, Colorado (1913-14), and Herrin, Illinois (1922). In Logan County, West Virginia, Sheriff Don Chafin was the equivalent of Harlan's Sheriff Middleton. At the behest of the coal operators, both commanded large armies of "thugs" to keep the union out of their corners of the Southern Appalachian coalfields.

The outsiders were right on target in their evaluation of the Harlan situation. The Denhardt Commission also was correct in its assumption that before conditions in Kentucky's coal capital changed, Sheriff Middleton would have to go. Meanwhile, there were stormy days ahead for both Sheriff Middleton and the Laffoon administration.

STORM OVER HARLAN

Since he lived only a block from the county courthouse. County Attorney Elmon Middleton often walked to and from his office. At noon on September 4, he walked home to lunch with his young wife and nine-month-old baby girl. When he started back to his office, it was raining. Kissing his wife and baby daughter goodbye, he climbed into his Ford coupe parked outside his Mound Street home. When he turned on the ignition, a terrific dynamite explosion shook the entire town. Windows in nearby buildings shattered, one piece of the car's engine landed a quarter of a mile away, the car's radiator came to rest twenty-five yards down the street. Without regaining consciousness, the thirty-year-old prosecutor died at 1:20 p.m.[1]

Within forty-eight hours, officers had arrested seven Harlan youths in connection with the crime. Because the murder caused tremendous local excitement, authorities whisked four of the men, Otis Noe, Fred Howard, Bill Leonard, and Bob Farmer to undisclosed jails.

The Harlan Fiscal Court posted a reward of five thousand dollars for information leading to the arrest of Middleton's assassin.

Governor Laffoon added a similar reward of one thousand dollars. At once Judge Gilbert empaneled a special grand jury to investigate the slaying. Quickly indicted and arraigned on charges of willful murder were Joe Hampton, Ernest Hampton. Otis Noe, Bob Farmer, Bill Leonard, and Bascom Huff.

In January, 1936, Otis Noe, 24, stood trial twice in Harlan Circuit Court. Hearing evidence in the first case was a Bell County jury which, after forty hours of deliberation, announced a hopeless deadlock. Immediately, a second trial began before a Clark County jury which found Noe guilty and recommended life imprisonment. There were no other convictions in the case; none of the remaining defendants went to trial.[2]

I

In the wake of the Denhardt investigation, hostility between the administration of Governor Laffoon and Harlan County authorities, and in particular Sheriff Middleton, flared in intensity. Conflict centered around the administration's decision to use National Guardsmen and state police in the county. First, General Denhardt ordered two National Guardsmen from the local unit to the Black Mountain coal camp following reports of disorder, including the dynamiting of the home of mine Superintendent Elbert J. Asbury. Later, fifteen state policemen showed up as observers at the Cloversplint Coal Company after Harlan labor leaders complained that the company had threatened local union officers.[3]

Apparently Denhardt believed that Black Mountain needed protection because Middleton allegedly had withdrawn three deputies from the camp.[4] At Cloversplint, mine Superintendent Armstrong R. Matthews decried the need for state police because his company had a deputy and had not threatened union officials.

Middleton, of course, discredited all charges made by labor leaders and state officials. The reports, said he, were just another attempt by so-called "agitators" to disseminate propaganda against Harlan's citizens and officials. Laffoon, on the other hand, warned the sheriff that while he did not wish to get embroiled in any controversy with Harlan officials, his intentions were to preserve law and order throughout the coal county. The local newspaper, meanwhile, observed that there was "peace and quiet" in Harlan despite several recent turbulent interludes.

"Peace and quiet," unfortunately, did not reign for long. When the state policemen appeared at the Cloversplint camp, Sheriff Middleton immediately asked Harlan Circuit Court Clerk Oscar M. Hoskins to enjoin their activities since neither the circuit judge, county judge, nor mayor had called for troops. Middleton also charged Denhardt with attempting to portray him as a biased, prejudiced, dishonest and incompetent official. The real reason behind the use of the troops, according to Middleton, was to fulfill a deal between organized labor and Laffoon, who was supporting Highway Commission Chairman Tom Rhea in Kentucky's upcoming governor's race. As part of the bargain, the governor allegedly had promised pardons for the union officials convicted following the "Battle of Evarts."[5]

The charge of a political deal apparently stemmed from the endorsement of Tom Rhea by five hundred and fifty-six delegates at a Kentucky Federation of Labor convention in Louisville. "The freedom of the mine workers in Harlan County is the price we have for the support of Rhea," President Turnblazer announced. "The mine workers are ready to once more become the shock troops of labor."

Laffoon and Denhardt promptly denied all of Middleton's allegations. The sheriff of Harlan County, observed the governor, had ignored union men in favor of HCCOA members, while Denhardt argued that state police could enforce the law anywhere in the state.[6]

As a follow-up to the Hoskins' injunction, Middleton on July third had the two guardsmen on duty at Black Mountain cited for contempt. Ordered to appear before Judge Gilbert, the soldiers faced possible penalty for violation of the restraining order. Meanwhile, fifteen state policemen obeyed the court order and remained in a Harlan hotel.

When Denhardt learned of the sheriff's action he ordered the state police detachment to the Black Mountain camp. The state policemen were at once charged with violating the injunction and ordered into Gilbert's court.[7] Thus a lengthy wrangle developed between local officials and the state administration over the use of state troops in Harlan County. Meanwhile, the *Louisville Courier-Journal*, the state's leading newspaper, criticized the state for sending troops into Harlan. The real problem in Harlan, it said, was political and countering force with force was not a solution. The *Courier-Journal* also criticized the Laffoon administration for failure to eliminate the mine guard system and reform election laws even though it had controlled four successive legislatures.[8]

2

At the height of the conflict over the use of state troops in Harlan, the Laffoon administration, on July 5, 1935, initiated ouster proceedings against Sheriff Middleton. The state's legal action followed affidavits by fourteen UMWA organizers and members charging the sheriff with: the appointment of deputy sheriffs with criminal records to harass, intimidate, and prevent members and field representatives of the United Mine Workers of America from organizing the miners of Harlan County; the wholesale arrest of organizers at Cumberland on February 9; the bombardment of Bill Clontz's house, the assault upon Carl Williams; the arrest and imprisonment of Marshall A. Musick in May, 1934; the attack on Musick at Shields in May 1934; and the "hemming-in" of the Turnblazer party in December, 1934. The administration also accused Middleton of entering into a conspiracy with the HC-COA to keep the UMWA out of the county since leading coal operators had signed his performance bonds. In return, the sheriff appointed deputy sheriffs used by the coal companies as mine guards. Middleton had also neglected his official duty, according to the administration, by refusing to serve warrants on deputies accused of crimes, by failing to investigate alleged atrocities, and by declining to give official protection to UMWA leaders in Harlan County. BCLB Chairman Charles B. Barnes offered an additional statement in which Middleton had said he was going to help the operators keep the United Mine Workers of America out of Harlan County.[9] Ordered to appear in Frankfort on July 31, the embattled Harlan sheriff now had to show why he should not be removed from office.

On learning of the ouster proceedings, Middleton, apparently undaunted by action which he regarded as political chicanery in behalf of Tom Rhea, commented succinctly, "I have nothing to say."[10]

Arguing that the ouster attempt was politically motivated, the *Middlesboro Daily News* called the Harlan sheriff a pawn in the hands of a "state machine" which was seeking the support of Harlan's labor element. "If Sheriff Middleton would play ball with Governor Laffoon and his regime, the charges against him would vanish," the paper predicted.[11]

Originally scheduled to begin on July 31, the hearings were postponed because Laffoon underwent an emergency appendectomy on July 26 at St. Joseph's Hospital in Lexington.[12]

Finally, on August 29, the ouster proceedings got underway at the state capitol in Frankfort. At the outset, after explaining that he could "take care of himself," Laffoon ordered a number of armed, uniformed state police from the Senate chamber. On the first day prosecution witnesses, mostly union leaders, repeated testimony given early on at the BCLB hearing in Pineville. Nine of about forty witnesses had testified when Laffoon abruptly ended the hearing by announcing that he could not be present for an afternoon session, and that one of the sheriff's attorneys could not attend the following Monday. The sessions never reconvened.[13]

John Young Brown, a Lexington attorney and UMWA counsel, later revealed that Laffoon had left office without resuming the hearings or taking any action in the case. Then, during a concentrated union campaign in Harlan County, Governor A.B. (Happy) Chandler, who succeeded Laffoon, had dismissed the charges with the comment that Middleton was a high-class and efficient official. When he took office, Chandler said, the records of the ouster proceedings either were lost or destroyed and efforts to locate them were fruitless. Since there were no additional charges, and since those who had initiated the original case had not insisted upon a trial, Chandler ordered the matter dropped.[14] Were these records really missing? Hardly, since the transcripts of the Middleton ouster proceedings turned up in the office of Kentucky's Secretary of

State in Frankfort after Chandler became governor. Based on reliable evidence, the Chandler claim about "lost" or "destroyed" records does not seem plausible.

3

While the state administration considered the Middleton case, the courts debated the use of state police and National Guardsmen in Harlan. Initially, Judge Gilbert sustained the temporary Hoskins injunction. The state then took the matter before the Kentucky Court of Appeals which heard arguments in the case on July 18. Appearing for the state, Louisville attorney Richard Priest Dietzman argued that state police could act as peace officers in any county of the Commonwealth. On the other hand, Pineville lawyer Cleon K. Calvert, who represented Middleton and Gilbert, spoke in favor of the temporary injunction and against the indiscriminate use of state troops in any county of the state.

The next week the Court of Appeals announced its opinion. Agreeing with Calvert, Judge Wesley Vick Perry, speaking for the court, ruled that the state could exercise police powers only if local officials failed to uphold the law. The indiscriminate use of state police in any county of the Commonwealth would be harmful, Judge Perry concluded.[15]

Upon learning the court's ruling, Middleton commented, "I feel mighty good about it. In fact, I'm tickled to death."[16] However, Middleton's joy was short-lived. Additional trouble in Harlan during the summer of 1935 made the controversy over the use of state troops a much more volatile issue.

4

Kentucky's torrid gubernatorial campaign provided the spark which refueled the Laffoon-Denhardt-Middleton imbroglio. In neighboring Bell County on June 27 "Happy" Chandler opened his campaign at the courthouse in Pineville by denying that he had made a "deal" to pardon certain Harlan County men. "Labor," said he, "had a voice of its own and would not be delivered to any candidate."

A month later, Pineville was the scene of a giant political rally in support of Chandler's opponent, Tom Rhea. A carnival atmosphere permeated the town as three loudspeakers, blaring simultaneously, produced music ranging from "hill-billy" to "cha-cha." Street jug bands and string music groups provided "live" entertainment, while several itinerant preachers told the people to "get right with God." The Rhea bandwagon, composed of three trucks, continuously circled the courthouse, announcing a 7:30 p.m. speaking. A large banner which read, "President William Turnblazer, the United Mine Workers of America of District 19, are for Rhea and Roosevelt—They are right," hung between two massive pillars of the county courthouse. Arriving in state-owned trucks and in private conveyances, hundreds of highway workers joined miners to form a crowd estimated at between fifteen hundred and ten thousand.[17]

The rally's principal speaker was General Denhardt who substituted for the ailing Ruby Laffoon. Emotionally, Denhardt castigated Sheriff Middleton and "Happy" Chandler, called for the ouster of the sheriff, and urged the miners to support Tom Rhea. Promising to do everything within his power to seek the removal of Middleton, he cautioned Harlan citizens to see that "they" did not steal the election.[18] This rally, which took place a week before the primary, removed all doubt that the union supported Tom Rhea.

The climax to the campaign for governor, as well as the legal battle over the use of state troops, came on the eve of the primary. Before midnight Friday, the day before the election, National Guard officers from across the state gathered at Pineville's Continental Hotel, where Colonel John A. Polin informed them that they were acting under sealed orders. Near midnight, about a thousand guardsmen from the Louisville area and from central and eastern Kentucky poured into Pineville. When Denhardt arrived during the pre-dawn hours, the men received orders and ammunition, then piled into trucks for an invasion of Harlan County.[19]

The troop movement was shrouded in secrecy. Before leaving Frankfort, Denhardt denied that troops would be used in the Harlan primary election and Laffoon, from his hospital bed in Lexington, neither confirmed nor denied the military activity. In Frankfort, General Ellerbee W. Carter knew nothing about it, the governor's secretary was unaware of it, and the secretary of state's office disclaimed knowledge of the mobilization order.[20]

Although the troop deployment developed secretly, Laffoon's Executive Journal contained an order of August 5, which authorized mobilization under General Denhardt's command. In issuing the call for troops, the governor cited alleged terroristic acts committed against Harlan citizens; the denial of free speech and assembly; a contemplated election fraud by the sheriff's political faction (some 15,400 ballots had been printed for the Democratic primary when Harlan County had never voted more than one or two thousand Democrats); the alleged theft of more than a hundred ballots from the Harlan County courthouse; and a general condition of lawlessness.[21] Through the use of the state's military power, the administration hoped to safeguard the chances of Tom Rhea in Harlan County.

By daybreak on August 3, the entire county was under military occupation. When Harlan citizens arose, troops had encamped in the county's seventy-one precincts. Arrayed in full battle dress, including rifles, pistols, and bayonets, from six to fifty-five soldiers appeared at various polling places. At mid-day Louellen had fifty-five troops on duty, while eighty policed three Verda precincts. Each commanding officer carried a large blue-print map with precincts and roads marked. A mimeographed pamphlet headed "Honest Election League of Harlan County," read:

> Armed deputy sheriffs have no right to act as election officers or enter voting places; voters should not be permitted to be intimidated by armed election officers. Voters have a right to cast their ballots without fear and without being molested by (so-called) officers of the law. Any persons, whether deputy sheriffs or not, will be arrested who attempt to, or do threaten to intimidate voters.

Every guardsman received instructions to inspect ballot boxes and other election paraphernalia at each precinct.

During the day there were incidents at several precincts. At Kildav soldiers suddenly suspended voting after forty-seven Democrats had voted in four hours. They gave no reasons for their actions. There was no voting at Mary Helen, home precinct of County Democratic Chairman S.J. Dickenson, when soldiers refused to vacate the premises. At Shields, soldiers took coal operator and election challenger Tom Holmes into custody. Because so many soldiers were present at the courthouse, election officials postponed voting until 11:00. At other polling places election officials refused to allow voting until soldiers had moved at least fifty feet away from the polls.[22]

Sheriff Middleton called the affair "an invasion by a band of outlaws masquerading as soldiers." He charged General Denhardt with using high-handed, militaristic tactics to intimidate the citizens of Harlan County. Said he, "The answer to Denhardt will be found in the ballot boxes when they are counted. It is not the nature of the people of the mountains to let soldiers from the outside tell them whether they can vote..." Citing improved conditions, the sheriff also called Denhardt's contention of a proposed election "steal" ridiculous, and insisted that irresponsible agitators like Denhardt were causing all the trouble.[23]

In Harlan, Denhardt, assisted by Captain Diamond E. Perkins and County Attorney Elmon Middleton, established a command post at the armory. From this vantage point, the general directed several hundred troops.[24] About two and one-half hours before the polls closed, local authorities attempted to enjoin and cite Denhardt with contempt for leading the troops into the county. When Constable Merle Middleton arrived at the Armory to serve the injunction, troops blocked the door. Going around to the side of the building, Middleton threw the documents in, shouting "Here's some papers for you, General." Immediately, four guardsmen seized the constable and punched him with pistols. Replied Middleton: "You're too late, boys, the papers are served." Both Denhardt and County Attorney Middleton agreed that the constable had not followed a proper legal process by tossing the papers in the window.

Granted in mid-afternoon by Judge Gilbert, the injunction restrained the National Guard from further interference in the election. In leading more than five hundred troops into Harlan, Denhardt had acted without authority and without executive order. (Laffoon's Executive Order, which apparently authorized the troops to go to Harlan, was dated August 5, two days after the primary election.) According to the restraining order, soldiers reportedly had disturbed the peace by patrolling precincts, by acting as election inspectors, and by invading voting booths. In short, the guard had disrupted an otherwise quiet and orderly election day.

Despite the injunction, soldiers remained on duty until the polls closed. Obviously pleased with the day's work, Denhardt commented, "You can quote me as saying the expedition was entirely successful. We kept off the most gigantic election steal ever planned in Harlan County. I do not believe that more than three thousand Democratic votes were cast. If we had not been here, they would have voted fifteen thousand votes in the Democratic primary."

Leaving Harlan following the closing of the polls, Denhardt ordered fifty guardsmen "to stand at the courthouse and protect those ballot boxes from being stuffed or changed just as we did two years ago at the earnest solicitation of Judge (James M.) Gilbert and Sheriff (Theodore) Middleton, when they were elected. We had ample power then to preserve the sanctity of the ballot and to safeguard it from a few thieves and gunmen. We have the same power now."

When the vote tabulation began the following Monday, Sheriff Middleton barred guardsmen from the counting room. In the official tabulation, Lieutenant-Governor Chandler swept the county by a five to one majority and won fifty-six of the county's seventy-one precincts, including several large mining camps.[25] Statewide, he did not emerge a clear-cut winner and faced Tom Rhea in a September 7 runoff election.

After the election Harlan authorities took legal action against the remaining National Guardsmen in Harlan. With affidavits from the sheriff in hand, Judge Gilbert issued a temporary restraining order barring the troops, including two captains, from exercising police duty, displaying badges or emblems, and acting as bodyguards. About the same time, Commonwealth's Attorney Smith summoned Denhardt to tell a special grand jury about the alleged election "conspiracy." The general responded that he would be delighted to testify.[26]

When the grand jury convened. General Denhardt was absent. Thereupon, the grand jurors indicted him, Captain Perkins, and nineteen other guardsmen on charges of unlawfully obtaining possession of ballot boxes, interfering with election officers at various precincts, and intimidating voters. The indictment also cited Denhardt with contempt of Harlan Circuit Court by ordering guardsmen into the county. Subsequent to the indictments, Judge Gilbert sent bench warrants for Denhardt's arrest to the sheriffs of Franklin and Jefferson counties.[27]

A week later Denhardt surrendered to Franklin County authorities and posted a bond of ten thousand dollars. Disavowing that he had been a fugitive from justice, Denhardt offered to sacrifice his life for the sake of decent government in Harlan County. He concluded:

> I have been required to execute bond...for my appearance in Harlan County an (sic) answer two alleged indictments. I shall probably be tried there. If tried in that county, I shall, of course, be convicted, or probably assassinated before or during the trial.

Because of a crowded court docket. Commonwealth's Attorney Smith postponed the scheduled hearing. Denhardt did not appear in court.

The final disposition of Harlan's case against Denhardt came just ten days before a scheduled hearing in Harlan. Calling the indictments a result of "political passion and prejudice," and citing a statute granting officers civil and criminal immunity for acts done pursuant to duty, Governor Laffoon declared his adjutant-general "forever acquitted, released and discharged" from the Harlan charges. Laffoon later pardoned twenty-eight National Guard officers on the grounds that they had committed no criminal act.[28]

5

In the interim between the August primary and the September runoff, Judge Gilbert predictably sustained the latest injunction against Denhardt and the National Guard. The governor, Gilbert ruled, had neither power nor authority to call the guard into service for indefinite periods. Such orders, concluded he, should be for a definite purpose.[29]

Once more the administration requested the Kentucky Court of Appeals to decide the question which had raised a storm of protest in Harlan all summer long. With the entire court participating, Judge James W. Stites delivered a unanimous opinion overruling Gilbert for enjoining guardsmen and state police from acting as peace officers in Harlan County. It was the court's opinion that state military forces could not interfere with elections in Harlan County, but could act as peace officers. The sheriff, the court declared, was not the exclusive guardian of peace, because guardsmen on active duty possessed the same right. Since both the sheriff and the guardsmen had an obligation to uphold law and order, the court ruled that the state's police powers extended to any county.[30]

To climax the long, drawn-out controversy, the special Harlan grand jury made its final report on August 23. In addition to returning indictments against state military personnel, grand jurors disputed the existence of a reign of terror. Most witnesses, the grand jury noted, denied that lawlessness was rampant in the county. Some misconduct, according to the grand jury, had taken place and indictments returned, but it emphasized that no one knew anything about the Black Mountain dynamiting nor other alleged disorders in the county. Finally, the grand jury cricitized county attorney Middleton for his role as legal adviser to the guard during the August 3 primary.[31]

In an anti-administration and anti-Denhardt editorial, the Harlan Daily Enterprise lauded the grand jury's report. Calling the reign of terror a figment of the imagination, it asserted that the state policemen and militia were unnecessary because crime in Harlan was down by more than fifty percent.

County attorney Middleton criticized both the newspaper editorial and the grand jury report. Asserting that he had acted clearly within his rights as the guard's legal counsel, he accused Commonwealth's Attorney Smith of attempting to discredit him. Middleton pointed out that miners were frequently initimidated, deputies had disrupted mass rallies on three occasions in 1934, intoxicated officers had beaten and assaulted union men, and the presence of the National Guard had averted bloodshed when UMWA organizers were "hemmed in" on the night of December 8, 1934.

It was Elmon Middleton's contention that two principal causes lay at the root of Harlan's troubles: (1) wholesale election frauds; (2) the use of deputy sheriffs to harass union organizers and to disrupt union rallies. Middleton defended the use of troops by noting that their presence had curtailed a gigantic election steal in 1933 and prevented civil strife on several other occasions. Deploring the lack of indictments by grand juries, Middleton said that local peace officers had failed to protest constitutional rights of all the county's citizens.[32] A week later the youthful county attorney died.

Harlan officials disclaimed any link between the murder, the Rhea-Chandler political feud, and Middleton's advisory role to the National Guard. They jointly attributed his untimely death to the prosecution of local gambling interests. On the day he died, Middleton had planned to provide the grand jury with further evidence about Harlan's gambling and slot-machine operations.

Ironically, the assassination of county attorney Middleton occurred about five weeks following almost unanimous assurances from Harlan's political leaders that no disorder or unrest prevailed in the county.[33] Speaking out against the intimidation of labor, election corruption, and gambling, Elmon Middleton stood nearly alone among Harlan officials. Perhaps it is not unrealistic to view him as a martyr for honest elections and for justice to "Bloody Harlan's" persecuted miners.

Two days following the murder of Elmon Middleton, the Laffoon administration once again ordered troops into Harlan. Their mission: to safeguard the gubernatorial runoff election and to protect the people from a "reign of terror" which now had claimed a public servant.[34]

The election of September 7 was devoid of all the furor of the August primary. Seven hundred guardsmen, commanded by Lieutenant-Colonels Roy W. Easley and John A. Polin, entered Harlan under the authority of the court decision that they could act as peace officers as long as they did not interfere with the election. From eight to thirty soldiers inspected ballot boxes before voting commenced at each of the county's seventy-one precincts. Remaining at least fifty feet from the polls throughout the day, the troops escorted the ballot boxes to the county courthouse after the polls had closed. Little dissension accompanied the presence of the soldiers, and Sheriff Middleton commended their deportment.[35]

In the runoff, Chandler repeated his convincing Harlan primary victory over Tom Rhea. Winning fifty-six precincts and capturing the county by a 4-1 margin, he recorded staggering majorities at Mary Helen, Yancey, Three Point, and Tway.[36] Statewide he received a majority of twenty-six thousand, one fourth of which came from Harlan County.

There were two reasons for Chandler's impressive primary and run-off victories over Tom Rhea. First, the Laffoon administration had passed a sales tax bill which Chandler opposed and Rhea defended. Mountain residents of lower income status, including Harlan Countians, did not like paying the sales tax. A second and more important factor for Chandler's success was the support of Herb Smith, long-time political boss and administration man in Harlan County. Early on Smith largely supported the Republican party. In the 1930s, however, he switched to the Democratic party, supported Laffoon and was instrumental in getting the coal operators to do the same. Opportunely, in 1935, Herb Smith transferred his allegiance from the Laffoon administration, and Tom Rhea, to Chandler. In that year's Democratic primary and run-off elections, Chandler, with Smith's blessing and heavily supported by the coal operators, carried Harlan County convincingly.

Chandler's run-off victory over Tom Rhea was tantamount to his election as Kentucky's next governor. Still ahead was the November general election with token Republican opposition. The political storm, which had swept across Harlan during the summer of 1935 like a sudden thunderstorm, had now passed. The dispute over whether the state could exercise its police powers in the county had also ended, at least for the moment. Passing, too, was county attorney Elmon Middleton who became a victim of the deep rift between state officials and county authorities. Gone was a true friend of labor and the union. Although the union had lost a champion in the county courthouse, it could look forward to renewed efforts to unionize the county's miners. For, in Washington in 1935, Congress passed the National Labor Relations Act which eventually would become labor's emancipation proclamation.

HARLAN SHALL BE ORGANIZED

On Sunday July 7, 1935 Harlan County miners rallied near the site of the "Battle of Evarts." The purpose of the meeting was to acquaint the workers with their rights under the Wagner Act, which Congress had recently passed. With field representative Marshall A. Musick heading a list of speakers, the rally commenced in an atmosphere of calmness. Suddenly, as if by some prearranged signal, Harlan deputies converged on the scene. First they attempted to drown out the voices of the union speakers by the incessant blowing of automobile horns. Next, Deputies George Lee, whose son, Otto, was slain in the area in 1931, and John P. Hickey waded into the crowd, waving guns and shouting threats. Striding up to the rostrum, Lee attacked sixty-six-year-old William (Rockhouse) Munholland , an emaciated, one-eyed veteran of the mines, who was the speaker of—the moment. Munholland later recalled:

> He come over and slapped me...and I staggered over again to the bank, and a lady by the name of "Miss" Lane was thar; she went to screaming and hollering and they went on to make me hush hollering; so I just squatted down there, so I don't know what all took place.

The "Miss" Lane was 67-year-old Mrs. Belle Lane, who lived nearby. She recalled the horn-blowing, named George Lee, Merle Middleton, Frank White and John P. Hickey among the armed deputies present, and accused Lee of slapping Munholland. According to "Miss" Lane, when Lee attacked the elderly man, she screamed: "Lord of Mercy, stop that. Stop hittin' that pore old man." Hickey suddenly whirled around, made several poorly aimed efforts to hit her, and shouted: "God-damn you, go to the goddamn house where you belong!"[1]

George Lee and John P. Hickey later related their versions of the events at Evarts that Sunday afternoon. Both men swore that Sheriff Middleton had ordered them to Evarts as observers, to preserve order, and to see that there was no trouble or violence at the union meeting. Lee recalled that as he walked into the crowd the speaker, apparently Munholland, pointed a bony finger in his direction, and remarked, "There is one of them thugs now." Suddenly, said he, I "thought of my boy being killed there," and I "flew mad" and "slapped him before I thought of myself." As he walked back to his car, a fellow standing on a storehouse porch wanted to know "what the hell I did that for." A heated exchange followed and Lee struck the man. Hickey swore that he just lost his head when a man called him a "gun thug." He admitted that he had heard "Miss" Lane scream "Don't hit that man," but that he neither hit at her nor said anything to her.

Eight other Harlan lawmen explained their presence and actions at Evarts on July 7. Each one denied that Middleton had ordered them to the meeting. According to their stories, they just happened to show up at the rally and became snarled in a monumental traffic jam. Most of the officers said they did not leave their cars except to try to clear the road. They noticed that several persons blew their horns because of the heavy traffic but only one of the deputies, Merle Middleton, admitted blowing his horn. Several of the lawmen saw Lee and Hickey move into the crowd, noticed some excitement, saw people scattering, but did not see the deputies strike anyone.[2]

From the confused and conflicting accounts of the second "Battle of Evarts," several conclusions can be drawn. First, by self-admission, Deputies Lee and Hickey attacked two men at Evarts on July 7; second, some horn-blowing had occurred. Union spokesmen said it was intentional; deputy sheriffs attributed it to the "traffic jam;" third, at least fourteen armed deputy sheriffs attended the rally despite claims by some that no one had ordered them there. Finally, this display of armed force and physical abuse by Harlan's "gun thugs" effectively dispersed the crowd and terminated yet another union rally.

I

Two days before the second "Battle of Evarts," Harlan County miners supposedly received new life in their struggle to organize when President Roosevelt signed into law the Wagner Act.[3] On endorsing the new law, the President noted that it guaranteed workers the right of collective bargaining. It also established a National Labor Relations Board to hear cases in which the right of collective bargaining was abridged or denied, and to hold fair elections to determine the bargaining representatives of employees. The new law, the President said, was an important step toward the achievement of just and peaceful labor relations in industry.[4]

In addition to setting up an NLRB of three presidentially-appointed members and guaranteeing workers the right of collective bargaining, the Wagner Act made it illegal for an employer to: (1) interefere with, restrain or coerce employees in the exercise of their rights of self-organization and collective bargaining; (2) dominate or interfere with the formation or administration of any labor organization, or contribute financial or other support to it; (3) discriminate against an employee because of union membership or activity; (4) discharge an employee because of union activity; and (5) refuse to bargain collectively with representatives of employees.

Passage of the law augured new hopes for Harlan's miners, who had not derived many benefits from NIRA, because most operators had mocked the coal code. In fact, President Turnblazer had filed ninety-two complaints of alleged violations with the BCLB. One of the chief offenders was the Harlan-Wallins Coal Corporation, headed by bespectacled, owl-faced Pearl Bassham, a vehement anti-unionist. When hearings against his company took place in May, 1934, Bassham ignored a summons to appear before the board. Several months later he again refused to attend a board session in Cincinnati. Going on with the scheduled hearing, the BCLB learned from affidavits furnished by company employees, that Harlan-Wallins had interfered with the right of workers to organize and had refused to respect the coal code's maximum hours provisions. The board ordered the company to cease intimidation of workers, comply with the seven-hour work day, and reimburse employees who had worked over seven hours a day since April 1, 1934. Black Mountain Coal Corporation and Cornett-Lewis Coal Company also had violated the coal code in 1934. At Black Mountain local unions 6659 and 4493 had adopted resolutions which condemned operators for ignoring the existing contract by discharging men for union affiliations, using gunmen methods, denying freedom of assembly, and enforcing long hours.[6] Cornett-Lewis workers supposedly had voted secretly on the question of union affiliation and had rejected union membership by the overwhelming margin of 261 to 5. R.E. Lawson, the mine's general manager, remembered that the men had turned down the union by voting "Yes" or "No" on blank pieces of paper which they had signed. Reportedly he had called the miners into the company theater, and was present for both the voting and for the tabulation of the votes.[7]

Difficulty also arose during NIRA days at the Harlan Central Coal Company, located at Totz on Poor Fork where President C. Vester Bennett had apparently ordered the eviction of several local union officials. Pending further inquiry, the BCLB ordered suspension of the eviction notices, but three local union officials charged that the company had gone ahead and evicted them anyway.[8]

2

Although several Harlan operators, as noted, refused to honor the coal code, union contracts covered a portion of the county's mines while NIRA was in effect. During autumn, 1933, as discussed earlier, many operators had agreed to a contract under the NIRA.⁹ On its expiration in March, 1934, a work stoppage occurred. In conferences at Knoxville in early April, Turnblazer and an operators' committee met to negotiate a contract, calling for a seven-hour day, a five-day week, and a basic wage scale of $4.60 per day. In announcing the idling of three thousand miners, Turnblazer warned that they would not return to the pits until operators agreed to a new pact.

In less than a week, most District 19 mine owners had accepted an agreement incorporating terms of the national contract. Harlan operators, recalcitrant as ever, refused to come to terms. Turnblazer fumed, "They failed to put their cards on the table."

A week later two hundred District 19 delegates met in Knoxville to discuss the stalemate. Turnblazer immediately dispatched a telegram to NIRA chief Hugh S. Johnson, urging a thorough investigation of coal code infractions, including intimidation and coercion of miners, discharges for union activity, and evictions. Also restated were the complaints that many companies used "gunmen" methods and denied miners the right to elect a checkweighman. W. Arthur Ellison, a member of the operator's committee, stated that while he would welcome a federal inquiry, the divisive issue was the "check-off" system.

Most importantly, convention delegates unanimously authorized Turnblazer to negotiate individually with operators who were willing to sign contracts in line with the national agreement.

Meanwhile, the Harlan impasse continued. Four thousand miners, representing about fifteen Harlan mines, refused to work. Organizer Bill Clontz commented, "They are not striking, but just waiting." They waited until May 20, when Turnblazer divulged that the signing of a new contract in Cincinnati had broken the deadlock. Although the pact's terms were not officially published, "so complete was (John L.) Lewis's victory that even a majority of the Harlan operators signed the new agreement."¹⁰

The new agreement was in effect until April 1, 1935. Before it expired, Turnblazer, who was a member of a twelve-man union committee, went to Washington to confer with a similar operators' group. When the talks failed to produce an agreement, the federal government urged the extension of the existing code until June 16 to avert a crippling strike. The UMWA agreed but Southern Appalachian Coal Operators, which included the Harlan owners, balked. "Southern operators do not look with favor upon the code extension, but we do not go on record as opposing it," emphasized Secretary L.C. Gunter. Turnblazer disagreed. More than five thousand miners in the Kentucky-Tennessee field were idle, he said, because operators had rejected a code extension which President Roosevelt had requested. W.G. Polk, first vice-president of the Southern Appalachian Coal Operators' Association, had a change of heart: "We are," said he, "not refusing to cooperate with the NRA, and we have no fight with the union. We are anxious to cooperate." On hearing the news, a grateful Turnblazer pledged to cooperate fully in the formulation of a new wage agreement.[11]

In June, 1935, a nationwide coal strike appeared imminent, but a second extension of the code postponed it for two weeks. Both Turnblazer and Southern Appalachian operators, including Harlan owners, agreed to the extension when President Roosevelt requested it.[12]

Despite the two code extensions, negotiations did not produce a new contract until late September. Providing for a seven-hour day, five-day week, the new pact, which Harlan operators did not sign, sent four hundred thousand miners back into the pits. Scheduled to run until April 1, 1937, the agreement increased the basic wage rate to $5.50 but the miners lost their fight for a six-hour day.[13]

Back in Knoxville in late September, 1935, talks resumed between UMWA conferees and representatives of the Southern Appalachian operators. While owners were apparently willing to grant the fifty cents per day wage hike, they hesitated to accept the eighteen-month term of the contract. In the face of the deadlock, Turnblazer announced plans to sign up individual operators who would go along with the national pact.

Meanwhile the Southern Appalachian coalfields remained idle. Finally, at the end of October, Southern Appalachian operators endorsed all the provisions of the contract. A throng of miners from throughout District 19 later gathered in Jellico to consider the new document. Turnblazer explained that the agreement extended only to April 1, 1937, and that the operators could call for a joint conference before that date if economic conditions prevented payment of the new wage scale. The miners then accepted the contract and returned to work.[14]

Although the Wagner Act had gone into effect, the new contract did not cover all Harlan County miners. In what seemed to be a typical move to circumvent the agreement, George S. Ward announced on September 29 that the HCCOA had acceded to a wage increase in line with the new contract. Most Harlan operators were still unwilling to accept the "check-off" because that would mean acceptance of the UMWA.[15]

3

While these difficult contract negotiations were taking place, the UMWA was busy conducting mass meetings throughout Harlan County. On April 21, 1935 miners at Alva, mining camp of the Black Star Coal Corporation, heard A.T. Pace predict that the day of freedom was just around the corner. At Cumberland on June 15, a smaller crowd, composed mostly of miners from Letcher, Perry, and Leslie counties, listened as International representative Dale Stapleton forecast that the union would organize the Harlan field. Although Cumberland Police Chief Talton Hall was on hand to guard against violence, one organizer watched as gunmen ripped UMWA banners off two cars and chased a school bus containing twenty-five men from the city.[16]

A week later, fifteen thousand miners from Districts 19 and 30 rallied at Jenkins. Attended by Governor Laffoon and other state officials, the keynote of this meeting was "Harlan shall be organized." Laffoon expressed his support to the miners; General Denhardt reviewed the highlights of the Denhardt report; Tom Rhea pledged to support New Deal labor policies; and International Secretary-Treasurer Thomas Kennedy enthusiastically offered the aid of the international organization.

With these rallies providing the spark, UMWA officials launched a new organizing campaign in Harlan County. Turnblazer kicked it off with this stirring challenge:

It is a new day for the miners of Harlan County: it is a day of freedom...Now we have the opportunity. It is a golden opportunity, it is a wonderful opportunity, an opportunity you have been praying for, and your prayers have been answered by that Great Leader of the United States, Franklin D. Roosevelt. He has presented you this opportunity, and we ask...Are you going to fail him?

Organizers and field representatives, he said, would give the miners an opportunity to establish the best union in eastern Kentucky under the protection of the United States government.[17]

The July 7, 1935 rally at Evarts marked a new beginning of UMWA efforts to organize Harlan's coal miners. That meeting, as mentioned earlier, was broken up by armed, abusive Harlan deputy sheriffs. Undaunted, the union continued to organize and Harlan's "gun thugs" kept on harassing union men.

Several weeks after the second "Battle of Evarts," gunmen, at midnight, kidnapped a Cloversplint union leader. According to reports, at the peak of a strike called when the company refused to renew a union contract, three armed men broke into the home of Howard Williams, the black local union president. After Williams dressed, and while his wife and children cringed, deputies led him away. As the captors drove their captive toward the Virginia state line, they constantly badgered him for being dissatisfied with current working conditions and for getting involved with the union. On top of the mountain, the kidnappers stopped the car and threatened to kill Williams. Tearfully, the union leader begged for mercy. Finally gunmen put him out of the car with a warning that he never return to Harlan County. Happy to escape with his life, Williams remained in the mountains until daybreak, then walked to the home of a friend near St. Charles, Virginia.[18]

Lutishea Williams, the wife of Howard Williams, verified her husband's account. Almost hysterical about her husband's safety, Mrs. Williams called in neighbors who unsuccessfully searched the area. Next day word came that Williams was safe at UMWA headquarters in Middlesboro. While not recognizing any of the gunmen on the night of the kidnapping, she later pointed out two men in London, Kentucky, identified by a friend as Ben Unthank and George Lee.

A tense atmosphere enveloped the Cloversplint camp the day after the kidnapping. Armed deputies, including John P. Hickey, patrolled the streets and would not let residents go to the company store. Superintendent Matthews later confirmed that he had asked Sheriff Middleton to send additional officers to keep order.

Meanwhile, a UMWA delegation headed by T.C. Townsend and Howard Williams conferred with Governor Laffoon and General Denhardt about the kidnapping. Williams reviewed the story of his abduction and Townsend presented affidavits which portrayed general lawlessness in Harlan County. Troops, he said, were necessary to restore order. Granting the UMWA request, Laffoon once again ordered National Guardsmen into Harlan County.[19]

The governor decided to send the troops because deputy sheriffs had assaulted, molested and abused innocent persons, blocked highways and kidnapped Howard Williams. As justification for his actions, Laffoon also pointed to the assassination of Elmon Middleton and the failure of authorities to keep the peace. The guardsmen left the state capitol on Saturday, September 29, with instructions to investigate conditions thoroughly and to quell the worst reign of terror in Harlan County's history.[20]

Almost incredibly, Judge Gilbert rejected the "reign of terror" charges. He declared that conditions were quiet and peaceful,[21] and that neither Judge Saylor nor County Attorney Fuson[22] had received reports of disorders in the county.[23] In an attempt to disprove the "reign of terror," Gilbert ordered a court of inquiry in Harlan Circuit Court for Monday, September 30. With four national guardsmen patrolling the courthouse, about twenty witnesses testified. Joseph J. Timko[24] and Bill Clontz disputed the "reign of terror," as rumors and hearsay[25] although ironically, Ted Creech, son of operator R.W. Creech, early on had ordered Clontz from his home in the Twila camp.

Harlan officials and business leaders characteristically repudiated the "reign of terror." Captain Perkins received a telephone call from Denhardt reporting the beating of several persons, but was unable to locate any person allegedly beaten. Reports of evictions at Cloversplint, he said, were only rumors. Sheriff Middleton stressed that local authorities had the situation under control and the troops were unnecessary.

Commonwealth's Attorney Smith also discounted the "reign of terror" since the present administration had reduced crime by sixty-five percent in twenty months. County Judge Morris Saylor reported that he had not issued any eviction notices. Ted Creech denied that he had harmed organizer Bill Clontz. R.E. Lawson knew of no unusual disorders in Harlan. Law enforcement, said he, was better than for any of the twenty years he had lived in the county. Dr. W.P. Cawood had not treated any persons in a beaten condition at the Harlan hospital. Deputy Sheriffs Lon E. Ball and Jim Black Howard, Jailer Clinton C. Ball, businessmen Orville Howard and C.C. Bowling, coal operator J.S. Greene, and bankers A.C. Jones and W.W. Lewis also denied that there was a "reign of terror" and defended the county's law enforcement agencies. With the conclusion of the inquiry, the *Harlan Daily Enterprise*, in a banner headline proclaimed: "COURT PROVES NO REIGN OF TERROR HERE."[26]

Organizer Joseph J. Timko later gave a far different version of Harlan conditions. On the day of the court hearing, he said the sheriff of Bell County provided an escort to the Harlan County line, where National Guardsmen met and accompanied him to the Harlan courthouse. Outside the courtroom before court convened, Timko said he counted about thirty deputy sheriffs, and George Lee trailed him so closely that contact with witnesses was impossible. Timko claimed that Gilbert did not permit Howard Williams to identify his kidnappers, although both Lee and Unthank were in the courtroom at the time.

Timko also described a conference with Gilbert in Pineville on July 8, where Turnblazer had outlined organizational plans for Harlan County under the Wagner Act. After the meeting, the judge said that while conditions in Harlan were not as bad as previously, it was still unsafe for organizers to enter the area.[27] Unfathomably Gilbert refuted the "reign of terror" allegations even though "gun thugs" had beaten several persons at Evarts on July 7, had broken up that unon rally, and had kidnapped Howard Williams. If that was not enough evidence to substantiate the "reign of terror," someone had murdered County Attorney Middleton.

In the wake of the court of inquiry, Gilbert placed Howard Williams under a $300 bond to appear before the November grand jury. When Williams could not post bond, Gilbert sent him to the county jail.[28] Backed by the UMWA, Williams later brought suit in Federal District Court of Eastern Kentucky charging Gilbert with false imprisonment. In that case, Federal Judge H. Church Ford ruled that Williams had not been legally committed to jail and that Gilbert had exceeded his authority by requiring bond with surety. Nevertheless, the judge directed the jury to find that Gilbert was not civilly liable to damages because he had jurisdiction in the subject matter of the base.[29]

Meanwhile, National Guardsmen in Harlan were generally inactive. Major Oren Cain, commander of the detachment, said that was because the troops had found that Harlan was as peaceful and law-abiding as his home county of McLean.[30]

4

As the new union campaign sputtered, Kentucky went about the business of electing a new governor. Opposed in the general election by Lexington attorney King Swope, Republican, Lieutenant-Governor Chandler this time had the surprise backing of the UMWA. First, UMWA leader Sam Caddy, on October 7 announced that the union wholeheartedly supported Chandler because of his excellent labor legislation record.[31] Later, at a District 30 UMWA rally at Pikeville, Kentucky, International President John L. Lewis called on twenty-five thousand miners, including those from Harlan, to elect Chandler by an overwhelming margin.[32]

With solid UMWA support, Chandler handily won the election. While his resounding majority in Harlan did not equal his primary and runoff victories, he triumphed by 2,222 votes. Chandler swamped his opponent in the Three Point, Yancey, Mary Helen, Benham, and Wallins precincts, while Swope swept two Verda precincts, High Splint, and Tway which had previously gone to Chandler.[33]

The *Harlan Daily Enterprise* hailed Chandler's victory and at the same time called the quashing of the indictments against Denhardt and other national guardsmen an insult to the Harlan Circuit Court.[34]

On December 10, 1935 "Happy" Chandler was inaugurated as Kentucky's new governor. His administration began a quadrennium devoid of much of the strife and turmoil between state and Harlan officials which had occasioned the final year of Laffoon government. The hopes of the miners which had burned brightly after the passage of the Wagner Act flickered faintly at the end of 1935. With the end of the Laffoon administration the union now wondered if the Chandler regime would support their cause, for on the day of his inauguration, Sheriff Middleton, a Republican, and several of his deputies personally escorted Chandler.[35] A few weeks later Chandler cleared Middleton of all charges brought by the Laffoon administration.

Eventually the Wagner Act would be the miner's ticket to freedom, but in the meantime, there would be more trouble and more harassment by Harlan deputy sheriffs.

7

THE FEUDAL LORDS OF HARLAN

Into unfriendly and militantly anti-union Harlan County during the summer of 1935 came Joseph J. Timko to lead an organizational drive. Since only Black Mountain, Black Star and Cloversplint were operating under union contracts, Timko, organizer Jim Allen of District 30, and several co-workers met at the Pine Mountain Inn near the Harlan-Bell line to plan union strategy. Although mine guards were everywhere, union leaders then scattered throughout Harlan coal camps to contact miners. In efforts to evade gunmen, organizers sent advance men to set up as many secret meetings as possible.[1]

Tension always surrounded Timko and his assistants. One hot July night at the Cloversplint school, Timko was addressing two hundred miners on the benefits of union membership. Suddenly two cars containing armed deputies drove up outside and doused their lights. Timko quickly adjourned the meeting. With members of the local union on each side, Timko and Allen walked to their car, and with two men on each running board, sped away. Enroute to Bell County, the harried organizers stopped in Wallins to pick up A.T. Pace, only to learn that George Lee had already driven him from the town. When a car occupied by five men appeared, the organizers headed toward Bell County and outran the "thugs" on U.S. 119 to Pineville.

A few days later the UMWA made an attempt to re-establish headquarters in Harlan. Accompanied by Timko and Pace, the organizers were travelling toward Harlan when a car occupied by six armed men overtook them, passed, then stopped and blocked the highway. Armed with sawed-off automatic shotguns and pistols, three men jumped out and came running toward the union men. At gunpoint, the mine guards surrounded the organizers' car and ordered them to turn around and "get the hell out of here." Pace turned to one of the men whom he addressed as "Ben, " and asked if they could proceed to Harlan. In a threatening tone, Ben Unthank snapped, "I am warning you, Pace." The organizers then turned back toward Bell County.

Reaching Pineville, Timko told Turnblazer and Judge Gilbert about the incident. When Gilbert offered no relief, the organizers did not make another attempt to re-enter Harlan until August 3 when National Guardsmen, ordered into the county by Laffoon, provided protection. Even then they entered Harlan in cars that were not easily identifiable.

Timko later met with County Attorney Elmon Middleton to discuss the possibility of a grand jury investigation into the intimidation of the organizers. Middleton nervously said he would do all he could to help the union, but that he was on the "spot" and must not be seen with union officials. Middleton did not live to fulfill that promise.[2]

I

While the Wagner Act offered Harlan County miners new hope, they did not realize immediate benefits from the new law. First, strong anti-union hostility of leading Harlan operators had to be overcome.

Among the operators who opposed unionization was R.E. Lawson, general manager of Cornett-Lewis Coal Company. Lawson did not like union because it promoted hatred and divided the work-

Coal tipple, anti-union Harlan Fuel Company mine, Charles S. Guthrie, operator. (Courtesy: Knoxville News-Sentinel)

ers into classes. Charles S. Guthrie, secretary and general-manager of Harlan Fuel Company, Bryan W. Whitfield, vice-president and general manager of Harlan Collieries, and A.F. Whitfield, Jr.,[3] secretary-treasurer of Clover Fork Coal Company, opposed the union because of its involvement in the coal mine war of 1931-32. Although organizers could not contact workers at the High Splint camp, T.E. Mahan, Williamsburg attorney and operator of several coal properties in Harlan, basically followed a non-discriminatory union policy.[4]

C. Vester Bennett, president and general manager of Harlan Central Coal Company, refused in May, 1937 to bargain with the UMWA because its officials allegedly had told his men during a 1934 strike to damage and destroy mechanical mine equipment. Creech Coal Company would not allow union meetings although its employees had worked under a union contract until September, 1935. The company did not renew the agreement, according to

George Creech, vice-president and general manager, because the UMWA had charged it with code violations before the arbitration board in Knoxville. George S. Ward, speaking for the powerful HCCOA, declared, "The Wagner Act would not change conditions in Harlan County, and...they (the Association) would continue to block organization of the county."[5]

Several Harlan operators appeared to be more tolerant toward the union. William H. Sienknecht, operator of the Blue Diamond mine at Chevrolet, apparently attempted to work with the union. C.B. Burchfield, general manager of the Black Star Coal Corporation, swore that his company had never opposed the union while Elmer D. Hall, president of Three Point Coal Corporation, professed to have favored the organization all the while. According to a recent book *Growing Up Hard in Harlan County* by G.C. Jones, who was an undercover UMWA agent in the 1930's, Hall may not have had a pro-union attitude. Jones, for example, mentions that Hall built barracks near his mines to house state troops who came in to harass miners and union organizers.[6] While Bardo Coal Company had never operated under a union contract, President Kenes Bowling said it had never restrained workers who wanted to join the union. Similarly, Joe Stras, superintendent of the Kentucky Cardinal Coal Corporation, revealed that his company did not discriminate against the union and F.E. Gilbert, general superintendent of the Southern Mining Company, said that his company had the "check off" until January, 1937.[7]

2

With its organizational efforts temporarily stalled, the UMWA brought suits against Harlan authorities in federal court at London. Fourteen former Kentucky coal miners, who were arrested and jailed at Cumberland on February 9, charged Middleton and Gilbert with illegal imprisonment and demanded twenty-five thousand dollars damages each. UMWA attorney T.C. Townsend cited Middleton and his deputies with having denied the miners their civil rights by assaulting, arresting, and abusing them. Pointing to conditions which were strikingly similar to the Palmer raids during the Red Scare of 1919, the plaintiff's petition alleged that eleven men were crammed into two unventilated Cumberland jail cells measuring twelve square feet.[8]

The *Harlan Daily Enterprise* defended Gilbert and Middleton for suppressing lawlessness brought in by organizers and contended that it was the operators who had a genuine interest in the welfare of Harlan's miners. Likewise, the *Pineville Sun* criticized "imported troublemakers" for suing a judge who had followed the law and predicted that the litigation would intimidate neither Gilbert nor Middleton. Approving the legal action, the *United Mine Workers Journal* commented that the real purpose of the "reign of terror" in Harlan County was to prevent the union from gaining a foothold.[9]

In one of the suits, the UMWA won an impressive victory when a federal court jury awarded James Westmoreland $1,500 damages against Sheriff Middleton. In celebration of the verdict, T.C. Townsend announced that while the court kept on trying the cases, the UMWA would keep on organizing Harlan County.

The *Harlan Daily Enterprise* remained strangely silent on the court decision. The *United Mine Workers Journal* echoed the rejoicing of UMWA leaders by accusing Middleton, who had completely cooperated with anti-union coal companies, with having done more to discredit Harlan County than any other public official. Times are changing in Harlan, it opined, because for the first time the "Harlan County system had been 'cracked'."[10]

Encouraged by the federal district court decision, Townsend and Turnblazer laid the union's case before the LaFollette Civil Liberties Committee in Washington in spring, 1936. In a preliminary committee session, apparently held to determine if a full-scale inquiry was warranted, the union officials related that coal operators and their privately-paid deputy sheriffs had denied free speech, free assembly, and freedom of political rights in Harlan County. As examples, Townsend cited the Cumberland raid on UMWA headquarters on February 9, 1934, the subsequent imprisonment of twenty-five unionists in two dirty jail cells, and the kidnapping of Howard Williams. Only a thorough clean-up of conditions, said he, would bring industrial peace to Harlan County.[11]

Turnblazer, who had presided over District 19 for fourteen years, confirmed that UMWA organizers enjoyed no basic civil rights in Harlan County. To illustrate, he recalled the December 1934 "hemming-in" of the union delegation at the Lewallen Hotel and the apprehension of Timko, Pace, and Allen on a public highway in June, 1935 by Brutus Metcalf, Unthank and Lee. Referring to the Denhardt report, Turnblazer declared: "Our people in Harlan are not free. They are assaulted, evicted from their homes, and a universal blacklist exists. All these come from the fact that the deputy sheriffs are paid by the operators."[12]

The *United Mine Workers Journal* condemned the denial of free speech and assembly and the verbal and physical abuse heaped upon Harlan's miners and organizers by "gun thugs." Assigning responsibility for terroristic acts to various coal companies, the Journal concluded: "It is a story that, for sordidness, has rarely been equaled in all the decades of American history."[13]

Back in Kentucky, UMWA districts 19 and 30 called for a special session of the General Assembly to outlaw Harlan's privately-paid deputy sheriff system. Supportively, the executive committee of Labor's Non-Partisan League of Kentucky challenged Governor Chandler and the legislature to end "this disgrace to the fair name of our commonwealth."[14] To publicize the horrors of the deputy sheriff system, the union sponsored a series of statewide radio broadcasts over WHAS, Louisville.

Sam Caddy and John Y. Brown, a UMWA attorney in Lexington, organized the radio talks to inform the public about Harlan's "reign of terror." Brown assembled the data and arranged an impressive list of speakers, including Kentucky legislator Roy Conway of Pikeville, State Senator Joseph P. Tackett of Prestonburg, and the Reverend Adolphus Gilliam. The theme of the broadcasts was the denial of basic human rights to Harlan's miners. The Denhardt report furnished the basic source of information.

Beginning the broadcasts, Senator Tackett denounced the privately paid deputy sheriff system as "a sale of government itself." The sovereignty of the Commonwealth, he asserted, does not belong to public officials who sit in high places; nor to the capitalist nor to labor but to all the people of the state. Therefore, said he, public officials should be paid out of public funds alone.

Following Tackett, John Y. Brown, in a speech entitled "The Feudal Lords of Harlan," delivered a ringing indictment of the mine guard system. While impassionedly pleading for abolition of the system, he singled out denial of civil rights in Harlan County:

> The right to enjoyment of life and liberty has been abridged, reprisals have been effected against churches whose pastors criticized the system of privately-paid deputies, guaranties of the right to pursue safety and happiness have been vitiated, free dissemination of thought and opinion has been abolished, private property of individuals has been denied protection, and the right to peaceful assembly had been destroyed.

No properly informed legislature, Brown warned, could refuse to abolish a system that had denied at least six of the seven inalienable rights guaranteed by the State Constitution. The bottom line, according to Brown, was that "no feudal lord ever rode more ruthlessly...than the coal barons of Harlan County with their roving bands of deputies," whose sole purpose was to prevent men from joining labor unions.

Also appearing on the broadcasts were P.H. Callahan, a Louisville civic leader and industrialist; George C. Burton, a Jefferson County commissioner; and T.C. Carroll, vice-president of the Brotherhood of Maintenance of Way Employees, of Covington. Callahan, like Brown, condemned the mine guard system and demanded its abolition. Burton repeated Brown's charges that freedom of assembly did not exist in Harlan, and called for the state to banish forever the sale of police power to special interests. Carroll depicted Harlan as the only county in the state where UMWA representatives did not enjoy freedom of assembly. Harlan's coal barons, said he, used an army of deputies to abuse many of the county's citizens and anyone else who passed through the area.[15]

Incensed by the WHAS broadcasts, the Harlan grand jury, which was in session at the time, subpoenaed Roy Conway and John Y. Brown to tell all about the "reign of terror." Brown took to the air again to castigate Harlan officials for "making a grandstand

UMWA Attorney John Y. Brown; made "Feudal Lords of Harlan" speech, 1936. (Reprinted by permission—Knoxville News-Sentinel).

play" with the summons. Declaring that neither threat nor subpoenas nor summonses could intimidate future radio speakers, he once more assailed Harlan operators for hiring deputy sheriffs with full power of arrest off company property.

Despite Brown's protests, both he and Conway testified before Harlan's grand jury. First to appear, Conway, who co-authored a bill to outlaw the privately-paid deputy sheriff system in the 1936 Kentucky General Assembly, reported little personal knowledge of conditions in Harlan. The real purpose of his talk was to garner support for a special legislative session to reconsider the anti-mine guard bill. Brown, who made a symbolic appearance on Labor Day, 1936, revealed little firsthand information about Harlan conditions.

The grand jury report dismissed the radio addresses as political propaganda conjured up by persons prejudiced and antagonistic toward Harlan County. It noted that Brown had no direct information, but as an employee of the Non-Partisan Labor League, had made a speech for political purposes. Conway's talk, the grand jury opined, was delivered to promote interest in anti-mine guard legislation. In stark contrast to the theme of the radio talks, another Harlan grand jury called conditions in the county quiet and peaceable, acknowledged that business generally was good, and concluded the miners were as economically well off as those in any other section of the country.

The *Harlan Daily Enterprise* deprecated Brown's knowledge of circumstances in Harlan. Peace officers, it said, protected jobs held by Harlan County miners and the out-lawing of the mine guard system would deprive industrial operations of self-protection. The newspaper, whose editor was an ally of the HCCOA, rejected the complaint that mine guards had barred organized labor as it reasserted that living conditions in Harlan's non-union coal camps were more trouble-free than in most unionized fields. Once more the *Daily Enterprise*, as expected, praised local law enforcement and refuted Brown's characterization of the coal operators as "Feudal Lords" who, assisted by armed guards, treated their employees like medieval serfs.[17]

The grand jury investigation destroyed the labor radio series. According to Brown, the inquiry had intimidated speakers and made it impossible to obtain others. There was an impression throughout the state, he said, that Harlan "is a nation within itself," and that local authorities could do almost anything they wanted there. In planning the radio broadcasts, John Y. Brown and others probably erred in using the Denhardt report as a basic resource for the programs. Early on Harlan officials had considered it biased and used it to stop the talks.

3

Unalarmed by continued opposition from Harlan County officials, and undeterred by lack of success in getting the mine guard system outlawed, UMWA stalwarts, in late December, 1936, made plans for a massive organizational campaign. First, Turnblazer informed Governor Chandler about the union's plans to hold a District 19 rally at Evarts on January 3, 1937. The union, said he, would keep order and comply with the law. In return he asked the governor to protect the union's exercise of the basic rights of freedom of speech, press and assembly.[18]

Announcement of the January 3 rally appeared in the December 30 edition of the *Knoxville News-Sentinel*. Citing the case, *United States vs. Cruikshank* (92 U.S. 542), which affirmed the people's right to assemble peacefully and to petition Congress for a redress of grievances, the UMWA invited Harlan miners to the Evarts Methodist Church where organizational plans would be outlined. The union was not expecting trouble, Turnblazer suggested, and it was going into the county this time to stay.[19]

The Evarts rally never took place. Three days before the scheduled meeting, Dr. W.P'. Cawood, county health officer, placed Harlan under quarantine because of a meningitis outbreak. While the prohibition on public gatherings came at an inopportune time for the UMWA, health officials claimed it had nothing to do with union plans.[20]

Immediately Turnblazer voiced determination to proceed with the rally if the health department edict did not apply to churches. From the operating room at the Harlan hospital. Dr. Cawood replied that the ban included churches. The union, the district union chief responded, would abide by all health laws and "be good little boys," but UMWA plans to organize Harlan County were still on. "They can't stop us," he declared.[21]

With the cancellation of the Evarts rally, the UMWA leaders switched the district convention to Middlesboro where pro-union Middlesboro and Bell County officials welcomed one hundred and twenty-five delegates. Turnblazer, Caddy, William Mitch, president of Alabama's District 20, and other union luminaries militantly called the miners into the union fold. Now was the time to organize, said Turnblazer, and if a majority of the miners signed up, unions would be planted in every mine in the county.[22] Warning that the task would not be easy, and would take time, money and courage, Sam Caddy advised that the UMWA would provide both funds and organizers. Although Governor Chandler, he said, had earlier killed a bill to outlaw the mine guard system, Harlan miners would no longer be detained from joining the union by that vicious system. William Mitch compared the Harlan fight to an earlier struggle in Alabama, and pledged the cooperation of District 20.

Also challenging the miners in stirring speeches were P.T. Fagan, district president from Pittsburgh; Peter Campbell, secretary of the Kentucky Federation of Labor; Hugh Lyons, District 12 representative from Illinois; and William Blizzard, District 17 vice-president from West Virginia. Harlan must be organized, Fagan emphasized, because it is a "black eye," the last barrier of resistance to the union cause. The workers, he said, should rise up like "men of courage" and join a union built by "men of courage." Campbell called Harlan the "stink hole of America," a blemish on America's union map. Chandler, said he, had misled labor, and "if he betrays us again, if I am the last man in Kentucky to do it, I'll tear off his pants and give him a licking." Lyons offered District 12 support to the new organizational campaign and Blizzard cautioned that it would take only time to re-establish the organization in Harlan over the opposition of company-paid deputies and company-controlled officials. "If the men...want to belong to the United Mine Workers of America, he exclaimed, all hell can't keep them out."[23]

Closing the convention, T.C. Townsend brought up the meningitis ban. "Unionitis" and Middletonitis," he argued, "cannot exist in the same case, and I know unionitis will win out." Following these rousing speeches, the convention, swept by enthusiasm, voted the moral, financial, and legal resources of nine UMWA districts to the Harlan County campaign.

Even before the miners had gathered in Middlesboro, UMWA officials had entered Harlan to organize the miners. Directed by L.T. "Tick" Arnett, who was one-fourth Cherokee Indian and a fine organizer though highly nervous, organizers met with enthusiastic miners at Harlan, Evarts and Black Mountain. Since Arnett and the miners doubted the genuineness of the meningitis quarantine, the union continued to send organizers into Harlan, and planned a mass rally as soon as the ban on public gathering ended.[25]

The nascent Harlan campaign coincided with the expiration of contracts in all unionized soft coal fields. District 19 leaders believed, therefore, that a robust Harlan organization would lead local operators to accept a contract in accord with the national agreement. Predicting victory for the new campaign, Townsend and Turnblazer listed five reasons for its probable success: (1) the re-election of President Roosevelt whose administration had sponsored the Wagner Act; (2) UMWA organizers, if harassment continued, could appeal both to Congress and the Kentucky General Assembly; (3) the La Follette Civil Liberties Committee could be summoned to Harlan if violations of the civil rights of UMWA leaders continued; (4) a federal court jury recently had awarded James Westmoreland $1,500 damages against Sheriff Middleton; (5) the Harlan movement expected to receive extensive support in men and money from at least nine other districts.[26]

Thus the union looked to the January, 1937 campaign as the decade's brightest opportunity to organize Harlan County. But first there was additional violence and murder, before the union came to Harlan to stay.

MURDER!

I

The new campaign to organize the miners of Harlan County began in earnest on January 9, 1937 when Vice-President Arnett and a delegation of fourteen organizers visited Evarts and Wallins. Almost at once the unionists realized that several deputies, including George Lee, were on their trail so at nightfall, they returned to friendlier Bell County. Two days later Arnett and his fellow organizers returned to Harlan and established headquarters at the New Harlan Hotel, because, according to Turnblazer, Governor Chandler had promised protection.[1]

The *Knoxville News-Sentinel* appealed for cool heads during the campaign. It admonished both union leaders and coal operators to permit the miners freely—with no coercion or compulsion from either side—to make their own choices in the American Way. If the operators restrained "gun thugs," said Turnblazer, the UMWA would convene a meeting and allow the men to decide for or against the union. If the workers rejected the union, the UMWA would withdraw. If the miners voted for the union, the HCCOA should accept it. George S. Ward refused comment on Turnblazer's proposition.[2]

With failure of compromise efforts, the UMWA broadened its efforts. From its Harlan headquartes, organizers, handicapped by the meningitis quarantine and constantly spied upon by the sheriff's office, approached miners on an individual basis. In mid-January, Arnett informed an old acquaintance, Deputy Allen Bowlin, that the organizers were going about their business peacefully and were not drinking or carrying weapons. Replied Bowlin: "You are a damned fool if you think you can do it peacefully." Slipping into Arnett's room the next day, the deputy offered to become an undercover agent for the union. Arnett vetoed the proposition. Later Bowlin informed Arnett that organizers faced death, dynamitings, and burnings by the "outfit you call thugs."

During the opening phases of the campaign, Arnett asked Sheriff Middleton for protection. Middleton, however, hesitated to protect the UMWA because of the false imprisonment judgment the union had obtained in Federal Court.[3] So for a time the sheriff followed a middle-of-the-road policy by neither protecting nor harassing the union and its leaders. After Governor Chandler had dismissed ouster proceedings[4] against Middleton in mid-January, Harlan's deputies noticeably expanded anti-union activities. Appearing in large numbers, gun "thugs" impressively displayed sidearms, talked abusively, and told organizers to get on the hard road and keep moving.

On January 22, Arnett called UMWA organizers together to warn that "things were getting awfully tight." They should, said he, remain in their rooms on hearing any disturbances in the hotel or outside in the streets. The warning was not in vain. At about three o'clock the next morning, Arnett was suddenly aroused by the rattling of his door and a disturbance in the hotel hallway. On hearing a hissing, sizzling sound and assuming that dynamite was about to explode, he opened the window and jerked out the screen. While attempting to alert his companions, he detected the odor of tear gas. Looking out into the hallway, Arnett spotted three tear gas bombs which he immediately raked away from his door. Suddenly two explosions in the street outside rocked the hotel. About three minutes later, hotel guests, including screaming women and crying children, streamed into the gas-filled corridors and downstairs to the lobby. When efforts to summon city policemen and Sheriff Middleton failed, Arnett called "Peggy" Dwyer in Pineville and asked that information about the attack be passed on to Governor Chandler.

On learning of the hotel gassing, Adjutant-General Lee McClain ordered Sergeant Clyde Jones, commandant of Harlan's state highway patrol unit, to investigate the episode. Jones allegedly refused because it would put him on the "hot-spot" and "they would bump him off." Finally, pro-union Bell County Sheriff James W. Ridings, accompanied by his brother, Deputy Chester Ridings, escorted the organizers out of the county. In Harlan for a little more than a week, the beleagured union men had to continue organizational efforts from Pineville's Continental Hotel.[5]

When Middleton got around to investigating the disorders,"[6] he concluded that neither threatened to "take human life," and surprisingly laid the blame on the UMWA.

In a letter to the sheriff, Turnblazer condemned the continued harassment of organizers by Harlan deputy sheriffs. Once again he requested protection. This time Turnblazer's plea failed to reach Middleton. Deputy Lee Ward intercepted the letter and inscribed: "Refused by W.L. Ward, Deputy and Office man to Sheriff Middleton." Unopened, the letter, along with several others which demanded security for UMWA leaders, was returned to Turnblazer.[7]

On a quiet Sunday afternoon a week later, Marshall A. Musick and his wife walked to the homes of several Evarts church members to discuss removal of the meningitis ban so that church services could be held. Along the way they noticed that cars occupied by Deputy Sheriffs Bob Eldridge and Hugh Taylor, and coal operator Tom Holmes, of Cook and Sharp Coal Company, passed several times. While visiting a parishioner, Musick, who was Arnett's assistant, noticed three cars parked across the valley from the house. Later, as the Musicks returned home down the railroad tracks which paralleled the highway, gunfire broke the Sabbath calm and bullets, spraying all around the couple, caused dust and gravel to fly in all directions. Miraculously the Musicks escaped serious inju-

UMWA organizer L.T. (Tick) Arnett who led the 1937 UMWA organizing campaign in Harlan (Reprinted by permission—Knoxville News-Sentinel).

ry, although Musick reported feeling a sting on the back of his neck and his hat flying off his head. Friends recalled that as the Musicks started home, cars occupied by Deputies Fayette Cox, L.E. Ball, Lee Fleenor, Bob Eldridge, Hugh Taylor, and Frank White drove slowly down the road behind them.[8]

Apparently Tom Holmes had prior knowledge about the attack. James H. Brewer, a Baptist deacon, former coal miner, and Holmes' brother-in-law, recalled that the coal man had warned him to remain inside while "they" gave Musick a "enouncing." While Brewer watched the events leading up to the attack and heard the shots, he did not see the actual shooting because of a curve in the highway. A few days later, Deputies Lee, Fleenor, and Bowlin ransacked Brewer's house "for meat," without a search warrant.[9]

Despite these attacks, organizers, at the direction of "Tick" Arnett, entered Harlan during the day and returned to Pineville at night. Near the end of January the union made another attempt to re-establish headquarters at the New Harlan Hotel. The management refused to provide rooms. On these frequent visits. Deputies Bowlin, Lee, White, and Wash Irwin shadowed the organizers.[10]

MURDER!

2

On February 6, the Harlan County Health Department finally lifted the meningitis quarantine. Within forty-eight hours six organizers had visited the Evarts vicinity to plan a mass union rally. Securing a plot of ground, they conducted a union meeting in early afternoon in order to be out of the area by nightfall. As the organizers drove through the community of Verda, about three miles from Evarts, they saw Deputy Frank White seated in his car by the side of the road. As the union caravan passed, two short horn blasts sounded. Immediately, a barrage of gunfire rained down on the cars from the wooded hillside. One bullet punctured the radiator of organizer W.M. Hall's car, another ripped Arnett's hat from his head, while a third struck organizer Matt Bunch's automobile. Pursued through Harlan to Baxter, the organizers unsuccessfully sought protection from two state patrolmen. Sheriff Middleton also passed by but refused assistance. Stranded, the organizers boarded a bus for Pineville.[11]

The most seriously wounded organizer was Thomas Ferguson, a UMWA veteran of thirty-seven years from New Lexington, Ohio. Ferguson later displayed clothing worn on the day of the attack and furnished these details: a soft-nosed bullet struck his shoulder, tore a hole of about three inches in his coat, passed through his hip, and left a large hole in his underwear. Arnett described the wound as a "nasty hole" in Ferguson's back. Hospitalized in Pineville for about five days, Ferguson was under heavy guard for two nights. Incapacitated for more than a month, he did not return to the field until mid-March.[12]

Meanwhile, Marshall Musick continued to be a "marked" man. In early February several friends warned him to leave the county. While in Evarts to transact union business on the morning of February 9, he noticed that Unthank, White, Fleenor, Lee, Irwin and Ball were shadowing him more closely than usual. Recalling the earlier warning, Musick went home, discussed the situation with his wife, and decided to leave. Before boarding a train for Pineville late in the afternoon of February 9, Musick called his family together and told 19-year-old Bennett to take care of his mother and the other children. He never saw his son alive again.[13]

Following the departure of the elder Musick, the family, according to one report, gave a small party for some neighborhood children whom they had entertained by making candy. By 8:30 the party was over and the children had gone home. Suddenly, without warning, bullets began flying through the air into the Musick home located about two hundred feet from State Highway 38. Mrs. Mallie Musick vividly remembered that terror-filled night: She recalled reading the paper in the living room while the radio was playing. A daughter, Pauline, was ironing and the three boys were playing checkers. Suddenly she heard a sound like "something popping in the grate" following by several similar sounds. When she realized that bullets were crashing into the house, she told the children to run toward a back bedroom. The family crouched for several minutes in a darkened corner of the room. When the firing stopped, Mrs. Musick called out to each of the children. In turn three answered. When Bennett did not respond, she crawled over and discovered him dead. Another son, Bert, suffered minor injuries from flying splinters while Mrs. Musick received similar wounds in the neck. According to a neighbor, there were three slow-moving automobiles in front of the Musick house at the time of the attack, and as soon as the shooting stopped, all three headed rapidly toward Evarts.[14]

A coal miner for about a year and a union member since age fifteen, Bennett Musick apparently died instantly from bullet wounds in the head.[15] While the night-riders intended to kill Marshall Musick, they shot instead Musick's son who became Harlan's first victim in the unon campaign of 1937.

Marshall Musick learned of the tragedy on arrival at UMWA headquarters in Pineville. Concerned about the safety of his family, Bell County Sheriff Ridings and Deputy Chester Ridings, went to Evarts, found the terror-stricken family in their darkened home, and brought them and Bennett Musick's body to Pineville.

On Friday, February 12, Bennett Musick was laid to rest near St. Paul, Virginia, the Musick family homeplace. Raised later at the gravesite was a massive monument.

UMWA District 19 President William Turnblazer (L) and UMWA Attorney T.C. Townsend (R). (Reprinted by permission—Knoxville News-Sentinel).

The Musick family resided in Pineville for about a year, then moved to Jellico, Tennessee, where Musick continued to work as an UMWA organizer in East Tennessee and in Whitley and McCreary Counties in Kentucky.[16]

3

Immediately following the murder, Judge Gilbert ordered an investigation by Judge Saylor, Sheriff Middleton, and County Attorney Bert O. Howard. Middleton at once offered a reward of five hundred dollars for information leading to the arrest and conviction of the person or persons responsible for the assassination. Howard visited the murder scene the next day. An estimated twenty-five shots struck the house and young Musick was hit in the lip by a bullet which penetrated his brain. Also interviewed were neighbors, who were of little help because they were asleep at the time of the shooting. Citing the murder, the shootings, and the hotel gassing, Gilbert ordered a special term of court and a special grand jury. The charge to the grand jurors included two matters in particular: (1) the slaying of Bennett Musick; (2) the ambush-shooting of organizer Tom Ferguson.[17]

Following assurances from Harlan officials that witnesses would receive complete protection, the grand jury, headed by Harlan businessman Homer Highbaugh,[18] began deliberations in mid-February. Apparently, after the grand jury made a genuine effort to provide immunity, "witnesses did not hesitate to tell freely all they knew."[19]

The grand jury reported on four cases: the Musick murder, the ambush of organizer Ferguson, the gassing of the New Harlan Hotel, and the assault on Marshall and Mallie Musick. Its report disclosed that there was insufficient evidence to warrant indictments because witnesses, who told both of hearing shots and seeing cars at ambush scenes, and of seeing masked men at the New Harlan Hotel before tear gas bombs exploded, could not identify any assailant. The grand jury reckoned that since most of the crimes were committed either from ambush or at night, witnesses either were asleep or were otherwise unable to name persons responsible for the felonies.[20] Later, however, several persons who testified before the grand mry related far different accounts of these crimes.[21]

Meanwhile, UMWA representatives, and counsel, including T.C. Townsend and Turnblazer, assembled photographs of the Musick home, of Bennett Musick's body, and affidavits from Mallie Musick and other persons for presentation to the La Follette Civil Liberties Committee which was meeting in Washington. Alleging "industrial autocracy" in Harlan County, and attributing the murder of Bennett Musick to the mine guard system, Townsend again called for the end of "gun thug" rule. On behalf of the UMWA, he asked the La Follette Committee to investigate Harlan where union representatives could not enter to organize coal miners who want to be organized.[22]

Before the end of the month, five La Follette Committee representatives, armed with subpoenas, arrived in Pineville. Headed by Benjamin Allen and Felix Frazer, the delegation also included John Y. Brown and L.T. Arnett. Calling for a thorough investigation of conditions in Harlan County, Frazer and his associates summoned Sheriff Middleton, Pearl Bassham, R.E. Lawson, Tom Holmes, and

Bryan W. Whitfield, Jr. So that they might be easily recognized, committee agents drove automobiles bearing red, white and blue decals inscribed with the words, "U.S. Senate Civil Liberties Committee."[23]

Following four years of almost continuous industrial turbulence, Harlan County conditions now faced exposure by a federal agency. Unlike previous investigations, the La Follette inquiry had official status. The Dreiser group, and other inquirers of the 1931-32 period, had conducted unofficial investigations: the Denhardt commission, as noted, became involved in a political tempest. Beginning in spring, 1937 the La Follette probe marked the entry of federal authority into the Harlan conflict.

Monument erected at Bennett Musick's gravesite by UMWA. (Bennett Mustek's grave is located in the vicinity of the 1989 dispute between the UMWA and Pittston Coal Group.) (Courtesy: Marshall A. Musick).

INQUIRY IN WASHINGTON

I

On Monday, March 22, 1937, the La Follette Civil Liberties Committee opened its investigation into the labor turbulence of the Harlan County coalfields. The scene was a small hearing room in the Senate Office Building in Washington, half of which was available for spectators. Taking up the other half of the room was a magnet-shaped rostrum at which sat Senator Robert M. La Follette, Jr., Senator Elbert Thomas of Utah, attorney John Abt, and Robert Wohlforth, the committee's executive secretary.[1]

The committee first looked into the weapons and ammunition bought by Harlan coal companies after January 1, 1933. Several companies, on request, produced invoices which showed purchases of revolvers, shotguns, rifles, tear gas grenades, sickening gas grenades, riot guns, both long and short range projectiles, and Thompson sub-machine guns. Kept in company arsenals, several Harlan coal operators admitted that these weapons were necessary to combat UMWA efforts to organize Harlan County.[2]

2

A highlight of early committee sessions was incriminating testimony offered by two of the principals in Harlan's long and stormy coalfield warfare. A dour, bespectacled George S. Ward, HCCOA Secretary since 1931, in a matter-of-fact manner, disclosed that the Association's monthly financial statements came from penciled notations of checks and cash vouchers later destroyed. When a shocked Senator La Follette inquired, how long has that been your practice?, Ward responded about three or four years because he feared an investigation.

The average annual income of the HCCOA, according to Ward, was about sixty thousand dollars derived from an assessment on coal mined by its members. Normally a half cent per ton, an increase to one cent per ton came during the reorganizational campaigns of July—November, 1933, November 1935—January 1936, and January—February, 1937. The reason for the increase, he said, was to fight UMWA organizing efforts.

Strangely vague about Ben Unthank's activities for the HCCOA, Ward, when pressed, revealed that the Association had disbursed more than $2200 to its "field man" or "chief thug,"[3] during the January—February, 1937 organizing campaign. Asked what Unthank did. Ward commented that the HCCOA had provided the money without asking what he (Unthank) did with it. Significantly, the disbursement to Unthank had come at the time of the gassing of the New Harlan Hotel, the Ferguson ambush, and the murder of Bennett Musick.[4] Uncertain about Unthank's work for the HCCOA, Ward positively remembered not ordering the terroristic acts allegedly committed by the "field man" and his associates.

Ward insisted that the HCCOA did not dabble in local politics during the 1930's. La Follette refuted that notion since Ward, a former Harlan sheriff, was county GOP Chairman, and Silas J. Dickenson, operator of the Mary Helen mine, was Democratic boss.[5]

Following Ward as a witness was Harlan's controversial sheriff, Theodore Roosevelt Middleton, who had risen from relative obscurity to the county's chief law enforcement officer. Before becoming sheriff, Middleton had operated poolrooms at Wallins and Evarts, run a grocery at Evarts, worked in mines owned by his mother, worked as a real estate agent in Tacoma, Washington, and operated a restaurant in Harlan. Immediately before taking office as Harlan's police chief, he had acquired ten shares of stock in the Green-Silvers Coal Corporation, and as chief, had operated a dairy farm near Harlan. Once, during the 1920's Middleton had spent six months in prison for violating prohibition laws.[6]

The La Follette Committee examined at length four areas of the sheriff's Harlan County administration: (1) ties with Harlan coal operators; (2) reputations of more than three hundred Middleton-appointed deputy sheriffs; (3) accumulation of a large personal fortune while in office; (4) unorthodox use of Harlan tax funds.

1. TIES WITH HARLAN COAL OPERATORS: As mentioned above, several of Harlan's leading coal operators had signed the sheriff's performance bonds. Confronted with this information, Middleton denied any connection between the sheriff's office and the coal men. Conversely, La Follette argued that there was a direct link between Middleton and the operators who had saved him a considerable sum of money. When Middleton stuck to his story. La Follette rejoined: "Well, the record will speak for itself."

2. REPUTATIONS OF MIDDLETON'S DEPUTIES: Records furnished the committee revealed that from January 1, 1934, to March 1, 1937, the sheriff had appointed 379 deputies, of whom one hundred sixty-three still held commissions on March 1, 1937. Middleton disagreed, saying he did not believe there were more than ninety deputies, some of whom were inactive. Unsure about the number he paid, Middleton finally concluded that nine lawmen received their salaries from the sheriff's funds. The remaining officers were on the payrolls of Harlan coal corporations.

When campaigning for sheriff, as noted above, Middleton had promised to appoint "sober and discreet deputies." Four years later, the sheriff admitted that the characters of some were fairly good, while the reputations of others were not so good.[7]

Indeed the reputations of several Middleton-appointed deputies were not so good, for Harlan court records revealed that grand juries, in 1934 and 1935, had indicted several deputies, including the sheriff's brother and first cousin, for obstructing justice, drunken driving, carrying concealed deadly weapons, flourishing dangerous weapons, stealing a ballot box, detaining a female, illegal voting of ballots at one county precinct, willful murder, robbery, malicious shooting and wounding, and malicious striking and wounding.[8]

The most blatant example of the appointment and reappointment of a deputy with a criminal background was Lee Fleenor. Indicted, tried, and freed on two counts of murder in 1932, Fleenor finally went to the state penitentiary in 1934 following a conviction for murder. After serving slightly more than a year, he returned to Harlan and became an active deputy in January, 1937.

In fact, the reputations of seven deputies were so bad that a 1934 Harlan grand jury had recommended dismissal. Although each man had been indicted on at least one felony charge, the sheriff failed to discharge any of the seven.

Other documents showed confinement of thirty-six Harlan deputies in the Kentucky State Reformatory at Frankfort. Six officers had served time for manslaughter. A Federal Bureau of Investigation transcript revealed the conviction of one Harlan officer for using the mails to defraud and the sentencing of at least ten other deputies for such crimes as white slavery, arson, and automobile theft and transportation across a state line.

Armed with abundant evidence, La Follette successfully challenged Middleton's previous contention that the reputations of his deputies were "fairly good." When asked if he had any further comment to make about the character of his deputies, Middleton replied, "No, Sir."[9]

3. ACCUMULATION OF PERSONAL FORTUNE: The evidence also documented substantial business ties between Middleton and his wife, leading coal operators and county officials. Partners of the Middletons in Verda Supply Company, the company commissary of the Harlan-Wallins Coal Corporation, were Mrs. Morris Saylor, wife of the county judge, Mrs. Pearl Bassham, and Bill Bassham, brother of Pearl Bassham. Allies of the sheriff at Harlan Bourbon and Wine Company, which controlled liquor franchises throughout the county, including those in the unincorporated mining camps, were County Judge Saylor, County Treasurer W.W. Lew-

is, and Attorney H.M. Brock. Both business ventures were highly profitable for the sheriff.

On assuming office, Middleton had these assets: ten thousand dollars, a herd of dairy cows valued at five thousand dollars; ten shares of Green-Silvers stock worth one thousand dollars; stock market investments of three thousand dollars and one thousand dollars in his personal account at Harlan National Bank. From his annual salary as sheriff, limited by law to a maximum of five thousand dollars, Middleton received $3,094.95 in 1934; $4,234.32 in 1935; and $4,460.09 in 1936.

When the La Follette investigation opened, Middleton's financial empire had increased tenfold. For example, as president of the Green-Silvers Coal Corporation, in which he owned thirty shares of stock, he received a monthly salary of $650; he also owned 160 shares of stock in the Crummies Creek Coal Company; one-fifth or fifteen thousand dollars interest in a La Follette, Tennessee coal firm; and one-half or twenty-five hundred dollars interest in a Rockcastle County "wagon mine." Mrs. Middleton owned an additional forty-five shares of stock in the Green-Silvers mine and fifty shares in Verda Supply Company.

In 1937 the sheriff also owned the following stocks:

Gold Seal Electric	100 shares
Remington Rand	100 shares
Allegheny Corporation	100 shares
Commonwealth and Southern	100 shares
Cities Service	100 shares

Other assets included a 409-acre farm, stocked with over 100 head of dairy cattle, some sheep, hogs, and horses, near Pennington Gap, Virginia, and one-third interest in about 600 acres of coal land leased to the Harlan-Wallins Coal Corporation. Middleton and his wife also owned a house, a lot containing their dairy, and a residence lot and one-story business building in Harlan. In summary, then, from January 1, 1934, the day he took office, to spring of 1937, Middleton had amassed a fortune exceeding one hundred thousand dollars while receiving annual salary limited by law to five thousand dollars.[10]

Interested in this sudden accumulation of wealth, Senator La Follette began to probe into the sources of Middleton's income. Uncertain about annual dividends from his Green-Silvers Coal stock, Middleton admitted receiving about two thousand dollars from his Crummies Creek Company stock and, at least two hundred dollars a month from Verda Supply stock in 1936. For the coal land leased to Harlan-Wallins, Middleton and his wife had received ten thousand dollars per year. If the company mined more than ten thousand dollars worth of coal, it paid a royalty of nine cents per ton, netting the sheriff an additional four thousand dollars. Daily his dairy had sold around seven hundred quarts of milk, for about twelve cents a quart, to coal company stores in several coal camps. Finally, annual rents totalling $3,425 from two Harlan stores, purchased in 1936, added to Middleton's fortune.

When the committee began to look into the sheriff's stock market speculations, legal counsel, including Cleon K. Calvert, of Pineville, advised that additional revelations about his personal finances might result in income tax litigation with the Federal government. From that point Middleton refused to provide further details about his personal worth.

In truth, Middleton's testimony revealed that since 1934 his annual income, exclusive of the sheriff's salary, stock trading accounts, the wagon mine, and dairy, amounted to $20,075. La Follette asked why the sheriff had found the office so lucrative, especially since his annual income had never equaled the statutory limit of five thousand dollars. Replied Middleton: "I am just as puzzled about it as the Senator is."[11]

The committee concluded correctly that the sheriff had used his connections with Harlan's business community and coal operators to line his pockets. In turn the sheriff was an ally of operators who wanted to keep the UMWA out of the county.

4. USE OF HARLAN TAX FUNDS: In handling the state's monies, Middleton opened four accounts in the Bank of Harlan: (1) the sheriff's general account principally for general funds and tax monies; (2) a general tax account primarily for the deposit of tax money; (3) a special account for delinquent tax collections; and (4) the sheriff's personal account. Because he was bondable, Mid-

dleton assumed the right to convert money to personal use and to interchange money in the various accounts at any time. Both W.W. Lewis, the president of the Bank of Harlan, and vice-president Pearl Bassham apparently closed their eyes to these unconventional banking practices while Sheriff Middleton interchanged the four accounts at will.[12] For example, from January 1, through February 28, 1934, he transferred $59,000.07 in tax monies to his personal account although fiscal court reports allowed him only $25,783.31 as tax collector for that period. Unable to account for the remaining $33,216.76, the record showed that the sheriff had probably used tax money to pay personal stock-trading debts to Westheimer and Company, a Cincinnati brokerage firm, and to repay personal loans to Harlan banks.

Cosigning the sheriff's personal notes during his tenure in office were coal operators such as Pearl Bassham. It also seems apparent that Middleton had secured coal operators as personal bondsmen because some of them were willing to ignore his financial free-wheeling at banks in which they were officers and stockholders. Incredibly he perceived no irregularities in the handling of four bank accounts, nor did he believe that his financial machinations obligated him to anyone.

In sharp contrast, Senator La Follette pointed out that operators and business leaders had aided the sheriff by signing his notes and by helping him accumulate a large personal fortune. From the evidence, the senator's conclusion was right on target.[13]

There were additional inconsistencies in Middleton's testimony. Earlier the sheriff had told committee agents Jack B. Burke and Ernest Dunbar that the serial numbers of the burned gas shells recovered from the New Harlan Hotel were illegible. Refuting Middleton's allegations, Thomas Franklin Baughman, a special FBI agent and a firearms identification expert, reputed never seeing shells damaged so extensively.[14]

Finally, to climax Middleton's often vague and contradictory testimony, the La Follette Committee produced his military record. It seems that for four years the sheriff first saw duty as an enlisted man in the United States Army, then took the oath of an officer on June 19, 1917. After the war, when he applied for appointment as a regular officer, the Army vetoed the application because of lack of personal veracity. Asked to comment on the military report, Middleton tersely replied: "No comment."[15]

3

The La Follette investigation also disclosed that Morris Saylor, the 38-year-old Harlan County judge and Commonwealth's Attorney Daniel Boone Smith had extensive business connections with the coal operators. Saylor, a former Harlan merchant, and his wife, like the Middletons, owned one-fourth interest in Verda Supply Company and at one time the judge owned twenty shares of stock in Harlan Bourbon and Wine Company and fifty shares of stock in the Bank of Harlan.[16] Since Judge Saylor, who heard cases involving coal operators and mine guards, was a business associate of the coal mine owners, that may account for both his expressed unfamiliarity with the criminal records and sordid reputations of Harlan County lawmen and his failure to recall a 1934 grand jury report which had recommended dismissals of seven deputy sheriffs. The sheriff, said Saylor, could appoint any deputy he wanted and he (Saylor) had no voice in the matter.

Elected in Kentucky's 26th judicial district with UMWA support in 1933, Commonwealth's Attorney Smith, after assuming office, received monthly retainers from Harlan-Wallins Coal Corporation, Mary Helen Coal Corporation, and R.C. Tway Coal Company and was legal adviser to Black Mountain Corporation and Black Star Coal Corporation. If a conflict of interest arose, said Smith, he fulfilled his role as a prosecutor. On the other hand, since the HCCOA was "a very powerful thing, " and because both he and Unthank were employees of the operators, Smith admitted subconsciously believing one witness more than another.[17]

The composition of two Harlan grand juries during the critical months of February and March, 1937 came to light during the Senate inquiry. The foreman of the February panel was Homer R. Highbaugh, insurance agent-deputy sheriff and the son-in-law of A.B. Cornett of the Cornett-Lewis Coal Company, and broth-in-law to W.W. Lewis. The foreman of the March jury was Hens

Bennett, brother of C. Vester Bennett, operator of Harlan Central Coal Company. Other March jurors included: Deputy Sheriff Jim Black Howard, M.L. Wright, a Southern Mining Company official; Grant Saylor, the county judge's father; Deputy Sheriff Ben Gilbert; W. J. Metcalf, first cousin of Deputy Brutus Metcalf; and Matt Carter, an R.C. Tway Coal Company employee. While both George S. Ward and Smith were incredibly vague about the identity of some of the jurors mentioned above, relatives either of county officials or coal operators packed both grand juries. When the Musick murder case and the other anti-union crimes of January—February, 1937[18] were under consideration, nepotism dominated the selection of Harlan grand juries.[19] Harlan families, Smith confessed, were so inbred, had intermarried, and were so interrelated that an impartial jury was almost impossible to obtain.[20]

4

Vice-President Pearl Bassham of the Harlan-Wallins Coal Corporation was one of the few Harlan operators who showed up to testify before the La Follette Committee. His company, he said, controlled access roads into the camps, and despite the passage of the Wagner Act, enforced the "yellow-dog" contract. Although Harlan-Wallins was the largest single contributor to the Operator's Association in 1936, Bassham questioned neither Ward's reckless financial system nor the destruction of Association records. While he had attended nearly every HCCOA executive board meeting from 1933 to 1937, Bassham did not know what Ben Unthank had done with HCCOA funds because the board never discussed the matter.

According to Bassham, Harlan-Wallins made substantial profits off its employees. One profitable scheme was a monthly car "raffle" system in which the company sold around eight hundred chances, at one dollar each, on old, second-hand cars belonging to a company or county official, or a leading businessman. The holder of the lucky number got the car. In this way, the company had disposed of about two hundred cars over a ten-year period. The company also deducted from its employees between eighteen hundred and

Coal operator Pearl Bassham who headed the strongly anti-union Harlan-Wallins Coal Corporation. (Reprinted by permission—Knoxville News-Sentinel)

twenty-four hundred dollars per month for medical services. After compensating three physicians a total of $1,250 each month, the balance of the money went into the company treasury.[21]

Almost unconscionably Bassham admitted that he was unfamiliar with HCCOA by-laws which called for "the establishment and maintenance of cordial and peaceful relations between the employer and employee," but opposed all "movements to force the coal operators to recognize or adopt the so-called closed shop policy or practice." Asked if company towns, "yellow dog contracts," munitions, deputies, and business dealings with county officials constituted effective instruments for carrying out the by-laws, Bassham replied, "I guess that is right."[22]

Following Bassham's testimony, the La Follette Committee heard descriptions of terroristic acts allegedly committed by Harlan deputy sheriffs. First, two Harlan youths, twelve-year-old Markham Clouse and John Clouse, his thirteen-year-old uncle, were out hunting scrap iron on the afternoon of the Tom Ferguson ambush. Both boys said they had heard Frank White's "horn signal," and recognized Bill Lewis, Melvin Moore, Luke Hubbard, and Lee Hubbard on top of a cliff firing at the organizer's caravan. After-

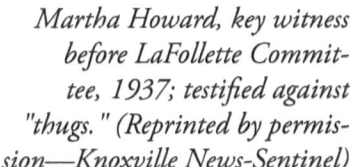

Martha Howard, key witness before LaFollette Committee, 1937; testified against "thugs." (Reprinted by permission—Knoxville News-Sentinel)

wards Pearl Bassham and Deputies Wash Irwin and Luke Hubbard warned the boys against telling the grand jury what they had seen. On a cold, dark February night in 1937, Kelly Fox, a twenty-nine-year-old automobile mechanic, who lived near the Musicks, had watched Deputy Frank White lean out of a car, and in the glare of its headlights, fire several volleys into the Musick house.[23]

Married in Washington during the La Follette investigation, Lawrence and Martha Howard described a Harlan cafe scene on the afternoon of the Bennett Musick slaying: Merle Middleton, Frank White, George Lee, and several other deputies had gathered in the Harlan Grill to drink. While the bourbon flowed, the laughter became raucous and the conversation risque. After a while, the white-haired Lee pulled out two pistols and tossed them on the table. A startled onlooker inquired: "Whatcha goin' to do, George, bump off old man Musick?" There was more laughter, drinks, jokes. Around seven o'clock, the deputies shoved back their chairs and reeled to their feet. Lee slammed his two pistols back in the holster. "We're going up to see Old Man Musick now. Come on, join us," he shouted to Lawrence Howard. Howard refused to go.

Deputy John P. Hickey offered Mrs. Martha Howard, a comely brunette, one hundred dollars for each organizer lured to a lover's lane. "I'll get him then," the deputy said. Mrs. Howard rejected the proposition.[24]

Two Harlan peace officers, William C. Johnson and Hugh Taylor freely discussed their anti-union activities. A former Baldwin-Felts guard, Johnson unabashedly referred to himself as a "thug" because he was always going "thugging." When Senator La Follette asked what that meant, the deputy said it meant "catchin'" union organizers, takin' 'em for a ride, and bumpin' 'em off. Johnson hastily confessed that while he had killed no one in Harlan County, he had followed orders to beat up union men and "bust up their meetings."

Although Hugh Taylor frequently trailed organizers, he declined to go see "old man Musick" in February. Later, after remarking that the murder of Bennett Musick was a "shame," Deputies Frank White and Wash Irwin followed Taylor, shot him in the hands and arms and left him for dead in a roadside ditch near High Splint. Deception saved his life. Although suffering intense pain, Taylor remained alert, raised a bleeding hand, allowed blood to drip on his chest, and then dropped the hand to his side. White and Irwin, their guns ready, cautiously drew near the body. Bending over and seeing the blood-soaked chest, White murmured, "We got him." Eventually Taylor landed in the Harlan hospital where a friend warned him to get out of town before Ben Unthank's gang killed him. Removed to the Pineville hospital, Taylor recovered but never returned to Harlan County.

Earlier Sheriff Middleton and Harlan businessman Clarence Poer allegedly offered Taylor two thousand dollars to "get lost" until the "heat" was off. Poer denied making this offer. Wash Irwin's only comment on the alleged attempt to murder Taylor: "I ain't got no compliments to say about it."[25]

Several Harlan citizens suffered remarkable lapses of memory in Washington. One, Merle H. Middleton, declared that he knew nothing about "thugs," had not helped break up union meetings, and did not recall that "thugging" meant hunting organizers. Nor did he remember being at the Harlan Grill on the night of the Musick murder. Apparently Middleton first had offered to go to Washington to refute the testimony of Lawrence and Martha Howard. Later he ignored two telegraphic summonses because he was "too busy," "was in a hurry," and "did not want to fool" with the committee aide who handed him the subpoena because he "looked like a kid."

At the conclusion of Merle H. Middleton's testimony, an exasperated and irate Senator La Follette declared:

> May I say for the benefit of the record and those who read it and may not see the attitude and appearance of this witness on the stand, that your memory has been so blank and your testimony so evasive that, for those who read it in the future, I would say that it was not worth serious consideration.

Like several other Harlan residents who testified in Washington, Merle H. Middleton seemed vexed by voluntary collective amnesia.[26]

5

While the committee listened to accounts of abuse and harassment at the hands of Harlan officials inside, two witnesses were roughed up outside the Senate hearing room. First, four burly men attempted to beat up Lawrence Howard in a Senate office building washroom. Then, after he had implicated several Harlan deputies in connection with the Bennett Musick murder case, Howard received a threatening telephone call in which a voice warned him to leave the capitol or be buried either in Arlington Cemetery or in Harlan's Resthaven Cemetery. On hearing this report, Senator La Follette admonished the Harlan crowd that "the city of Washington, the Capitol of this nation, is not in Harlan County, Kentucky, and the witnesses of this committee are not going to be intimidated with impunity if this committee can prevent it."

In a second incident, Ted Creech, the son of Harlan operator R.W. Creech, and an alleged ring leader in the "reign of terror," told Richard C. Tackett, "You've put the operators in a fine fix. Wait till we get you back in Harlan and we'll send you up for another eight or ten years." When Tackett reported this threat, Creech denied it as several lean, gaunt miners threw the hearing room into an uproar by jumping to their feet and shaking their fists at him. Tackett later testified against Creech, who was indicted and acquitted of perjury by a District of Columbia grand jury.[27]

6

With the completion of testimony local officials, business leaders, and the local press almost unanimously condemned the La Follette hearings. Judge Gilbert branded the inquiry one-sided, unfair and charged that witnesses who testified about acts of terror in Washington revealed no such information in his court.[28] Gilbert was right. Some of the same persons who told all in Washington were unresponsive and taciturn in Harlan. That was not so surprising since Harlan deputies thronged to the court house and to the court rooms when hearings and trials were in session. Their presence undoubtedly intimidated many witnesses who, out of fear for their lives, remained silent.

Clifford Dotson, president of the Harlan Kiwanis Club, agreeing with Gilbert that the investigation was unfair, criticized the handpicking of witnesses. The pro-operator *Harlan Daily Enterprise* proclaimed "The World Should Know the Truth," called the investigation a fiasco and lamented that both sides had not received a fair trial. While some things have gone on that should not have, the paper judged the operators blameless and sounded the old refrain that the miners were better off than in other coal counties.[29]

Recent studies have attempted to show that the La Follette committee had an ax to grind with its probe into the Harlan controversy. For example, Jerold Auerbach has said that the Committee was "biased," hand-picked its witnesses, and did not attempt "to tell both sides of an often sordid story."[30] More recently, John W. Hevener has subscribed to the Auerbach thesis.[31] Perhaps the La Follette Committee did have an ax to grind, perhaps its investigation was slanted toward organized labor, perhaps, as Auerbach has suggested, La Follette used the hearings to promote industrial unionism. While it may have had all these things in mind, nevertheless it appears that the committee made a genuine effort to get the operators and their accomplices to Washington to relate their side of "an often sordid story." For various reasons the committee failed. Ben Unthank, Harlan's "chief thug," dropped out of sight to avoid a committee summons. Other principals either did the same or simply refused to go to Washington. The fact of the matter is that George Ward was there, as was Sheriff Middleton, Daniel Boone Smith, Merle H. Middleton, Pearl Bassham, and Morris Saylor. These pro-operator witnesses all too often offered vague, obscure and contradictory testimony. On the other hand, pro-union witnesses freely related in detail the machinations of Harlan gunmen subsidized by the coal operators.

This is not to suggest that the union had clean hands. Of course, union men harassed non-union men, a fact of life in all industrial areas during the 1930's. That union fallacy does not alter nor obscure the fact that, in Harlan, the operators controlled the county courthouse and paid "gun thugs" to keep the union out of the county. The gunmen did their job well. The Hays-Bablitz Commission, the Denhardt Commission,[32] and the La Follette Committee documented that there was indeed a "reign of terror" in Harlan County. The La Follette Committee, as had its predecessors, publicized it in all its horror and apparently made a decent attempt to hear both sides of, an "often sordid story." To those persons not completely familiar with the demography of Harlan County, its environs, its politics, and the life-styles of its people, the evidence uncovered by the La Follette Committee may seem one-sided, unfair, biased. Local politicians who collaborated with the coal operators naturally believed that the investigation was unjust. On the other hand, many a local citizen admitted that it was dangerous to profess allegiance to the union during the terror-filled days of the 1930's. The La Follette inquiry exposed that unhealthy climate and in so doing, became the catalyst which ultimately pointed the way to the emancipation of Harlan's blue collar class.

The La Follette Committee ended its inquiry into Harlan's labor conflict on May 5, 1937. A while later it released a report which castigated Harlan's "thug gangs," who, with the knowledge, consent, and approval of the HCCOA, had perpetrated a "reign of terror" on Harlan's miners. Throughout the 1930's the HCCOA had subverted the office of sheriff and had used Ben Unthank and Merle H. Middleton to direct two "thug, gangs." Denied to Harlan's miners were basic civil liberties, such as free speech, free press, and free assembly. In essence, industrial policemen, furnished industrial munitions by the coal companies, prevented Harlan County's miners from joining the UMWA. A conspiracy by the operators, "abetted by a venal county administration," had kept Harlan's miners from enjoying the right of self-organization guaranteed by Section 7a of the National Industrial Recovery Act and Section 7 of the Wagner Act.

According to the La Follette Committee, the miners of Harlan were kept in a state of subservience by the company town system. A case in point was the unincorporated town of Lynch, owned by the United States Steel Corporation. Containing twelve thousand persons, the company controlled the miners, their families, relatives and friends who came to visit. Industrial policemen in "the kingdom of Lynch," acting as company agents, effectively suppressed attempts of UMWA organizers to solicit members. This repression continued despite the passage of NIRA and the Wagner Act. In short, in a single-spaced four-page report, the La Follette Committee discovered that Harlan County was closed to the UMWA despite passage of federal laws guaranteeing workers the right to join a labor union.[33]

7

While the La Follette Committee was preparing its report on Harlan conditions, the Federal Bureau of Investigation swung into action. In the summer of 1937, twenty bureau agents conducted an on-the-scene inquiry in Harlan County. Interviewing coal miners, organizers, and other prominent individuals, the FBI obtained detailed affidavits of anti-union policies and practices of Harlan coal operators and officials. For example, Sheriff Middleton told one Green-Silvers employee, discharged for loading "dirty coal," that you have been stung by that old union bee and I don't know if you will ever get it out of your system." The sheriff ordered another Green-Silvers worker, who had joined the union, off company property. Deputy Sherman Howard knocked a Harlan Collieries employee unconscious after learning that he belonged to the union. Mine Superintendent Harry Bennett, of Harlan Central Coal Company, switched an employee from brakeman on an electric coal hauler to coal loader because he had joined the UMWA. Later Bennett told the worker that he would never work another day because he had attended a union meeting. UMWA organizers James Bates and Robert Childers recalled numerous acts of terror by Deputies Unthank, Lee and White during the years 1933 to 1935.[34]

The FBI investigation, combined with the earlier La Follette inquiry, culminated in the indictments of twenty-two coal companies, twenty-four operators, and twenty-three peace officers by federal grand jury at Frankfort on September 27, 1937.

Naming sixty-nine defendants, the indictment charged that they

> did unlawfully and feloniously conspire, confederate and agree together and with each other and with. other persons and corporations to the Grand Jurors unknown to injure, oppress, threaten, and intimidate certain citizens of the United States...in the free exercise and enjoyment of certain rights and privileges secured to the said citizens by the Constitution and laws of the United States, to wit, the right and privileges of the said employees to self organization and to form and join and assist labor organizations and to bargain collectively through (sic) representatives of their own choosing and to engage in concerted activities for the purpose of collective bargaining and other mutual aid and protection, and secured to the said employees by Section 7 of the National Labor Relations Act of July 5, 1935.[35]

Alleged in the indictment were several acts of conspiracy: first, the HCCOA's policy of direct oppression and intimidation of unionists; second, the employment of Ben Unthank's gunmen to oppress, injure, and intimidate miners; third, Sheriff Theodore R. Middleton's appointment of deputy sheriffs, to threaten, beat, and kill pro-union miners. Other charges included false arrest and imprisonment of miners, disruption of union meetings, discharge of miners for alleged union activity, and annoyance of union organizers who sought to recruit members in Harlan County.[36] Alleging a conspiracy among the HCCOA, George S. Ward, Sheriff Middleton, and twenty-three deputy sheriffs, the federal grand jury charged this powerful coalition with preventing the organization of the Harlan coalfield by the UMWA.

The scene now shifted, in spring of 1938, to a tiny federal court room in London, Kentucky, where Harlan coal company executives and peace officers went to trial on charges of conspiring to keep the UMWA out of Harlan County.

THE MARY HELEN CONSPIRACY TRIAL

I

On May 16, 1938, the Laurel County seat of London, a farming community of about two thousand, became the scene of the great conspiracy trial, *The United States vs. Mary Helen Coal Corporation, et al.* After years of turmoil and terror, sixty-nine Harlan County coal corporations, coal operators and peace officers appeared in Federal court charged with conspiring to deprive Harlan miners of their right to join the United Mine Workers of America. Presiding was Federal Judge H. Church Ford, named to the Eastern Kentucky District by President Roosevelt in 1935.[1]

In 1938 London's business district, which ran along Main Street for about four blocks, consisted of the Federal Building, the town's tallest structure, the tri-level Laurel County courthouse and jail, three elevatorless hotels, each containing fewer than one hundred rooms, and a motion picture theater which opened only at night and on Sunday afternoons. Located in the town was Sue Bennett Memorial College, a Methodist-affiliated junior college. The principal denominations were evangelical, including Baptist and Methodist churches. Episcopal and Catholic communicants travelled to Corbin, about fourteen miles south, to worship.[2]

Despite the existence of a few area "wagon" mines, London mainly served as a shopping center for a farming area. On court days, bewhiskered and overalled farmers came to town to lounge and loaf on the streets with an occasional peek into courtroom happenings. They spent the day sitting around the courthouse, arguing politics, whittling, and spraying the area with tobacco juice.

As the Mary Helen conspiracy trial opened, London's Main Street sparkled with red, white and blue lights, and the American flag draped every building. In the dining room of the London Hotel, Old Glory occupied one corner, but nearby stood the Stars and Bars of the Confederacy, a silent reminder that states' rights were not dead in London. Next to the Federal Building a vacant lot was a beehive of activity. Operating there was a patent medicine man, a trailer equipped with an automatic picture-taking machine, a pottery salesman, and a hot dog and cold drink stand. The central attraction was a marathon checker game played by two solemn-faced negroes. Occasionally the sonorous monotone of a mountain exhorter or the nasal twang of a hillbilly singer who regaled the crowds with old mountain ballads disrupted the town's otherwise quiet atmosphere. On Saturday, May 21, at the end of the trial's first week, a concert performed by twenty-six high school bands from mountain communities added a festive touch to the little town.

The more than five hundred visitors, who were on hand for the courtroom litigation, transformed and modernized London's lifestyle. Just before the trial opened, for example, one of the town's first electrically refrigerated drinking fountains was installed in the Federal courtroom. Chief prosecutor Brien McMahon, of the Civil Rights Section of the United States Department of Justice, and his battery of lawyers leased an entire house and established direct teletype service to Washington.[3] A group of New York and press service correspondents took a lease on an apartment in a home near the Federal Building.

According to both the local and national press, the huge crowds who gathered for the trial severely taxed London's accommodations. Persons attending court rented practically all the town's available rooms, apartments and cottages. Several local families moved out of their homes and turned them over to visiting witnesses, attorneys and newspapermen. Sue Bennett College dormitories housed about half of the Government's two hundred-fifty witnesses. Visitors reserved the town's three hotels to the eaves and homes within "four gavel throws" of the courthouse prepared extra rooms to take care of the overflow crowd. Former Federal Judge Charles I. Dawson, who was chief defense counsel, several of his assistants, and clerical help occupied much of the Wilbur Hotel in Corbin, while more than two hundred defense witnesses shared an entire tourist camp at London's eastern limits. Joseph C. Harsh noted that London's hotels and rooming houses were doing a "land-office business" and its eateries were "flooded," yet by nightfall during most days of the trial, there were not enough strangers in town to turn a couple of dozen heads.[4] In short, London was enjoying a boom which it hoped would not end soon, observed F. Raymond Daniell in the *New York Times*.

2

The small courtroom in which the trial took place contained the massive elevated bench of Judge Ford. At the front, directly below the judge's bench, was the jury box. A curved railing running the entire length of the room separated the jurors from benches reserved for spectators. Inside this enclosure were several long tables reserved for counsel and for the press.[5] Judge Ford ordered newsmen who came from Chicago, Cincinnati, Louisville, New York and Knoxville to speak in subdued tones and to take no pictures.

At the outset, the defendants, attorneys and the special venire of one hundred twenty talesmen packed the small room to capacity. After the selection of the jury, one hundred seats were available for spectators.

At nine o'clock on Monday morning, May 16, Judge Ford gaveled court to order. Well known for his courtroom decorum, the judge put into effect a no smoking order[6] and limited access to the courtroom to United States marshals and deputy marshals, regular officers of the court, defendants and their attorneys, government counsel, jurors and prospective jurors, witnesses, and authorized representatives of the press. Ford also ordered marshals to disperse large gatherings of people in adjacent hallways or stairways and to search persons entering the courtroom for deadly weapons.

With these procedural matters out of the way, the clerk called the roll of defendants. Two were missing. One, Homer (D.Y.) Turner, a former Harlan County peace officer, had died. Former Deputy Hugh Taylor, who early on had electrified the La Follette Committee with his account of Harlan terrorism, was unaccountably absent. Judge Ford immediately ordered FBI agents to find, arrest, and escort the missing defendant to London.[7] Joining the defendants belatedly, and pleading not guilty, the court assigned counsel to defend Taylor.[8]

During the afternoon of Monday, May 16, the tedious process of jury selection began. For the remainder of the week, for the government, and Charles I. Dawson for the defense, carefully examined prospective jurors from about ten minutes to half an hour. According to a news report:

> The defense inquired whether the prospective juror had received any money from the government on any type of relief or benefit payment program. It wanted to know if the prospective juror had any opinion about capital and labor, whether he thought labor was the underdog, whether he had ever worked for any concern where there had been a strike, or whether he had employed labor himself. It inquired whether the prospective juror had any ill feeling or hostility toward any peace officer, or whether he had ever been a peace officer himself.[9]

Counsel also inquired into the relationships among jurors and their kinsmen, and the corporations and individuals on trial.

For the most part the process went smoothly and by the end of the week both sides had accepted a twelve man jury and two alternates from a total venire of two hundred seventy. Made up largely of southeastern Kentucky farmers and tradesmen from a rural non-industrial background, the jurors included:

L.F. Johnson, foreman, Clay County general storekeeper
W.B. Johnson, Whitley County farmer and ex-deputy
Arch Baldwin, Laurel County farmer
Alex Powell, Rockcastle County farmer and deputy
J.M. Hibbard, Laurel County farmer
T.N. Roberts, Clay County farmer
Edwin Bell, Wayne County farmer
Denton Campbell, Clay County merchant
Ellie Chestnut, Clay County farmer
Richard Hopper, Knox County carpenter
Walter Sizemore, Clay County farmer
Charles Evans, Knox County treasurer and school board treasurer

Added as alternates because the court expected a lengthy trial, were W.H. Main, a Knox County realtor, and A.B. Sams, a Clay County farmer.[10]

3

Following the selection of the jury, McMahon, a "thickset, black-haired Irishman," and Dawson, "square-jawed, stern, and sharp-spoken," delivered opening statements. Pointing a finger at the HCCOA, McMahon declared that the main bond that drew these men together was their common hatred of unions. He noted Ward, Ben Unthank, T.R. Middleton, and various operators had gathered in the Association's offices, located across the street from the county courthouse, to discuss ways and means of preventing coal miners from joining the union. The government, said McMahon, also expected to prove that these men and others, including deputy sheriffs, had secretly huddled in a back room of the courthouse, called a "whispering room," to map anti-union strategy.

In support of the conspiracy charges against the defendants, McMahon mentioned the involvement of the HCCOA in the increase of tonnage assessments, destruction of Association records, in employment of Ben Unthank as "field man," and collaboration between the HCCOA and former Sheriff Middleton who had become a coal operator after taking office. He summarized the violent events which had hindered organizational efforts in Harlan County and called the outbreak at Evarts on July 7, 1935, "a forerunner of things to come." McMahon closed by stating that

> the government would prove...that the defendants had indeed violated the laws of the United States, and the evidence would support the conspiracy charges.[11]

Speaking impassionedly and pacing back and forth so vigorously that his sock garter came unfastened, Dawson implored the jury not to try the defendants for the alleged acts of violence and terrorism which government counsel had depicted. The principal charges against the defendants, said he:

> were that they conspired to deprive the employees the right to join a labor union and to engage in collective bargaining through representatives of their own choosing.

In response to that charge, Dawson pointed out that the HCCOA, from October 2, 1933 to September 22, 1935, had agreed to union contracts which excluded the closed shop. Emotionally he exclaimed, "I say, gentlemen of the jury, when you hear this testimony, you will know—they talk about not dealing with the unions; that is the purest kind of drivel and poppycock."

Defense strategy intended to show that the sheriff's office wanted only to prevent a recurrence of 1931-32 when "outside agitators" had overrun the county. Theodore Middleton, said Dawson, had seen that the county was "not submitted to another outrage like that."[12]

Following Dawson's opening statement, the government began its attempt to prove collusion between the HCCOA and county officials. For about three weeks one hundred forty-eight witnesses, including Federal Bureau of Investigation agents,[13] and several Harlan County officials implicated a conspiracy among the defendants, while miners and organizers explicitly described anti-union activities by the defendants.

Among the first to testify, FBI agent George A. Stevens revealed that George S. Ward had said that the purposes of the HCCOA were to combat freight rate differentiation, establish an uniform system of accounting, and prevent the unionization of coal miners in Harlan County. Association "field man," Ben Unthank, Stevens re-emphasized, had received additional funds during the first two months of 1937 because of increased union activity in Harlan County. FBI agent R.E. Paterson quoted operator Charles S. Guthrie with saying that "gun thugs" were sometimes hard to hold in check, and L.P. Johnson, of the Crummies Creek Coal Company, with confessing that we have had some unscrupulous operators and deputy sheriffs.[14]

Three surprise government witnesses were former Harlan County jailer Clinton Ball and former deputy sheriffs Henry M. Lewis and Clarence Middleton, the sheriff's brother. Ball, a Democrat and political enemy of Theodore Middleton, stated that he had seen Unthank, Ward, Pearl Bassham, and the former sheriff together "lots of times," and that on the day of the Musick murder, there were "at least twenty or twenty-five deputies," including Unthank, Wash Irwin, Frank White, and Allen Bowlin around the courthouse.[15]

Although Lewis, who was a deputy sheriff until February, 1937, had refused to get involved in anti-union activities, he reported seeing Unthank, Ward and Bassham in the "whispering room" very often. Clarence Middleton told the court that he, too, had seen his brother, Bassham and Ward in the "whispering room" frequently, but that he had refused Bassham's offer to harass UMWA members and organizers.[16]

Another surprise witness for the prosecution was Elbert J. Asbury, superintendent of the Black Mountain Corporation. A former defendant, against whom the government had dropped charges, Asbury remembered looking over and returning financial statements at executive board meetings without noticing disbursements to Ben Unthank. On one occasion he recalled that operator Elmer D. Hall had protested the use of Association funds to oppose the union, whereupon operator Robert C. Tway had called him (Hall) "thin-skinned." Despite Dawson's stern cross-examination, Asbury stuck to his testimony that the government had not made a deal with his company in return for a pledge to testify against the defendants.[17]

Former Harlan Methodist minister Carl E. Vogel testified that George S. Ward apparently had attempted to get a Methodist preacher at Black Mountain removed because he "was too actively engaged in union activities." Ward also had said, recalled Vogel, that the Wagner Act would not alter HCCOA policy to block organization of the county.[18]

The prosecution also produced Mrs. Martha Howard as a witness. After she described some of the anti-union antics of Harlan deputy sheriffs, including the proposal allegedly made by Deputy John P. Hickey, the defense bitterly assailed her testimony.[19] Harlan Mayor L.O. Smith, Police Judge E.L. Howard, Patrolman Hamp Howard and Police Chief Harmon Noe paraded to the witness stand to describe her reputation as "bad." Those four officials also testified that Martha Howard and her husband, Lawrence, were in jail instead of at the Harlan Grill, on the night of the Bennett Musick murder.

One source has speculated that this defense testimony successfully impeached Martha Howard as a witness for the government. In rebuttal, the prosecution brought out that the date the Howards entered jail was altered from February 6 to February 7 on police court records and that Chief Noe had calculated a date of release which was not recorded. Whether the defense completely destroyed Martha Howard's credibility appeared somewhat doubtful in light of the government's rebuttal. The defense witnesses who gave this questionable testimony also were part of the local political establishment which was against the union.[20]

In an attempt to buttress its case, the prosecution climaxed its presentation by introducing several witnesses who testified about the murder of Bennett Musick. Relating stories which closely paralleled earlier versions, Marshall Musick and Mallie Musick, who sobbed and dabbed at her eyes with a red handerchief, described the slaying of their son. Two brothers, known as the "Sargent boys," recalled that Deputies Wash Irwin and Homer (D.Y.) Turner had aroused them from their beds on the night of the Musick murder and asked them to go to the Musick home. After pleading that they ("Sargent boys") had to work the next day, they went home and were not present when the attack occurred. Later, according to one of the "Sargent boys," Irwin laughed and said, "you ought to have been with us." He (Irwin) said, "We shot that house all to hell." Said, "That old man wasn't there," said, "when I shot there was the damndest (sic) streak of fire run from the door up."[21]

Opening its case on June 18, the defense had three goals: to introduce witnesses, mostly coal operators, linking Harlan's labor problems to the events of 1931-32 and the famous "Battle of Evarts;" produce coal miners to repudiate government testimony about alleged intimidation of unionists by the defendants; and deliver rebuttal testimony that would place some of the most vicious acts of violence, notably the murder of Bennett Musick, on union leaders.

Eleven operator defendants either strongly denied the anti-union activities charged by the government and its witnesses or justified their opposition to the union. Charles S. Guthrie, of Harlan Fuel Company, said that several "atheistic," Communistic posters seized at the Evarts UMWA headquarters in 1931 convinced him that the union was "a bad moral influence." After he had opposed the use of HCCOA funds for anti-union activities, Elmer D. Hall said George S. Ward had assured that the Association would stop spending money for that purpose because Ben Unthank was no longer its employee. D.B. Cornett, payroll clerk for the Cornett-Lewis Coal Company, testified that after lodging a similar complaint. Ward had promised that there "would be no more of that."[22]

Over one hundred miners strongly defended their employers. To a man, they denied that their bosses opposed the union.[23]

Three defense witnesses tried to prove that Deputy Frank White was not involved in the murder of Bennett Musick. Government witness Kelly Fox, a young automobile mechanic, had placed White on a highway near the Musick home, firing shots toward the house. Not so, said the defense. Instead, Frank White had whirled through several Harlan County nightspots accompanied by Bettie Huntsman, Emily James Weaver, and Claudia Eaton. On cross-examintion, Welly K. Hopkins brought out that White was married at the time, but on redirect, Dawson established that White had made that social scene with the full knowledge of his wife.[24]

The defense of Deputy White was hardly necessary. On the evening of July 6, according to a news report, White was sitting in a rocking chair on the porch at Miles Tourist Court near Corbin. Suddenly two shots rang out. White fell three or four feet to the ground. Two bullets, apparently fired at close range, struck the deputy in the left temple. One bullet lodged in his brain, the other plowed through his head and tore a hole in his hat. He died a little over an hour later in a Corbin hospital.[25] Apprehended in connection with the murder and held without bond on a first degree murder charge was Chris Patterson.[26] While the government did not directly charge White with any violent crime against union men, the defense offered testimony in his behalf because allegedly he was part of the conspiracy to keep the UMWA out of Harlan County. The jury did not receive news of White's death until it began its consideration of the case.

The murder of White was only one of several violent events which occurred during the conspiracy trial. Judge Ford cancelled the July 6 morning session because Harlan County authorities had jailed defendant Lee Fleenor for shooting Charley Reno in what may have been a grudge assault.[27] Earlier during the month of June, the former president of a UMWA local union at Yancey was shot to death and a dynamite explosion had destroyed the home of a prosecution witness in the Green-Silvers camp. In the midst of these outrages, Sheriff Herbert Cawood, the nephew of former Sheriff Middleton, claimed that conditions were as "peaceful as Sunday School." In adopting a stance which had become standard in Harlan County, Cawood denied any connection between the crimes and the conspiracy trial. However, FBI agents once again entered Harlan in an attempt to learn if there was any connection between the attacks and the victims who were government witnesses.[28]

Fifteen Harlan peace officers denied participating in acts of violence and terrorism and in conspiring to keep the union out of the county. After spending nearly half a day uttering such denials, an exasperated Brian McMahon asked Deputy John P. Hickey:

> Mr. Hickey, was there another Deputy Sheriff in Harlan County who looked exactly like you?
> Mr. Hickey, plainly expecting a blistering cross-examination,

gasped in surprise. His already red face turned redder as he hesitated. Then he snapped:
No, not that I know of.
That is all, said Brien McMahon... as a ripple of subdued laughter swept through the courtroom.[29]

Defense counsel next threw a bombshell into the proceedings by attempting to blame the murder of Bennett Musick on the UMWA. Several witnesses, including a hotel desk clerk, swore that union organizer Belton Youngblood, from Alabama, and three other men had picked up some weapons from an Evarts hotel kitchen around eight o'clock on the night of February 9, 1937 and returned them after midnight. Two other witnesses, brothers John and Henry Bolin, testified that they had driven past the Musick home just as a volley of shots poured from two cars. Subsequently they followed the vehicles into Evarts, and saw Youngblood and Granville Sargent, one of the "Sargent boys," emerge from one of them. Two other witnesses reported that they were in an Evarts saloon just before the shooting, that Youngblood and Sargent had entered to buy whiskey, and had remarked to the owner as they departed, "We are going up the road a piece." Later the two men reappeared, purchased more whiskey, and commented, "Well, everything went off all right."

In rebuttal the prosecution offered eight witnesses, including some of Pineville's most prominent citizens, in an attempt to destroy this incredulous defense version of the Musick murder. Each one testified to seeing Youngblood in Pineville the night of February 9, either at the Continental Hotel or at the Hub Restaurant when a call came bearing the news of Bennett Musick's death.[30]

Successfully challenging defense efforts to lay the Musick murder on union officials, the government produced license receipts, a power deposit receipt, and meter readings of the Kentucky Utilities Company which showed that power service at Bryan Middleton's saloon had been cut off on January 23 and restored on February 18 with a meter reading of "1233" for both days.[31]

As the lengthy trial wound down, defendant Merle Middleton, along with several friends and relatives of the jurors, one day at noon paraded back and forth before the house where the jury was staying. On learning of this unconventional behavior, Judge Ford ordered three Clay Countians, including the father of juror Ellie Chestnut, into court for questioning. Each one told the judge that they had come to town with Clay County attorney A.D. Hall, who was Middleton's lawyer, and denied "parading" in an attempt to influence the jury. Because of this impropriety, however, Judge Ford delivered a stern reprimand to the defendants:

> If you men try to come up here and influence this case, I will deal severely with you. If you loaf around this court I will send you to jail promptly. And if I hear of any of the defendants indulging in this sort of thing again I will put them in jail also.[32]

He also confined the accused to the courtroom for the first time during the ten week trial.

As the contradictory evidence showed, the Mary Helen conspiracy trial was extremely complex and controversial. Not only was it disrupted by the murder of defendant Frank White, episodic violence in Harlan County, and the provocative "parading" stunt by Merle H. Middleton and others, several Harlan "perjury mills" threatened to disrupt the proceedings.

In the first incident, Merle H. Middleton and former Deputy Lee Hubbard rounded up fourteen-year-old Avery Eggers and Ernest Huff, a Harlan-Wallins miner, and took them to a Harlan garage where they attempted to force Huff to sign a statement that he (Huff) had played pool with them (Middleton and Hubbard) on the night of the Musick murder. After Huff testified about that incident, he was remanded to jail in London for safe-keeping. Eggers reported that Hubbard had offered him a job at five dollars per day if he (Eggers) would "tell lies for him" (Hubbard).[33]

Toward the end of the trial, evidence of a second "perjury factory" surfaced. Everett Fleenor, an uncle of defendant Lee Fleenor, allegedly took three Evarts youths to the office of Harlan attorney C.B. Spicer where they confessed that they had seen UMWA organizer Belton Youngblood in Evarts on the night of the Musick murder. The next day on returning to the lawyer's office, each one was paid twenty-five dollars. After relating a similar story in London, one of three boys, received an additional twenty-five dollars on a side street near the Federal Building. Later Hoskins' conscience began to bother him and in a dramatic moment of the trial, he returned to the witness stand and stunned the court with this admission: "I got to studying about it and knowed I done wrong."

On another occasion, Officer Bruce Cawood had escorted two Evarts women to Spicer's office where both had signed statements that they had heard L.T. Arnett remark on an Evarts street: "It's too bad the Musick boy got killed, but we thought they were all away from home. But maybe it will be all for the best because this will build up a lot of sympathy for us. Sometimes accidents are the very best things that can happen." Later Spicer offered both women transportation, expenses, and twenty-five dollars if they would go to London and repeat Arnett's statement in court. Both turned down the proposition. This defense ploy to use the testimony of five Evarts residents to lay the Musick murder on UMWA officials utterly failed.

Officer Cawood and Attorney Spicer unequivocally denied involvement in the second "perjury factory" episode. Admitting that he had escorted the two women to Spicer's office, Cawood denied knowing what had happened because he had remained outside. Attorney Spicer, whose office was the headquarters of the alleged "perjury factory," categorically refuted the women's testimony.[34] Nonetheless, Brien McMahon termed the episodes the "rottenest exhibition of perjury ever to be perpetrated from the witness stand."

4

Finally, eight weeks of conflicting testimony ceased and attorneys made closing arguments to the jury. Welly K. Hopkins, whose voice "shook with emotion" as he spoke for more than seven hours, summed up the government's case:

> The coal operators raised a wall of steel around Harlan County. Any union organiser who dared to enter did so at the risk of facing the blazing guns of Ben Unthank and his numbers men. The only way the miners had to learn of the rights that were being denied to them was for the information to be dropped from the heavens,

where the power of the otherwise all-powerful coal operators did not extend.

Attorneys Cleon K. Calvert, H.H. Tye, and W.W. Lewis closed for the defense. The lanky, bespectacled Calvert, who carried a cane with a gold head, told the jury: "The only time they (the government) ever produced two witnesses to testify about a single thing they paraded before you a pimp and a prostitute." Tye told the jurors to weigh the evidence carefully, and not be swayed by the emotionalism of government counsel. The HCCOA, proclaimed Lewis, had been formed "nineteen years before the Wagner Act was ever heard of" and "it was ridiculous to assume that it had been formed to deprive miners of their rights under the law."

Brien McMahon and Henry Schweinhaut spoke the last words for the prosecution. "If it had not been for the investigation the Senate made of Harlan County conditions," declared McMahon, "the death of Bennett Musick would not have ended the "reign of terror." Martha Howard, said Schweinhaut, "was a woman with strength of character to tell her story, knowing in advance that she would be set upon, ridiculed and made the target of slings and arrows of people who stood without sin."[35]

With the completion of the final arguments, Judge Ford charged the jury to consider "overt acts" against individual defendants only as they might tend to prove a conspiracy. Jurors, said he, could not render a verdict of guilty against only one defendant because a single defendant could not have participated in a conspiracy alone. The jury received the case at 2:16 p.m. on Saturday, July 30. The end to a complicated trial that had filled fifty-seven days in eleven weeks had finally come.

Initially, the jury deliberated for five hours and fourteen minutes without reaching a verdict. On learning about the stalemate at 9:00 p.m. Saturday, Judge Ford confined the jurors to quarters throughout the weekend. Deliberations resumed on Monday, August 1. Following a one-hour recess for lunch, the jury announced a hopeless deadlock at 2:50 p.m. Judge Ford then questioned each juror individually. Foreman L.F. Johnson responded: "Your Honor, we stand just like we did Saturday night." "Is there any possibility of agreement?" the judge asked. Johnson said no. In turn jurors Sizemore, Chestnut, Bell, Hopper, Sams, Campbell and Evans concurred that agreement was virtually impossible. Judge Ford brought an end to the controversial trial by discharging the jurors at 2:52 p.m. on August 1.[36]

An analysis of votes of the jurors is interesting. On every ballot, Chestnut, Sizemore, L.F. Johnson, Campbell, and Roberts, all Clay Countians, and Richard Hopper and Charles Evans, of Knox County, voted for acquittal of all defendants. The other five, Bell, Wayne County; Powell, Rockcastle County; Hibbard and Baldwin, Laurel County; and Sams, Clay County, consistently stood for conviction.

There seems to be a connection between the vote of the Clay County jurors and the intrusion of Clay Countians during the trial's final days. In a post-trial interview, juror Hibbard revealed pronounced conflict among the jurors from the beginning. The jury, he said, had originally stood at eleven to one for conviction, but a definite change had occurred about two weeks before, or about the time of the "parading" incident by Merle H. Middleton and the Clay County citizens. From the trial's second day, said Hibbard, one juror had stated that he would be against conviction, and had never wavered. At one point in the deliberations, according to Hibbard, the argument had grown so intense two jurors almost exchanged blows.

There did not seem to be much doubt about Hibbard's attitude concerning the case. "I knew I was right and I would have stayed in there 'til January before I would have given in," the sixty-year-old farmer exclaimed. Hibbard concluded: "The Government made out as good a case of conspiracy as ever was made in any court. I knew I couldn't be true to the oath I took and I couldn't go home and say I had done my duty unless I voted to find them guilty. I knew the Government wasn't trying to do any man wrong, and I know they were telling the truth.[37]

On hearing the verdict, Brien McMahon moved immediately for a retrial and Judge Ford set September 15 for consideration of the government's motion. With this legal technicality resolved, the curtain fell on the trial amid subdued rejoicing among most of the defendants. Covering two and one-half months, and including: testimony from 569 witnesses, the record of this massive litigation filled fifty-one volumes—more than twelve thousand pages—of transcribed material. From this vast array of conflicting and bewildering evidence, the court had asked a mountain jury of farmers and tradesmen to render a verdict. According to the *New York Times*, "even a jury of trained intellects might well be graveled."[38]

Meanwhile, the *Knoxville News-Sentinel* urged "Peace for Harlan." Echoing the remarks of defense attorney Forney Johnston, made immediately after the deadlock, it declared that

> all parties desired peace and fairness in Harlan County. Why not hold up the retrial, it asked, and give the coal operators time to show that they would accept and negotiate in good faith with the UMWA.

A retrial and favorable verdict for the union would be an "empty victory," the *News-Sentinel* said as it challenged Harlan to reconcile the conflict.[39]

5

In retrospect, the outcome of the Mary Helen Conspiracy trial was predictable. For almost three months a jury composed of rural farmers and small town businessmen had listened to the testimony of more than five hundred witnesses. What they heard day after day was mind-boggling. Government witnesses gave testimony in support of the conspiracy theory. Witnesses for the defense disclaimed the conspiracy. Which side to believe? Perhaps the *New York Times* was correct when it stated that this trial might well have confused a jury of intellectuals.

Not only was the jury befuddled by the conflicting testimony, it also had to sort through evidence about several Harlan County "perjury mills." The government attempted to prove that defense witnesses had offered perjured testimony. Predictably the defense denied that government contention. What could this jury believe?

Apparently the defense, as mentioned, used the "parading" stunt in an attempt to influence the jury. Notably all but one of the Clay County jurors voted for acquittal. The result was a "hung jury." It is the writer's observation that efforts to pressure juries was a rather

THE MARY HELEN CONSPIRACY TRIAL

J.N. Hibbard, juror, Mary Helen conspiracy case, voted for conviction of defendants. (Reprinted by permission—Knoxville News-Sentinel).

common occurrence in the Kentucky mountains and in Harlan County. The defense may have intentionally tried to sway the London jury. The fact remains that there was disagreement among the jurors early in the trial and that divisiveness increased toward the end of the lengthy litigation.

One fact about this trial seems certain. Neither the government nor the defense desired a repeat performance. Although the jury was unable to agree on a verdict, both sides were open to compromise an end to Harlan's long and bloody industrial conflict. The La Follette inquiry and subsequent FBI investigation were the twin forces which finally brought the operators and "gun thugs" to court. Before government and defense forces had convened in London, however, events which would ultimately lead to the reconciliation of Harlan's lengthy labor turmoil were unraveling.

6

What of the conspiracy? The London jury, of course, could not agree that there had been one. Juror Hibbard believed that the HCCOA and the county administration had connived against the union. A recent opinion discounts the existence of a widespread conspiracy among the operators and county officials. That view is based on the fact that a handful of operators, Hall, Matthews, Burchfield, protested the use of HCCOA funds to repulse the UMWA.[40] And as has already been pointed out, several Harlan operators, again a handful, said they could live with the union, even found it acceptable. While all this may be true, the hard, cold reality is that the HCCOA was an extremely powerful agency, and in collaboration with Sheriff Middleton and his army of over three hundred deputies, effectively prevented the union from organizing Harlan's coal mines until the La Follette Committee, the FBI, and the Department of Justice stepped into the conflict. While a few operators may have opposed HCCOA strategy, itis inconceivable that they paid money into its treasury, attended executive board meetings, saw its financial statements and were oblivious to its inner workings. It is quite possible that the so-called pro-union operators became more tolerant of the union only after they saw the long arm of the Federal government reaching into the Harlan controversy.

According to trial testimony, there was a "whispering room" in the county courthouse and HCCOA offices were just across the street. In these twin locales, operators, the sheriff, and other interested parties gathered to plan anti-union strategy. From these meetings, orders went to Ben Unthank and Merle H. Middleton to terrorize union organizers, their families, and union members. A plausible view would be that HCCOA-affiliated operators knew all about rampant anti-union terrorism and did nothing to stop it.

While there may have been a few operators who did not like what was taking place and were a little more tolerant of the union, a preponderance of evidence showed that the HCCOA backed Ben Unthank and Merle H. Middleton and that the county courthouse was under the aegis of the operators. The dissenting voices of a few operators, a small minority, does not alter that fact.

What then of the conspiracy? The very nature of conspiracies is their secretiveness and clandestine machinations. While the Mary Helen trial shed light on some of the conspirators, forever enshrouded in mystery, and history, is the extensiveness of the conspiracy and all those involved.

Company town houses, anti-union Mary Helen Coal Corporation, 1939 (University of Kentucky Photo Archives).

THE TRIUMPH OF THE UNION

I

Progress toward the complete and successful unionizaton of Harlan's coal mines began shortly after the La Follette hearings had ended in Washington in spring, 1937. An important first step came when Governor Chandler in mid-May announced the end of the county's privately paid deputy sheriff system, and sent state patrolmen to protect Harlan's unincorporated areas. The *Louisville Courier-Journal* called the governor's action "an excellent start in eradicating the provoking cause of violence and disorder in Harlan County," while the *Knoxville News-Sentinel* said the State of Kentucky is finally recognizing and accepting part of the responsibility for the outrages in Harlan.[1]

Before the La Follette hearings adjourned, Harlan's miners began to meet. With sixteen state patrolmen watching, they met on Sunday, May 2, at Cumberland, Wallins, and Insull. That same day at Verda four thousand miners heard Turnblazer speak. A week later at Verda, twenty-six state policemen observed an UMWA organizational meeting attended by six thousand men.[2] In charge of the new campaign was fiery George Joy Titler, whose grandfather had died in the Wilderness campaign in 1864 and whose great-grandfather had fought at Valley Forge. Five-feet nine inches tall and weighing 220 pounds, the brown-haired blue-eyed Titler later was secretary-treasurer of West Virginia's District 17 and president of West Virginia's District 29.[3]

The following week, to celebrate the end of the notorious mine guard system, an estimated ten thousand miners attended a morning meeting at Benham and about five thousand met at Wallins in the afternoon. At the two rallies Sam Caddy exhorted the men to exercise the right of free speech and collective bargaining guaranteed by "Uncle Sam" and the Wagner Act. Said he: "The union is here to stay."[4] Turnblazer commended Governor Chandler for ending the "gun thug" system: "Today marks the end of a rule of thuggery and terrorism in Harlan County." Calling attention to twenty-six local unions and a membership of eight thousand compared to one union mine a year ago, Turnblazer declared, "you can thank the Wagner Act, the nine old men and John L. Lewis for that." Following the meetings, union officials sent telegrams of gratitude to Senator La Follette whose committee was instrumental in ending Harlan's "reign of terror," and to Governor Chandler for sending state patrolmen to replace the mine guards.[5]

Meanwhile, union and operator representatives opened contract negotiations in Louisville. Although the sessions were amicable, talks were unsuccessful and the two groups decided to meet again a month later in Cincinnati.[6]

The day before the Cincinnati conference, an ecstatic George Titler announced an important break-through with the signing of a contract with Pearl Bassham's Harlan-Wallins Coal Corporation covering about one thousand five hundred miners.

On the heels of this union euphoria, contract talks resumed at Cincinnati. When the conference deadlocked, Governor Chandler called spokesmen from both sides to Frankfort where a three-hour conference failed to produce results. Apparently the chief point of conflict was the "check-off,"[7] which the union demanded for the entire contract, but which the operators wanted monthly. Neither side would compromise despite Chandler's insistence that peace in Harlan required concessions from both groups.[8]

In the meantime, County Judge Morris Saylor, reacting vigorously though belatedly to the charges made against Harlan deputies during the La Follette hearings, discharged several prominent peace officers. The ax first fell on Deputy Sheriff Lee Fleenor whom Saylor dismissed with this admonition: "It is time to purge the ranks of deputy sheriffs and get rid of any officer who is involved in trouble not necessarily in his line of duty."

To protest Fleenor's sudden dismissal, Wash Irwin, Allen Bowlin, and George Lee, three of Harlan's longtime lawmen, resigned. Fleenor appeared on Harlan streets without his hip holster, vowed that he "wasn't done right," and said the judge should have given him at least fifteen days notice. The white-haired Lee, eldest of the Harlan deputies, said he quit to protest the mistreatment of Fleenor. Bowlin echoed Lee: "We are quitting because we don't think Fleenor got a square deal."[9]

In the midst of Saylor's purge of peace officers, Wash Irwin was mysteriously shot to death. According to reports, Irwin, accompanied by Deputy Sheriffs Perry G. Noe and Bowlin, had gone to the top of Pine Mountain to listen to the Joe Louis—James Braddock heavyweight championship bout on the radio. Later that night, George Lee and Henry Metcalf, who were also on the mountain to hear the fight, found Irwin's body, slumped under the steering wheel with three bullet wounds in the back of the head.

County Attorney pro tem George R. Pope immediately ordered the arrest of Bowlin, Noe, Fleenor, Lee and Metcalf. Following examining trials of Noe and Bowlin before an overflow crowd and watchful state patrolmen, Judge Saylor ordered the two men held to the grand jury without bond. Fleenor, Lee and Metcalf later surrendered to Sheriff Middleton. Lee, spokesman for the group, remarked that they had gone fishing.[10]

Although Harlan authorities never successfully solved the Irwin murder, Judge Saylor fired Perry G. Noe and John P. Hickey and Henry Metcalf resigned. As replacements, Saylor unexpectedly named six men, including UMWA organizers Belton Youngblood and William Clontz, to the county patrol. While he had refused resignations of several other officers who were good deputies and an asset to Harlan County, Saylor acted to rid the ranks of troublemakers.[11]

2

Meanwhile, the UMWA continued its organizing efforts. In mid-July, more than one hundred delegates, representing thirty-six local unions, met at the county courthouse where Turnblazer pledged to continue the fight until the UMWA won a sweeping victory in Harlan County. At the same meeting, UMWA attorney James S. Golden called the Wagner Act the greatest benefit ever given to the working man. Said he: "The victory in Harlan County is within grasp, and before long a complete victory will be won."[12]

Additional federal intervention, however, was necessary before the union won a complete victory. On July 10 Turnblazer requested the National Labor Relations Board to investigate charges that twenty-seven coal companies had coerced and intimidated workers, promoted company unions, and discharged men for union activity.[13]

As a follow-up to Turnblazer's allegations, the National Labor Relations Board initiated several hearings in Harlan County. The board's first inquiry against the Clover Fork Coal Company featured HCCOA "chief thug" Ben Unthank, who early on had evaded questioning by the La Follette Committee. While acknowledging that he had employed upwards of fifteen men during January and February, 1937 because the UMWA was putting on an organization drive, Unthank explained that he had known his men only by numbers. Although some of his "numbers" men had obtained jobs in the mines to spy on union men and others had kept organizers Lawrence (Peggy) Dwyer and A.T. Pace under surveillance, Unthank denied that George Lee, Lee Fleenor, Wash Irwin and Hugh Taylor had worked for him. That denial prompted hearing coordinator Irving McCann to impugn Unthank's credibility as a witness: "The connection between these men and Unthank is clear."

At the Clover Fork mine in June and July, 1937, a wildcat strike broke out when non-union workers refused to work with UMWA miners. George Whitfield, company spokesman, ordered the union men to leave. On July 14, the "scabs" stretched a banner across the mouth of the mine: Although they call us yellow dogs, we are 100 percent Americans and will not work with union men." Later the non-union miners carried the standard in a parade and formally voted against the union. When the company supported the non-union men, George Titler, visibly upset, complained that it had sponsored the July 14 walkout in an attempt to discredit the UMWA.[14]

The Clover Fork hearing adjourned on August 12. The NLRB later ordered the company to reinstate sixty men discharged because of union activities and to "cease and desist" from interfering with the right of workers to organize under the authority of the Wagner Act.[15]

The NLRB directed four other hearings in Harlan during autumn, 1937. In October the board heard charges against Charles S. Guthrie's Harlan Fuel Company, which, as previously noted, was strongly anti-union. Testimony revealed the discharge of workers for union activity; the formation of a viable company union, the Yancey Workmen's Association, and the alleged scheduling of "strip-tease" shows by the company to compete with local union meetings. Apparently several Harlan operators used "strip-tease" shows in attempts to discredit the union. Bryan W. Whitfield, Jr., of Harlan Collieries, admitted that he had told his men: "Boys, whenever Mr. Turnblazer has a dinner on the grounds for you, we will have a leg show."[16] As in the Clover Fork case, the board ordered Harlan Fuel to "cease and desist" from unfair labor practices, to reinstate laid-off employees with back pay, and to withdraw recognition from the Yancey Workmen's Association.[17]

The NLRB late in 1937 investigated Green-Silvers Coal Corporation and Good Coal Company. While Green-Silvers allegedly had fired employees for joining the union, company witnesses said the real reason was for loading dirty coal. Witnesses also complained that deputy sheriffs had intimidated employees, a complaint denied by company president Sheriff Middleton.[18]

National Guardsmen on duty at Kitts (Clover Fork Coal Company), 1939 strike. (Reprinted by permission—Knoxville Hews-Sentinel).

In the Good Coal case, the company had fired workers for failure to work on Labor Day. Company spokesmen contended that since it was necessary to operate the mine on the holiday, they had not discriminated against union men. To no avail the NRLB ordered the reinstatement of 116 miners who were laid off and it ordered the company to disband the Wallins Creek Employees Association, a company union, in favor of the UMWA as exclusive bargaining agent for its workers.[19]

Harlan's final NLRB hearing involved the decidedly anti-union Harlan Central Coal Company, where miners claimed intimidation because of union activity. Company president C. Vester Bennett and George S. Ward, however, refused to testify on grounds of self-incrimination in face of the upcoming Mary Helen conspiracy trial.[20]

State legislation was also a significant contributing factor to the success of the new unionization campaign in Harlan County. On January 13, 1936 State Representative Roy Conway, of Pike County, had introduced a bill to prohibit the compensation of sheriffs and deputy sheriffs by private persons, firms or corporations. A substitute bill, presented on January 29, which barred private businesses from paying constables, deputy constables, and patrol officers, had passed the House by a 52-36 vote but had died in the Senate.

At the beginning of the 1938 session, Governor Chandler demanded the passage of a law that would completely abolish the company paid deputy system. Responding with fervor, the House overwhelmingly approved Bill No. 17 which outlawed the notorious system and while the Senate endorsed the measure by a vote of 28—1. On January 24, in the presence of a delighted UMWA delegation headed by Turnblazer, Governor Chandler signed the bill into law.[21]

At the same time, the General Assembly enacted a companion bill which prevented a person convicted or under indictment for a crime involving moral turpitude under the laws of the Commonwealth, or any other state of the United States, from appointment as a peace officer. Supported by the UMWA and the Chandler administration, both laws struck at the roots of two evils inherent in the Harlan County system: privately paid peace officers and those with criminal backgrounds. The *Louisville Courier-Journal* heralded "the doom of the monstrous system by which county peace officers are hired out" and concluded that the two measures "should put an end to the bloody record indexed by Harlan's appalling murder docket."[22]

Out of gratitude to the state administration, Harlan miners staged a gigantic "Chandler Appreciation Day" in Harlan on May 30. First, thousands of miners wearing Chandler buttons and UMWA ribbons marched through the narrow streets of the county seat. Then, in a crowded circuit courtroom, Turnblazer presented Chandler a framed testimonial. Acknowledging the honor, the governor responded that he had promised "Bill Turnblazer and these other men that their men would be protected."[23] As a direct result of state laws and federal intervention, said Turnblazer, five thousand Harlan miners were now in the fold.

3

The previously discussed La Follette hearings and Mary Helen conspiracy trial, together with the NLRB investigations, climaxed two years of Federal intervention in the Harlan labor controversy. Although the London jury, as mentioned above, could not agree on a verdict, in the wake of the trial came the first general contract for Harlan's coal miners. Negotiations leading to the pact had begun in early August, 1938 when John L. Lewis met with Turnblazer and Titler in Washington to discuss the terms of agreement. Later the union leaders conferred in Louisville with Charles I. Dawson who subsequently arranged a conference of both sides at Tate Springs, Tennessee. After two days of continuous negotiations, agreement came on the preliminary terms of a contract. When the meetings resumed in Cincinnati, UMWA representatives and an HCCOA committee, after three days of discussions, hammered out an agreement covering nearly twelve thousand Harlan miners and all mines, except the "captive" operations at Lynch and Benham and a few independent producers. Effective from September 1, 1938 to April 1, 1939 the contract provided for a seven-hour day, a five day week, a minimum wage of $5.60 per day, a minimum tonnage rate of sixty-five cents per ton, time and one-half for overtime, grievance committees at every mine, a checkweighman at every mine, and arbitration boards for hearing appeals.[24]

The new contract was a signal for jubilation at the Jellico, Tennessee district headquarters of the UMWA where band music accompanied a gala celebration by five thousand cheering miners. Turnblazer, standing beneath a huge banner inscribed "Harlan Signed Up 100%," announced a mammoth Labor Day program in Harlan to commemorate the significant event.

National leaders lauded the contract and the peace it brought to troubled Harlan. President Roosevelt heralded the agreement with bringing decent treatment to Harlan workers. In a radio address, NLRB Chairman J. Warren Madden said that Americans should rejoice in the reclamation of Harlan County. John L. Lewis called the Harlan pact "the end of a long struggle to establish collective bargaining in that area." Said he: "In every way, the agreement should be hailed as a constructive accomplishment for the coal operators, the coal miners, and the public at large."

Locally, spokesmen for the operators applauded the end of industrial strife in Harlan County. George S. Ward pledged the cooperation of the HCCOA. The coal operators, he said, were entering into the contract in good faith to make every effort to live up to it. W. Arthur Ellison, owner of the Mahan-Ellison mine at Stanfill, expressed personal satisfaction in the role he had played in bringing the labor troubles in Harlan County to an end. The operators, emphasized Blue Diamond executive William H. Sienknecht, were willing to do everything in their power to make the contract an instrument for real peace in Harlan County.

Turnblazer called the pact "the best thing that could happen," and pledged the cooperation of the district organization to the attainment of a "long sought for peace." In the hour of triumph, the district union chief commended the *Knoxville News-Sentinel* for the part it played in finally bringing peace to the Harlan County coal field.

The press also endorsed the new contract. The *News-Sentinel* acknowledged the statesmanlike conduct and the spirit of give and take on both sides and the *Harlan Daily Enterprise* called on both parties to work together in harmony.[25]

Delegates from thirty-seven local unions unanimously ratified the contract at a Louellen rally on August 28. There Turnblazer challenged the miners to abide by its terms and James S. Golden thanked the operators for having experienced a "change of heart."[26]

On Labor Day, September 5, thousands of miners thronged to Harlan to participate in a "victory celebration." In front of the county courthouse Mayor L.O. Smith welcomed the workers and urged that "we live like a happy family, keeping faith with the Christian religion." Phillip G. Phillips, regional director of the NLRB, told the cheering crowd: "You have won a great victory for democracy. You have earned the right to celebrate. The victory was won the American way." "There's going to be no more rough stuff in Harlan County," said Phillips, and "you can thank God for the New Deal, which is here to protect the working man and give him his right to join a union." George Titler told the celebrants:

"The union pledges 100 percent cooperation to the miners and the coal operators. I am firmly convinced the operators will meet the union halfway and peace will reign in Harlan County." Proclaiming a "great victory," Turnblazer said: "We want peace, the operators want peace. The bars are down, and it's up to you to get into the union."

The UMWA scored impressive victories during the next two months. On September 21 Theodore Middleton's Green-Silvers Coal Corporation and Creech Coal Company came to terms. In October the union notched its greatest success when Lynch's United States Coal and Coke recognized the UMWA as exclusive bargaining agent.[27]

The Green-Silvers agreement brought a dramatic exchange of letters between two former antagonists, ex-sheriff Theodore Middleton, and UMWA organizer Lawrence (Peggy) Dwyer. Middleton invited Dwyer to come and discuss with our people the purposes and problems of the United Mine Workers of America so that our local union will be 100 percent. Dwyer promptly accepted the invitation and congratulated Middleton for "a very fine spirit" which "will bring about lasting peace between employer and employee."[28]

4

The celebration of "peace at last" was somewhat premature because the new contract covered only a seven-months period. When it expired on April 1, 1939, Harlan's twelve thousand miners walked out. For ten days peace reigned. On April 12, pre-dawn violence flared at the Clover Fork camp when three to five hundred pickets, apparently UMWA sympathizers, attempted to shut down that mine. Injured in a wild melee were pickets and several company officials. At Brookside, a member of Harlan Collieries cleanup crew was shot and the next day pickets jerked one member of the Cornett-Lewis mine maintenance crew from the mantrip.[29] While there were only sporadic incidents during the remainder of the month, large numbers of pickets, often numbering into the hundreds, roamed the county to disband mine operations.

Turnblazer went to Harlan on April 17 to plead for peace and order. Speaking in the circuit courtroom, he said: "If there is any attempt to run the mines, we'll have pickets on hand. The present situation in Harlan County is highly satisfactory to the UMWA, and we'll do all we can to keep down strife and confusion."[30]

Turnblazer's appearance produced an interval of calmness. Ten days later, however, about fifteen hundred idled miners swarmed around the Kentucky Cardinal mine, near the Bell-Harlan line. Although there was no reported violence, Bell County Attorney Walter B. Smith suggested that many pickets seemed to be stretching peaceful picketing a little too far. The next day Harlan authorities arrested twenty-eight men and two women for "ducking" nine persons in the river at Evarts to the chants of: "We baptize you in the name of the father, the son, and John L. Lewis." At examining trials in Harlan on May 3, fourteen of the defendants were held to the grand jury on five hundred dollar bonds, seven on one thousand dollar bonds.[31] UMWA representative Paul H. Reed told the group to refrain from these baptizings because they would cause trouble sooner or later. James S. Golden also counseled compliance with law and order because the union had achieved success in that way. Said he: "Most of the harm that has been done has been caused by men who have lost their heads."[32]

Despite pleas for order, mass picketing continued. At 4:00 a.m. on May 3, about one thousand pickets gathered at the Clover Fork mine, taunted men who arrived for work with cries of "scab" and "yellow dog," and attacked two men who attempted to drive through the crowd. State Police Captain Carl Norman held off the unruly mob that day with a shotgun and a pistol.[33] The next morning seventeen hundred pickets gathered at Good Coal Company on Wallins Creek. They dispersed when the company shut down the mine. The pickets then roamed back to the Clover Fork mine, where once again Captain Norman and the state police chased them from the camp and from a railroad bridge, forcing them to the hills. Following that incident Clover Fork manager E.G. Whitfield warned that the mine would not reopen until the governor provided adequate protection. Chandler immediately reinforced the state policemen in Harlan with this warning:

The officers will see that the roads are kept clear, and if anyone tries to congregate along the highway, they'll keep them moving. They're to see that there's no violence. If anybody tries to make trouble, they'll put him in jail.

For the next week Harlan County was relatively quiet as contract talks continued in New York. Fifty state highway patrolmen kept the roads clear while operators debated reopening the mines. On May 8, William C. Burrows, the state industrial commissioner sent by Chandler to the scene, said that the mines would reopen "100 percent" if given troop protection. At the same time, George Titler warned that "peaceful picketing" would follow a resumption of operations.[35]

Chandler, on May 10, revealed tentative plans to send the National Guard back to Harlan. Publicizing a request from County Judge Cam E. Ball, Chandler disclosed that around seven hundred troops would replace state patrolmen to protect the miners who wanted to work.[36] Highly critical of the governor's action, Turnblazer declared that "troops and injunctions can't mine coal."[37] Titler agreed: "Those soldiers will have a devil of a time mining coal with bayonets."[38] Since most of Harlan's twelve thousand five hundred miners had joined the union, Titler asserted that operators could reopen their mines without troops if they signed a new contract.[39] Despite union protests, on May 14 National Guardsmen once more invaded Harlan County. Commanded by Brigadier-General Ellerbee W. Carter, the military force consisted of over eleven hundred troops and sixty-five officers.[40]

Following his arrival, General Carter divided Harlan County into four zones of military occupation. Zone 1 included the Poor Fork area, Benham and Lynch; Zone 2 encompassed the Clover Fork and Evarts district; Zone 3 comprised the Martin's Fork and Catron's Creek mines; Zone 4 embraced Wallins Creek and Puckett's Creek. Armed with hand grenades, tear gas and machine guns, the troops set up roadblocks, dispersed large caravans of pickets, and kept roads and bridges cleared. The troops also stopped attempts by striking miners to prevent "scabs" from entering the pits.[41]

National Guardsmen holding back pickets during 1939 Harlan coal strike. (Courtesy: University of Kentucky Photo Archive).

National Guardsmen arriving at Harlan during 1939 coal strike. (Courtesy: University of Kentucky Photo Archive).

Despite the military occupation there were several "trouble spots" in the county.[42] At Totz, pickets continually harassed, and on one occasion, exchanged blows with workers. General Carter at once demanded a decrease in the number of pickets, and ordered roadblocks established near Cumberland to prevent Benham and Lynch motorcades from reaching the Totz camp. On May 19, guardsmen forcibly cleared the Harlan Central Camp of pickets by marching women, children, the lame and the sick for a mile under a blazing sun.[43] Another trouble spot existed at Verda on Clover Fork where on May 18 between fifteen hundred and two thousand pickets attempted to pass through a roadblock.[44] Sporadic sniper fire, often coming from the heavily wooded hillsides, occurred throughout the week all along Clover Fork particularly at High Splint, Brookside and Kitts.[45]

During the first week of troop occupation, *Knoxville News-Sentinel* reporter Louis Hofferbert discovered that soldiers, who operated from behind fortified barricades, denied free passage on public highways. Stopped at Mary Helen, Three Point, Tway and Kitts, guardsmen allowed the newsman to proceed at Brookside and Verda following a conference on company property with national guard officers. Said General Carter:

> Yes, we are maintaining the road blockades and we will continue to do so as long as we believe it is necessary to prevent picketing in such large numbers as to constitute intimidation.

While road blocks continued during the pre-dawn hours and in mid-afternoon when workers were going to and from work, Carter emphasized that normal travel would not be disturbed. Despite some anxiety among the strikers over the presence of troops, guardsmen had largely restored order by the end of the first week and many mines had reopened.[46]

The first break in the ranks of Harlan operators came on May 18 when Turnblazer announced the signing of "a standard captive mine contract" with United States Coal and Coke Corporation.[47] Two days later Black Star Coal Corporation became the first commercial producer to come to terms, and on May 22 Clover Splint Coal Corporation signed a union shop agreement. Despite these initial successes, HCCOA ranks remained united against the closed shop.

Late in May Harlan-Wallins Coal Corporation[48] and Darby Coal Company agreed to union shop pacts. These contracts inaugurated new union strategy—that of concluding agreements with individual companies. Later Berger Coal Mining Company and Black Mountain Corporation signed similar contracts which placed, according to Turnblazer, six thousand six hundred and eighty men under contract.

While the union continued its efforts to sign individual companies, it began separate negotiations with the HCCOA. According to a spokesman, HCCOA-affiliated operators were ready to accept the UMWA as exclusive bargaining agent, but unequivocally opposed the closed shop. At the end of May, talks between the HCCOA and the UMWA moved to Harlan from New York. With the closed shop issue still the central point of conflict, John Conner, United States Labor Department mediator, and Emmett Durrett, Kentucky negotiator, joined the sessions as conciliators. When the impasse continued, the joint conference broke off indefinitely, and Connor left Harlan.

Meanwhile, except for minor sniper activity, relative quiet returned to Harlan and General Carter departed on June 5.[49] Governor Chandler, in an attempt to resolve the dispute, huddled with George Ward and Turnblazer in Frankfort. At the close of that session, Ward stubbornly refused to release HCCOA members to negotiate individually with the union. Turnblazer's position was that since ninety-eight percent of the industry had accepted the closed shop, Harlan operators should do the same. After a fortnight of futile deliberations, Ward surprisingly did an about-face and released HCCOA companies to separate negotiations with the UMWA. Turnblazer and Titler promptly suggested individual contracts for twenty-one "hold-out" companies.

On the heels of this sudden change in HCCOA policy the union rallied at High Splint on Sunday, June 18. Turnblazer appealed for loyalty to the UMWA: "There are seven thousand five hundred men now under contract in Harlan County, and no let-up" in the campaign to organize the county "will be made until the other five thousand are under contract."[50]

The first break in the united ranks of the HCCOA came on June 20 when Creech Coal Company signed a union shop pact. An impromptu celebration and parade followed at Twila, site of the Creech camp. Turnblazer called the Creech contract

> a notable event for the United Mine Workers, not only for Harlan County, but for the whole of the coal industry. It means that the first strong pillar in a strong anti-union labor section had been pulled down, leaving the UMWA a clear field to clean up further opposition.

The signing of Creech Coal Company paved the way for further troop withdrawals from Harlan County, which beginning in May, had decreased until only two hundred fifty nine soldiers and nineteen officers remained by July 1.[51]

The quietness which had pervaded Harlan County for over a month remained virtually unchanged until July 9 when the union held a spirited rally at Lenarue on Martin's Fork. There thousands of miners and their families heard Turnblazer label Happy Chandler "Strike-breaker No. 1 for the year 1939." Then he stirred the miners with this challenge:

> This fight is just beginning, and we are here to stay until it is over. We are going to take care of the situations as they arise and I am telling you that no miner, his wife or children, shall be thrown out on the mountainside. (Applause)...I may say that we have not begun the fight on this proposition yet. It is no Sunday School picnic...there are some strike-breakers in this county and we will have to...get those fellows out. We have to curtail this production a little bit...
> Keep your eyes fastened to the sun, don't become discouraged, stiffen up your backbone and by the eternal, we must secure this union shop.[52]

George Titler called for the resumption of "peaceful picketing" since the mines were recruiting men from the outside and bringing them across the state line.

In the aftermath of the emotional Lenarue rally, roving bands of pickets reappeared at Harlan's unsigned mines. Tension mounted.

Harlan County Courthouse, 1939; scene of many UMWA rallies; UMWA pickets upper-right hand windows jailed after "Battle of Stanfill." (Reprinted by permission—Knoxville News-Sentinel)

Three days later, on July 12, a pitched battle at Stanfill and a riot in downtown Harlan once again plunged the county into chaos. As dawn came at the Mahan-Ellison coal camp, several hundred pickets were jeering, insulting, abusing, attacking, and forcibly detaining "scabs" who had arrived for work. Several pickets tried to jerk miners off the mine's man-trip. Guardsmen, under the command of Captain John Hanberry of Hopkinsville, intervened and a shot rang out. Killed in the shootout which followed, was Dock Caldwell, a union miner and injured were Captain Hanberry, another trooper, and four miners.[53] After the shooting, guardsmen rounded up, arrested and marched the pickets about ten miles to the Harlan County jail. Also taken into custody were George Titler and his wife who had rushed to the scene following the battle.

The riot in Harlan followed an altercation between a soldier and a union miner. As guardsmen marched the pickets through the streets of Harlan, a soldier reportedly shoved a miner who was watching from a sidewalk. When the miner grabbed the soldier's rifle, a scuffle followed. There were shots, a bullet grazed the miner, and his mother was shot in the leg. Although Harlan seethed with tension as large crowds milled through the streets, guardsmen finally escorted the pickets to jail, placed the courthouse under armed guard, and restored order.[54]

The "Battle of Stanfill" brought General Carter back to Harlan along with eighteen officers, two hundred fifty enlisted men, two tanks and machine guns. If it became necessary, said Major Joseph Kelly, he would send the entire guard to keep order. Governor Chandler attributed the new outrage to the Lenarue rally, Turnblazer's "incendiary speech," and the resumption of armed picketing.[55]

Arraignment of the pickets took place on July 17 before County Judge Ball. When Turnblazer and Titler waived examining trials, Judge Ball bound both to the grand jury on charges of sedition, forceable rebellion, and banding and confederating. The court placed an additional two hundred and sixty pickets under peace bonds on concealed weapon and banding and confederating charges. Also held on the latter charge were Mrs. George Titler and UMWA organizer James W. Ridings of Bell County. At the conclusion of the hearings, General Carter, after requesting permission from Judge Ball, told the pickets to "get out of town and back to where you belong, for we won't allow groups to form and loiter about town."

Declaring that an "emergency exists" and that "a state of excitement exists among the people," Judge Gilbert on July 25 empaneled a special grand jury. Subsequent indictments named UMWA officials Wash Hall, James Westmoreland, Jennings Musick, Turnblazer, Titler, and Mrs. George Titler on a variety of charges ranging from aiding and abetting malicious shooting and wounding, conspiracy to hinder a military organization, banding and confederating, to hindering a member of the militia under orders of an officer. Pickets had gone to Stanfill, the grand jury reported, armed with pistols, blackjacks, brass knuckles, rifles, clubs, and at least one submachine gun.[56]

The "Battle of Stanfill" signaled the re-entry of the Federal government into the Harlan conflict. UMWA International President John L. Lewis called for federal intervention because Chandler "pursues and wounds them (the miners) with the same ferocity and lack of restraint that characterizes the habits of a Dominican dictator." Further,

> Chandler has violated his oath and prostituted the power of his state: a) to repay a political debt to a criminal band of coal operators, whose previous crimes are spread on the sworn public records of three authoritative governmental agencies; b) to exact vengeance upon the United Mine Workers of America and its members in Kentucky, for supporting Barkley and opposing Chandler in the senatorial election last year.

In response to Lewis's plea, Attorney General Frank Murphy ordered Henry A. Schweinhaut and Welly K. Hopkins, of his department's civil liberties section, to keep a close eye on the Harlan situation.[57]

Meanwhile, Harlan contract negotiations resumed. On receipt of a telegram from Secretary of Labor Frances Perkins, representatives of the operators and the union met in Knoxville in an attempt to restore peace, harmony, and justice to both sides. Attending the Knoxville parley were John Conner, UMWA officials T.C. Townsend, O.E. Gassaway, Earl E. Houck, and Robert Hodge, and HCCOA representatives R.E. Lawson, W.J. Cunningham, Charles S. Guthrie and George S. Ward. Standing by to lend assistance was John R. Steelman, director of the Department of Labor's conciliation service.

After four days of almost non-stop deliberations, involving both Conner and Steelman, the HCCOA finally agreed to a contract with the union. Omitted was the union shop clause since the operators accepted the UMWA as exclusive bargaining agent for Harlan County until March 3, 1941, expiration date of the new agreement. The new contract also called for immediate dismissal of all "house cases," elimination of the "penalty clause" and the submission of all disputes arising over dues collections to an arbitration board. The HCCOA promised to provide the union with adequate local meeting places, and let striking miners return to work without discrimination or prejudice.⁵⁸

Both federal mediators lauded the new contract. Steelman called the occasion a "red-letter day for the people of Harlan County," and commended both operators and miners for reaching an understanding. Said Conner: "I was never so happy as I am today to know that the Harlan County strike has come to an end."⁵⁹

In Washington, Secretary of Labor Perkins declared that the settlement of the Harlan controversy

> showed once more that peaceful collective bargaining is the proper and satisfactory instrument with which to adjust industrial disputes in the interests of the parties directly concerned and of the public.⁶⁰

State and local officials acclaimed the end of conflict. Governor Chandler announced the withdrawal of all troops as soon as both the union and the operators gave assurances that there would be no recurrence of disorder. General Carter was glad the contract had been signed, and hoped it would bring lasting peace to the coal fields. Judge Ball looked forward to an immediate end of troublesome times and the return of peace and prosperity to Harlan County. A relieved George Ward welcomed the peace and harmony which the contract should bring to Harlan County.

Saturday, July 22, 1939 was a significant day in the labor history of Harlan County. On that date one hundred seventy delegates representing twenty-seven local unions unanimously ratified the first two-year contract covering all of Harlan's coal mines. The date set for the resumption of work was Monday, July 24.⁶¹ The conflict, the trauma, the turbulence, the violence which had marked the Harlan coalfield for almost a decade had finally come to an end.

5

Although the HCCOA and the UMWA accepted the new contract, two unsettled problems of the coalfield conflict remained. Union officials and pickets faced indictments in connection with the "Battle of Stanfill," and a second conspiracy trial confronted operators in Federal court. In the interest of a final settlement of the controversy, Governor Chandler, Attorney-General Murphy, and Assistant Attorney-General McMahon conferred in Washington about the pending conspiracy trial. Murphy, too, wanted permanent peace for Harlan County, but strongly opposed any deal to settle the remaining issues.

Kentucky's governor took a second step toward a lasting peace in early August. Before departing for White Sulphur Springs, West Virginia, site of another conference about the Harlan situation, Chandler announced gradual withdrawal of the remaining three hundred troops from Harlan County.[62]

The meeting at the West Virginia resort brought together nine men whose purpose was to end at last Harlan's labor troubles. Brien McMahon and Welly K. Hopkins represented the Department of Justice, Charles I. Dawson was spokesman for the operators, T.C. Townsend, Ben Moore, Earl E. Houck, and James S. Golden were the UMWA delegates, and Lieutenant-Governor Keen Johnson represented the Commonwealth of Kentucky. In secret sessions the negotiators came to an understanding which resolved all the issues of Harlan's labor conflict.[63]

Approximately two months later the secret White Sulphur Springs agreement was made public. It included dismissal of indictments against Turnblazer, Titler, Mrs. Titler, and all others involved in the "Battle of Stanfill." In motioning for dismissal in Harlan Circuit Court, Commonwealth's Attorney Smith cited the settlement of the labor dispute and a written request from Captain Hanberry, the National Guard officer who had sustained wounds at Stanfill, that all charges be dropped. The court was dismissing the cases, said Smith, to promote industrial peace and harmony in the area for all persons.

As part of the White Sulphur Springs settlement, Welly K. Hopkins, in Federal court at London, made a motion to dismiss all cases against Harlan operators and peace officers. In his motion, Hopkins noted that "gun thug" rule had finally come to an end, discrimination against miners and their families had subsided, the militia had gone, the mines had reopened, and the Harlan contract was functioning.[64]

At last industrial peace had come to Harlan County. True, the peace of 1939 would last only until the two-year contract expired in 1941. Then a renewal of conflict, violence and bloodshed would once more trouble miners, their families, the operators, and all of Harlan County. "Bloody Harlan" would once again draw the attention of local, state and national authorities. But, for the moment, after nearly a decade of almost continuous turmoil, Harlan's miners, operators and residents welcomed the end of conflict and with that, an interim of peace.

epilogue

The actions of Harlan Commonwealth's Attorney Daniel Boone Smith and United States Assistant Attorney-General Welly K. Hopkins in autumn, 1939 brought a temporary halt to Harlan's decade-long labor turbulence.[1] The HCCOA finally had come to terms with the United Mine Workers of America. Much violence and disorder had occurred and the county, held in the grip of a "reign of terror," had become even more widely known as "Bloody Harlan." But, alas, the last major bastion of anti-unionism in the Appalachian bituminous coal fields had crumbled.

For two years most Harlan miners worked under the new UMWA contract. With the expiration of that agreement on April 1, 1941 a general strike once more spread violence throughout the Harlan coal fields. Again there were shootings, killings and more shedding of blood as gunfire blazed anew in "Bloody Harlan." The most tragic incident occurred at the Crummies Creek company store located on U.S. Highway 421 just outside Harlan. Four weary UMWA pickets walked into the store in quest of soft drinks to quench their thirst. Positioned behind the counter and manning a machine gun was Deputy Sheriff Bill Lewis who had played a conspicuous role in the events of the 1930's by reportedly killing several men. Opening fire on the union miners, Lewis gunned down organizer Virgil Hampton, who was George Titler's assistant in the organizing campaign of 1937-38, Oscar Goodlin of Lynch, and Ed Tye of Kenvir. Injured by the same blast of gunfire were five other men.[2] Unlike the earlier "Battle of Evarts," in the aftermath of the Crummies Creek massacre, Harlan's operators soon agreed to another two-year contract with the United Mine Workers of America. Law and order returned to "Bloody Harlan," but as long as the UMWA remained a viable force, strikes, violence and bloodshed marred labor-management relations in Harlan County.

Looking back, George Joy Titler who guided the union campaigns of 1937-1941 in Harlan County, and who later was UMWA vice-president under W.A. (Tony) Boyle at the time of the 1969 Yablonski murders, remembered those four years as the most vivid of his life. Experiencing his "real baptism in fire and blood," Titler recalled that the Harlan struggle taught him the real value of the UMWA to thousands of Appalachian coal miners.[3] As the "Crummies Creek massacre" of 1941 amply demonstrated, Harlan men continued to die for the union cause.

Since Harlan sheriffs and their deputies were largely responsible for the violence which dominated Harlan's labor history during the decade of the thirties, it seems appropriate to suggest the end to which many of them came:

Theodore Middleton died of a heart attack in 1942; "Chief thug" Ben Unthank reformed, settled down, became a deacon in the Baptist Church; Frank White, as noted above, died at the hands of a gunman during the Mary Helen conspiracy trial; George Lee reportedly operated a "jenny barn" in the 1950's and 1960's; Lee Fleenor moved just across the state line to become a coal operator in southwest Virginia; Lee Hubbard migrated to Tennessee and became a Church of God preacher; Allen Bowlin died of cancer; Perry G. Noe was killed by John Lee; Chris Patterson was assassinated by persons unknown; Bill Lewis, who killed four men at Crummies Creek, was slain in August, 1941 while guarding ballot boxes in the Harlan County courthouse; Earl Jones died in a gunfight; Wash Irwin. as mentioned above, was murdered by a person or persons un-

EPILOGUE

known; and Lon Ball committed suicide. These men are just a few of the principals in Harlan's labor warfare of the 1930's who either died violently or of natural causes.[4] Jesus said, "for all they that take the sword shall perish with the sword."[5] A suitable paraphrase for "Bloody Harlan's" long and turbulent labor history might be: for many of those who live by the gun shall also die by the gun.

As World War II came and passed and as emphasis began to be placed on synthetic fuels, Harlan's coal industry went into a lag and with the lull, the UMWA declined in importance. Replacing the UMWA in several mines was the Tennessee-based Southern Labor Union, regarded by UMWA members as a "scab" outfit. Lacking the membership, the organization, and the potency of the UMWA, several Harlan operators, such as Charles S. Guthrie of Harlan Fuel, switched to the SLU. The UMWA ceased to be an effective institution among the coal miners in Harlan County.

Yet as the Brookside strike of 1974, or second "Bloody Harlan," showed, there were Harlan coal miners still willing to stand up, testify, and fight for the UMWA. In the 1930's the Brookside mine was the property of Harlan Collieries presided over by Bryan W. Whitfield, Jr. As a member of the powerful HCCOA, Harlan Collieries was staunchly anti-union. Both the company and Whitfield were defendants in the 1938 Mary Helen conspiracy trial at London. When the HCCOA capitulated to the UMWA following the Federal court case, Brookside signed its first union contract with the UMWA. For the next two and one-half decades Brookside was a union operation. In the mid-1960's, the union lost a strike and from that point until 1970, Brookside was a non-union mine.

In 1970 Duke Power Company, with headquarters in Charlotte, North Carolina, purchased Harlan Collieries from Whitfield. At the same time it also acquired the High Splint mine located about nine miles from Brookside on Clover Fork. Shortly after the Brookside mine changed hands, the new owners, known as Eastover Mining Company, Norman Yarborough, president, signed a contract with the "scab" Southern Labor Union. The Brookside miners had no voice in the matter although the NLRB, established with the passage of the Wagner Act in 1935, gave workers the option to designate an exclusive bargaining agent.

Brookside women with "switches" picketing at Brookside, 1973-74 strike. (University of Kentucky Photo Archives)

For about three years, the Brookside workers were represented by the SLU. In spring, 1973, as the "scab" contract was about to expire, Brookside miners began appealing for an election in order that they might vote on the union of their choice. Although Eastover quickly fired several UMWA stalwarts, in May, 1973, the workers, by a 2-1 margin voted to switch unions. For about three months the UMWA tried to negotiate a contract with Eastover. By mid-summer contract talks had bogged down. On July 26, the UMWA struck Eastover at Brookside.

Thus the stage was set for a thirteen-months strike marked by scabs, picketing, violence, state troops, and murder. Suddenly it was the 1930's all over again in "Bloody Harlan." At first the strikers and picketers confined their activities to the Brookside mine of Eastover. While doing research in Harlan County in July, 1974, the writer had opportunity to pass the Brookside mine several times. Always there were several cars or trucks parked outside the company store post office and pickets standing nearby. Prominently displayed were large placards which read "UMW of A ON STRIKE Brookside."

EPILOGUE

During the strike a new twist appeared at the Brookside mine. Since the Harlan Circuit Court limited picketing to three miners, "scabs" marched bravely past without interference from the helpless strikers. Apparently the court order did not include women. So, armed with switches,[6] sturdy Brookside women, spouses and girlfriends of the miners, flailed away at "scabs" going to and from work.

The "switches" and "switching" soon caught the attention of the court which expanded the order to include women. Undaunted, the Brookside women continued "flailing" which landed a number of them in Harlan County jail.

As the strike continued throughout the last half of 1973, Eastover fired and ' evicted additional workers. When negotiations between the company and the union broke down completely, the Brookside men moved up Clover Fork to picket Eastover's High Splint mine. Ironically, the High Splint workers were not on strike and had not voted in favor of the UMWA. Nevertheless, a picket line went up on Kentucky 38 in the summer of 1974 and High Splint became a tension spot for several weeks.

While in Harlan in July 1974, the writer encountered the High Splint picket line. Travelling Clover Fork one dark, showery summer afternoon, a curve in the highway gave way to a straight stretch where pickets lined both sides of the road near a bridge which led to the High Splint mine. Traffic slowed to a crawl as the miners crowded around, peered into each car and questioned each driver. Obviously the pickets allowed no one to cross the bridge. After a few moments delay, they cleared the road, traffic proceeded, and a personal feeling of uneasiness subsided. Later that evening shots in the night wounded a "scab" who drove through the picket line and crossed the bridge leading to the mine.

Just as the tragic death of Bennett Musick in 1937 provided the impetus for UMWA recognition by Harlan operators to end first "Bloody Harlan," so it was a lamentable fatality that brought a climax to second "Bloody Harlan" in late summer, 1974. One hot August evening, Eastover foreman Billy Carroll Bruner, who had tried to break the strike by running a truckload of scabs across the High Splint picket line, met up with twenty-three-year-old Lawrence Dean Jones, an old friend and a UMWA miner at Brookside. After the two men passed a few words, Bruner pulled a revolver and shot Jones in the head. Married after the strike began and the father of a three-month-old daughter, Jones died at the Harlan hospital.

Although a Harlan County jury later acquitted Bruner, the murder of Jones and even more the threat of a lawsuit by a group of stockholders charging the company with "gross mismanagement, " led to the recognition of the UMWA by Eastover-Brookside. The thirteen-month-old strike which had attracted the attention of the national media and the Nixon-Ford administration had come to an end. The UMWA had achieved a hollow victory.[7]

The Harlan coal mine wars of the 1930's and 1970's were both similar and different. In the 1930's Sheriffs Blair, Middleton, Cawood strongly opposed the UMWA. During the Brookside-High Splint srike, Sheriff Billy G. Williams attempted to remain neutral but was sympathetic toward the miners. In the 1930's only the miners became embroiled in the controversy. In 1973-74, the wives, mothers, sweethearts, and sisters of the miners, armed with "switches," vocally and effectively picketed in support of the strikers. The war of the thirties ended with almost all of the county's miners under UMWA contract. In 1974 only the men of Brookside joined the UMWA. Finally, two martyrs for union were Bennett Musick, killed in 1937, and Lawrence Jones, gunned down in 1974.

In the 1980's, the writer escorted four American Labor History classes on field trips into Harlan County. On each occasion, each class learned that most of the young miners, whose fathers and relatives were UMWA miners, are not UMWA members and are indifferent toward the union. The young miners are content with the current labor situation and have more benefits than the union can provide. On the other hand, the retired pensioners still swear by the UMWA. As one elderly miner put it, "They (the young men) need to get hungry, then they'll change their mind about the union." Operator Clyde Goins, president of Great Western Coal, which has one operation at the old Mary Helen mine, maintains that his company provides more benefits, better wages, better working conditions, and has fewer accidents than union mines. Great

EPILOGUE

Western's workers endorse Goins' view. By contrast, in 1984, a UMWA miner at the United States Steel operation in Lynch said, "The UMWA is the only way to go."

Today the UMWA is a ghost from out of the past in Harlan County. Closed down, boarded up, and in deteriorated condition is the old Brookside-Eastover mine. At High Splint, the Bennetts, a long-time Harlan coal family, are now operating a non-union mine. At Yancey the old Harlan Fuel tipple is falling down while Great Western operates a surface mine nearby. Within the past year, U.S. Steel pulled out of Lynch and has been replaced by ARCO, a subsidiary of Ashland Oil Company. Presently, ARCO is the only UMWA mine in the county and according to its personnel director, the 1200 men there may soon give up the UMWA.[8]

The legacy of "King Coal" in Harlan: old, abandoned coal tipples and mines, run-down, ramshackled old company towns, one union mine, pensioners who are rabid union men, the young lions who do not need it. Yet, to the casual observer, the economy of Harlan suggests that while the UMWA may not be the way to go, for the people fortunate enough to have jobs, coal is still the way to go!

acknowledgments

While it is impossible to mention all those persons who made contributions to this book, sincere and deep appreciation is extended to each one. Special thanks is owed to Daniel Ball Pope, Harlan Circuit Court Clerk in the mid-1950's, who furnished valuable court records relating to the labor cases growing out of the 1931 "Battle of Evarts;" to the late Herndon J. Evans, one-time editor of the *Pineville Sun* and then editor of the *Lexington Herald*, who graciously turned over to me his private collection of materials relative to the Harlan conflict; to Mrs. Al Benson, wife of convicted Evarts policeman, Al Benson, who provided the pamphlet *The Shame That Is Kentucky's*; to Mr. and Mrs. Marshall A. Musick, who on a cold January day in the late 1960's, invited me into their comfortable Jellico, Tennessee home where Mr. Musick regaled me with conversation about Harlan's industrial dispute and Mrs. Musick fed my wife and me a delicious country-style fried chicken dinner; to Mr. Davis T. McGarvey and Mrs. Wavelyn Smith of the Federal District Court Clerk's office, Lexington, who acquired the complete fifty volume transcript of the Mary Helen conspiracy trial for my perusal; to Mrs. Ann Sweeney and Major Eugene Reynolds, of the War Records Division, Frankfort, who made available military records concerning troop movements into Harlan County during the decade of the 1930's.

Special gratitude is due Charles Hinds, and his assistants, of Kentucky State Archives; the reference library staff and the Special Collections staff of the Margaret I. King Library, University of Kentucky, Lexington, who provided microfilm, access to the Chandler papers, and excellent photographs pertaining to the Harlan controversy; and the staff of the National Archives in Washington who introduced this indefatigable researcher to the records of the LaFollette Committee and the National Recovery Administration. I am also indebted to Mrs. Idonna Brys'on, office manager at the *Knoxville News-Sentinel*, Knoxville, Tennessee, and to assistant librarian Miss Julia Shaver, who located some very good photographs of some of the principals involved in the Harlan labor warfare.

The Augusta College Foundation and the Augusta College Faculty Research and Development Committee funded travel which facilitated the search for photographs described above.

This book would not have been possible had it not been for the special assistance of my good friend, Professor John E. Wilz, Department of History, University of Indiana-Bloomington, who, despite experiencing serious health problems, edited and re-edited the manuscript along with encouraging me to "continue the march."

In the typing of the manuscript at various stages, I had the services of four typists: Carolyn Vickers, one-time Political Science secretary at Augusta College; Mrs. Delia L. Daugherty, who assisted with some of the early editing and typing as well as encouraging me to publish this book; Mrs. Carolyn Kershner, secretary to the Dean, School of Arts and Sciences, Augusta College, who, despite a heavy work load and domestic responsibilities, still found time to make sense out of what I presented so that the manuscript wound up in publishable form; and Miss Lien Hsieh, Augusta College student, who typed the index.

Financial assistance for the typing of the manuscript was provided by the Augusta College Research Center, Dr. Ralph Walker, director, by my department chairman, Dr. Ed Cashin, and by the Augusta College Foundation.

The Augusta College Computer Services Academic Support staff, especially Mrs. Maureen Akins, assisted in the printing of the manuscript.

Finally, my wife, Sue Ann, travelled many miles with me, helped in note-taking, and kept the home fires burning while the manuscript was in progress.

notes

NOTES TO CHAPTER I

1. See below, pp. 27-28.
2. The account of the Waldo Frank-Allan Taub episode is found in *Harlan Miners Speak: Report on Terrorism in the Kentucky Coal Fields Prepared by Members of the National Committee for the Defense of Political Prisoners* (New York. 1970), 318-322, 336-338.
3. John Fox, Jr., *The Trail of the Lonesome Pine* (New York, 1908).
4. Having lived in the area during early childhood, the author presents his own impressions of its physical aspects. As a youngster and later as a one-room school teacher at the head of Martin's Fork in Harlan County, he traveled into the county often, viewing the region in all seasons of the year.
5. This term was used as local vernacular for the county seat.
6. Kentucky state road 38 follows Clover Fork while U.S. Highway 119 followed Poor Fork. Puckett's Creek ran beside Kentucky 72. Today, Cumberland, Benham, and Lynch, located about twenty-five miles from Harlan on U.S. 119 and state road 160, are called "Tri-Cities."
7. "Bulldog" gravy was a fixture in the diets of many early Harlan Countians. During the period of labor disorder, when many miners were idle, it filled a prominent place in the diets of miners' families. Made from flour, water and grease, and noted for its thickness, it was not very appetizing nor nourishing.
8. Malcolm Ross, *Machine Age in the Hills* (New York, 1933), 50; Horace Kephart, *Our Southern Highlanders* (New York, 1922), 46; Frederick Law Olmsted, *A Journey in the Back Country*, 1853-54 (New York, 1970), 258. Much information regarding early life and customs in Harlan County was obtained from my father, Floyd Taylor (1884-1970), a former Pineville, KY attorney. A member of a pioneer Harlan County family, Mr. Taylor spent most of his early life in the county.
9. Journal of Dr. Thomas Walker, excerpts of which are

recorded in Howard N. Eavenson, *The First Century and a Quarter of American Coal Industry* (Baltimore, 1942), 18, 300.

10. J.C. Tipton, *The Cumberland Coal Field and its Creators* (Middlesborough, 1905), 11.

11. Millard Dee Grubbs, *The Four Keys to Kentucky* (Louisville, 1949), 427.

12. Ross, *Machine Age in the Hills*, 50. Harry M. Caudill, *Theirs Be The Power: The Moguls of Eastern Kentucky* (Urbana and Chicago, 1983), 90-91.

13. For example, Harlan-Wallins Coal Corporation, which operated three mines in the county, was absentee-owned while Harlan Fuel at Yancey and Creech Coal at Twila on Wallins Creek were locally owned. "Captive" mines were those which shipped their entire production of coal to the parent corporation or company.

14. Caudill, *Theirs Be The Power*, 87-90. Caudill details the activities of the Kentenia Corporation and quotes several letters written by FDR from the area in the early year of the twentieth century.

15. U.S. Congress, Senate, *Violations of Free Speech and Rights of Labor, Hearings*, before the La Follette Civil Liberties Committee, 75th Cong., 1st sess., on S. Res. 266, pt. 10, p. 3652. (Cited hereafter as Senate, *Violations of Free Speech and Rights of Labor*. The writer also has personal knowledge about the county's coal regions.

16. For a more complete discussion of Harlan's company towns, see Paul F. Taylor, "Coal Mine War in Harlan County, 1931-1932" (M.A. thesis, University of Kentucky, 1955), pp. 35-46.

17. United Supply Company, built in 1919 as the three-storied company store of the United States Coal and Coke Company at Lynch, still stood in 1987 and housed a small convenience store in one end of the building.

18. The camp at Lynch was above average in the 1930s and despite some decline is still better maintained than most in Harlan County. Caudill, *Theirs Be The Power*, pp. 93-102.

19. While engaged in oral history research in Harlan County in 1954, the writer visited many of these company towns and noted the cluttered environment. In spring, 1982, the author took his American Labor History class to Harlan where the students were dismayed by the litter in yards, on the sides of the roads, and in many streams and creeks.

20. "Sparkin'"—a mountain term which denotes courting.

21. Several UMWA organizers during this period were preachers or exhorters. For example, on Clover Fork Marshall A. Musick was a Baptist preacher and at Wallins Creek, William Clontz was a Methodist

preacher. The Lynch camp had Catholic, Methodist, Baptist and Presbyterian churches. Caudill, *Theirs Be the Power*, 96.

22. Ross, *Machine Age in the Hills*, 22.

23. A.F. Hinrichs, *The United Mine Workers of America and the Non-Union Coal Fields* (New York, 1923), 79, 53.

24. *Ibid.*, 53.

25. George J. Titler to Paul F. Taylor, November 26, 1972.

26. Titler, *Hell in Harlan*, 8-9, 16, 32-34. All the material relating to the early attempts to establish the union in Harlan were derived from Titler's book. On one occasion, "Peggy" carried $3,000 in the wooden leg from Indiana to the Cabin Creek-Paint Creek West Virginia area during the strike of 1912-1913. *Ibid.*, 33.

27. *Evans Collection*, Pineville, Kentucky. Herndon J. Evans, former editor of the Pineville Sun, permitted the use of a wide assortment of articles and papers relating to the conflict of 1931-32 which were unavailable elsewhere.

28. Interview X, at Evarts, Kentucky, August 16, 1954. During research for his Master's thesis, the writer interviewed several Harlan citizens, some of whom were central figures in the 1931-32 coal mine war. Some requested that their names not be used.

29. *Middlesboro Kentucky Daily News*, March 2, 1931.

30. Julia S. Ardery, ed., *Welcome the Traveler Home* (Lexington, Kentucky, 1983), 139-140.

31. *Evans Collection*, Pineville, Kentucky.

32. Interview with George Sweeten at Harlan, Kentucky, April 15, 1954. Mr. Sweeten was an active UMWA supporter during the 1930s, assisting in the establishment of four local unions in 1933.

33. Interview Z, at Harlan, Kentucky, August 24, 1954.

34. Interview with George Sweeten, April,15, 1954.

35. *United Mine Workers Journal*, February 15, 1931, p. 8; March 15, 1931, p. 2; *Louisville Courier-Journal*, April 19, 1935.

36. From the files, *United Mine Workers of America*, District 19, Middlesboro, Kentucky. This material was furnished by William Turnblazer, Jr.

37. U.S. Congress, Senate, *Conditions in the Coal Fields in Bell and Harlan Counties, Hearings*, before a subcommittee of the Committee on Manufacturers, on S. Res. 178, 72d Cong., 1st sess., May 11, 12, 13, and 19, 1932 (Washington: Government Printing Office, 1932) p. 204. Hereafter referred to as Senate, *Condition in the Coal Fields in Bell and Harlan Counties*.

38. Interviews with Al Benson, at Black Mountain, September 7,

1954; G. Wash Hall, at Harlan, August 11, 1954; and George Sweeten, at Harlan, April 15, 1954.

39. Hereafter, referred to as HCCOA.

40. The information regarding the viewpoints of Brock and Jones toward the union was gained from Interview U, at Harlan, August 10, 1954; Interviews X and W, at Evarts, August 16, 1954; and Interview V, at Harlan, August 10, 1954. The statement of Blair is quoted from *Louisville Courier-Journal*, March 28, 1932; that of Brock from *Lexington Herald*, August 17, 1931.

41. *Harlan Daily Enterprise*, April 3, 26-27, 29-30, 1931; Interview Y, at Harlan, August 23, 1954.

42. Indictment, Harlan Circuit Court Clerk's office.

43. E.J. Costello, *The Shame That is Kentucky's* (n.p., n.d.), pp. 11-12. This pamphlet, which contains a good account of the Burnett-Pace incident, was furnished by Mrs. Al Benson, Black Mountain. This incident was not reported in the *Harlan Daily Enterprise*. W.B. Jones furnished a few details on the witness stand at Mt. Sterling late 1931.

44. *Harlan Daily Enterprise*, April 19, 20, 28, May 1, 1931.

45. *Lexington Herald*, May 5, 1931.

46. No newspaper account mentioned the truck. Costello's pamphlet described it, and it was also mentioned during the Mt. Sterling trials.

47. That this signal was given was denied by the defense in the Mt.-Sterling trials. The defense version of the battle was that the miners were out to picket the truck since it was hauling the furniture of a "scab" to Black Mountain. Another version, which seems improbable, was that deputies from Harlan and Black Mountain were to swoop down on the picket line from two sides. This plan misfired when the Black Mountain deputies arrived at the scene first, while the deputies from Harlan were at Verda, about three miles from Evarts. The picket line may have been set up, but if so, it was concealed. Both versions are discussed in Titler, *Hell in Harlan*, 22-35.

48. *Lexington Herald*, May 6, 1931.

49. Interview Y, at Harlan, August 23, 1954.

50. Prosecution witnesses at Mt. Sterling testified that the miners opened fire first, killing Jones and Lee in the cars. The defense claimed that Daniels first started shooting with his submachine gun.

51. *Lexington Herald*, May 7, 1931.

52. *Harlan Daily Enterprise*, May 6, 1931; *Lexington Herald*, May 24, 1931. These indictments were the outgrowth of the disorders of April, 1931. Cusick spent five months and eleven days in jail. Benson stayed three months before being allowed a $21,000 bond.

53. Affidavits, May 20, 1931, in a box labelled "Evarts Labor Cases," Harlan Circuit Court Clerk's office; *Harlan Daily Enterprise*, May 20, 1931; *Lexington Herald*, May 23, 1931.

54. *Pineville Sun*, August 20, 1931; *Middlesboro Daily News*, August 26, 1931.

55. *Harlan Daily Enterprise*, December 4, 1931; *Louisville Courier-Journal*, November 20, 1931; *Lexington Herald*, December 29, 1931.

56. *Harlan Daily Enterprise*, November 22, 23; December 3, 1931. Although the writer examined transcripts of evidence for both the W.B. Jones and W.M. Hightower cases in the National Archives, no transcript of the Burnett case could be located.

57. The testimony of Commonwealth witnesses in the Jones case was excerpted from Kentucky, Montgomery County Circuit Court, *Commonwealth of Kentucky v. W.B. Jones*, trial transcript (NA/RG/60, Classified Subject Files, Enclosures), vol. 2, p. 179; vol. 2, p. 206, 269, 360, 312, 314; vol. 3, p. 369, vol. 5, p. 771. (Hereafter cited as *Commonwealth v. Jones*).

58. Interview with Al Benson, at Black Mountain, September 7, 1954.

59. William Turnblazer to W.B. Jones, April 3, 1931. A copy of this letter was contained in a box in Harlan Circuit Court Clerk's office.

60. Extracts of the lengthy testimony of W.B. Jones and defense witnesses were taken from *Commonwealth v. Jones*, vol. 7, pp. 978-1125; vol. 10, pp. 1542-1543; vol. 11, p. 1673; pp. 1689-1690. The Jones trial lasted sixteen days, included testimony from 178 witnesses, and cost the state $7,000.

61. *Lexington Herald*, December 2, 1931.

62. *Harlan Daily Enterprise*, December 11, 1931.

63. *Louisville Courier-Journal*, December 10, 11, 1931.

64. Kentucky, Montgomery County Circuit Court, *Commonwealth of Kentucky v. William Hightower*, trial transcript (NA/RG 60, Classified Subject Files, Enclosures), vol. 8, pp. 1052-1153; *Commonwealth v. Jones*, vol. 4, pp. 579-580.

65. *Lexington Herald*, January 13, 1932; *Louisville Courier-Journal*, January 14, 1932.

66. Kentucky Miners Defense, *Christmas Pardons for the Harlan Miners*, 3. This leaflet was furnished by Mrs. Al Benson, Black Mountain.

67. For a detailed discussion of communism and radicalism in Harlan County, Ch. VII, "Rendezvous of Radicals," in Taylor, "Coal Mine War in Harlan County, 1931-32."

68. Kathy Kahn, *Hillbilly Women* (New York, 1973), 3-11; Ardery,

Welcome the Traveler Home, 143-153.

69. John W. Hevener, *Which Side Are You On? The Harlan County Coal Miners, 1931-39* (Urbana, 1978), 59-61.

70. Tony Bubka, "The Harlan County Coal Strike of 1931," *Labor History* (Winter, 1970), pp. 56-57.

71. Taylor, "Coal Mine War in Harlan County, 1931-32," pp. 135-136; 141-150; 159; 174-175; 220; 222; 228-229. Also Hevener, *Which Side Are You On?* 84; Melvyn Dubofsky and Warren R. Van Tine, *John L. Lewis; A Biography* (New York, 1977), 172.

72. Paul F. Taylor, "London: Focal Point of Kentucky Turbulence," *Filson Club Historical Quarterly* (July, 1975); 257-261; Ardery, *Welcome the Traveler Home*, ch. 16. On the Dreiser incident at Pineville's Continental Hotel, also see W.A. Swanberg, *Dreiser* (New York, 1965), 387. Several of the author's delegation were surprised that Dreiser took Marie Pergain with him to Kentucky and prophetically predicted trouble over her presence. Swanberg, *Dreiser*, 384.

73. Taylor, "Coal Mine War in Harlan County, 1931-32," pp. 248-250.

74. Most of the information regarding these hearings was gleaned from the *Washington Post*, May 11-16, 1932, the *Christian Science Monitor*, May 12-16, 1932, and the *Cincinnati Enquirer*, May 12-20, 1932, and Senate, Conditions in the Coal Fields in Bell and Harlan Counties.

75. The testimony of Jim Garland and Mrs. Elizabeth Baldwin was taken from the Washington Post, May 12, 1932, and Senate, *Conditions in the Coal Fields in Bell and Harlan Counties*. Also used in regard to Garland's appearance before the committee was Ardery, *Welcome the Traveler Home*, 136, 173.

76. *Washington Post*, May 12, 13, 1932. Johnson earlier had spent thirty-seven days in a Kentucky jail on charges of criminal syndicalism. *Washington Post*, May 13, 1932.

NOTES TO CHAPTER 2

1. *Harlan Daily Enterprise*, August 4, 1933; *Louisville Courier-Journal*, August 4, 5, 1933.

2. *Knoxville News-Sentinel*, May 29, June 16, 1933; *United Mine Workers Journal*, June 15, 1933, pp. 3-5.

3. Titler, *Hell in Harlan*, 32-33; Senate, *Violations of Free Speech and Rights of Labor*, p. 3459-3461.

4. *Knoxville News-Sentinel*, June 12, 1933.

5. Senate, *Violations of Free Speech and Rights of Labor*, p. 3462;

Pineville Sun, June 22, 1933; *Knoxville News-Sentinel*, June 18, 21, 1933.

6. *Knoxville News-Sentinel*, June 16, 17, 1933. Apparently Dwyer had planned a meeting at the Harlan courthouse for June 18, and this was the proposed meeting to which Judge Howard referred here.

7. Dwyer's estimate of the crowd was reported in the *Knoxville News-Sentinel*, June 26, 1933, as 3,000 to 4,000; the *Harlan Daily Enterprise*, June 26, 1933, set the attendance at 500 to 800. The Harlan paper, operator-controlled, generally gave poor coverage to events connected with the labor troubles, while the *News-Sentinel* provided the best coverage.

8. Senate, *Violations of Free Speech and Rights of Labor*, pp. 3463, 3467. Middleton was armed with a loaded revolver. *Ibid.*, p. 3468. A local union was located in one or more coal camps and was an affiliate of the district and national organizations. Dwyer's nebulous statement regarding the number of local unions established in Harlan contradicts what he claimed at the June 25 Harlan rally.

9. The information about the new organizational campaign and the attacks on union organizers was gleaned from reading the Knoxville News-Sentinel, June 2, 1933; July 6, 7, 23, 1933.

10. Senate, *Violations of Free Speech and Rights of Labor*, pp. 3464-65, 3496.

11. *Harlan Daily Enterprise*, January 4, 5, 1933; February 8, 1933; April 16, 23, 1933; March 12, 30, 1933; May 28, 1933; July 2, 1933; *Knoxville News-Sentinel*, July 21, 1933; *Pineville Sun*, July 20, 1933.

12. Senate, *Violations of Free Speech and Rights of Labor*, p. 3466. Dwyer said that Saylor had promised protection to the miners in ' return for their endorsement and support.

13. Interview with William (Bill) Clontz, at London, Kentucky, October 17, 1966. Interview with Marshall A. Musick, at Jellico, Tennessee, January 4, 1967.

14. Senate, *Violations of Free Speech and Rights of Labor*, pp. 3499-3500. Under Kentucky law the county judge must approve the appointment of deputy sheriffs selected by the sheriff.

15. *Knoxville News-Sentinel*, August 5, 6, 1933; *Harlan Daily Enterprise*, August 6, 1933; *Louisville Courier-Journal*, August 5, 6, 1933. These two accounts differed on the number of fingers Cawood lost in the battle. The *Courier-Journal* stated that he lost one, but the *News-Sentinel* maintained that he lost two.

16. *Louisville Courier-Journal*, August 5, 6, 1933; *Harlan Daily Enterprise*, August 7, 11, 13, 1933; *Knoxville News-Sentinel*, August 13, 1933.

17. Interview with Claude Taylor, at Cumberland, Kentucky, December 30, 1966.

18. *Harlan Daily Enterprise*, May 28, 1933; November 17, 1933. The Harlan Democrats used the "New Deal" theme in announcing their slate of candidates.

19. James P. Johnson, "Drafting the NRA Code of Fair Competition for the Bituminous Coal Industry," *Journal of American History* LIII (December, 1966), 522-24; 524-31; Bernard Bellush, *The Failure of the NRA* (New York. 1975), 91-92.

20. *Knoxville News-Sentinel*, July 6, 1933.

21. Johnson, "Drafting the NRA Code of Fair Competition," 531-533.

22. A checkweighman was a mine employee who weighed coal at the tipple. Before the code was negotiated, the coal company appointed the checkweighman. The miners held out for the right to name their own. They felt that in times of labor difficulties, the checkweighman could discriminate against union miners.

23. Johnson, "Drafting the NRA Code of Fair Competition," 534-537.

24. United Mine Workers of America, *Proceedings of 33rd Constitutional Convention* (Indianapolis, Indiana, 1934), I, p. 111-113. Bellush, *Failure of the NRA*, 92.

25. *United Mine Workers Journal*, December 1, 1933, pp. 10-11.

26. *Knoxville News-Sentinel*, September 29; October 25, 26, 1933.

27. *United Mine Workers Journal*, October 15, 1933, p. 10.

NOTES TO CHAPTER 3

1. *Pineville Sun*, September 14, 21; November 30, 1933; *Middlesboro Daily News*, September 14, November 25, 28, 1933. A total of $250 in rewards was offered for information leading to those responsible for the first attack. Part of the money was set aside by the Bell County Fiscal Court. The impact from the two explosions severely damaged a number of homes and buildings in Pineville, including the Pineville School and the Pineville Methodist Church.

2. Jay H. Taylor was an uncle of the author. He was noted as a defense lawyer.

3. The account of the examining trial was drawn from the *Pineville Sun*, January 11, 1934 and the *Middlesboro Daily News*, January 11, 13, 1934. The author searched the Bell County Courthouse, including the attic, in an attempt to find trial transcripts. None was located and most

of those attorneys who were involved in the case are now deceased.

4. Bell Quarterly Court, Commonwealth Docket, January, 1934, 250-251.

5. Bell Circuit Court, Commonwealth Orders, No. 21, February, 1934, 536.

6. The author used the local newspaper accounts of the trial, which were quite detailed, because no trial transcripts could be located in the Bell County Courthouse. *Pineville Sun*, March 15, 1934; *Middlesboro Daily News*, March 13, 1934; Bell Circuit Court, Commonwealth Orders, No. 22, May, 1935, 510-511.

7. Bell Circuit Court, Commonwealth Orders, No. 22, May 1935, 510-511. On motion of Commonwealth's Attorney Smith, two additional cases, charging banding and confederating and conspiracy, were filed away with leave to reinstate. A third case against Patterson, Baker and Tackett was also filed away because "the indictment is lost, misplaced and cannot be found in the clerk's office." In November, 1936, on motion of Commonwealth's Attorney Pro-tern Cleon K. Calvert, cases against Tackett, Baker, and Unthank for banding and confederating to injure persons, and against Tackett, Baker, Patterson, and Unthank for conspiracy to injure persons and property, were taken from the docket and dismissed. Calvert was one of the leading lawyers for the operators during this entire period. Bell Circuit Court, Commonwealth Orders, No. 23, November, 1936, 569-570.

8. Senate, *Violations of Free Speech and Rights of Labor*, pp. 3471-78; 3479-3484. Patterson served 10 months and 6 days before being given a "full and free" pardon by Governor Laffoon. Tackett remembered that Ben Unthank had paid his salary about a year following his (Tackett's) release from jail. The testimony of Baker which linked Unthank to the assaults on Dwyer was presented to the LaFollette Civil Liberties Committee. All quotations are found in the Senate report on the committee hearings.

9. *Harlan Daily Enterprise*, November 13, 16, 19, 27, 1933. The *Knoxville News-Sentinel*, January 7, 1934, featured a full-page illustrated article by Kyle Whitehead, staff member of the *Daily Enterprise*, discussing Harlan's murder record, and presenting vignettes of the new officials and the steps they planned to take to improve conditions.

10. *Knoxville News-Sentinel*, January 4, 1934; *Harlan Daily Enterprise*, February 5, 1934.

11. *Harlan Daily Enterprise*, February 11, 1934.

12. *Knoxville News-Sentinel*, January 7, 1934.

13. Harlan County Court, Order Book, 1934, 165-170; Senate,

Violations of Free Speech and Rights of Labor, pp. 141; 3470. A check of the Harlan County Order Book for this period indicates that several deputies were appointed and released with such rapidity that it was often difficult to follow their careers. Some served only briefly before being relieved from duty.

14. Harlan County Court, Sheriff's Bond Book, No. 4, 83-88i 82-89; 162-66.

15. *Knoxville News-Sentinel*, January 7, 1934.

16. Interview with Marshall A. Musick, at Jellico, Tennessee, January 4, 1967.

19. John F. Day, *Bloody Ground* (Lexington, Kentucky, 1981) Ch. IX, p. 133.

20. *Harlan Daily Enterprise*, January 21, 28, 31, 1934.

21. *ibid.*, March 19, 28, 1934.

22. The account of Fleenor's indictment, trial, and conviction was obtained from the *Harlan Daily Enterprise*. April 16 to May 6, 1934. Trial transcripts were unavailable in this case. Also the *Knoxville News-Sentinel*, May 6, 1934.

23. *Harlan Daily Enterprise*, May 18, 1934; *Knoxville News-Sentinel*, May 27, 1934. Mr. Musick, on January 4, 1967, named George Lee and Ben Unthank as two of the deputies who arrested him on this occasion.

24. *Knoxville News-Sentinel*, March 23, 1934; *United Mine Workers Journal*, April 15, 1934, p. 10. A copy of the first resolution was sent to local officials; copies of the second were transmitted to the National Labor Board, the Secretary of Labor and General Hugh S. Johnson.

25. Harlan County Order Book for 1932 shows that Menefee was appointed a deputy sheriff by Sheriff Middleton. Several patrolmen at Lynch had served as Frick guards. Caudill, *Theirs Be the Power*, 100-101.

26. Senate, *Violations of Free Speech and Rights of Labor*, pp. 3967-69; 3971-72; 4113-4114. In 1984 the Lynch mine, which was still an United States Steel operation, was the only UMWA mine in Harlan County.

27. *ibid.*, pp. 3612-3616.

28. *ibid.*, pp. 3624-3625; 3626; 3630-3631; 3632. Gilbert's expression, "I cannot get my court waited on," was a common one in the hills, meaning that the court docket was overcrowded with cases waiting to be heard.

29. Interview with William Clontz at London, Kentucky, October 17, 1966.

30. Senate, *Violations of Free Speech and Rights of Labor*, pp. 3810-

3811; 3811-3812; 3815-3817; 3821.

31. The check-off was a system used to collect union dues. The men signed a card empowering the company to make the deduction from the payroll.

32. Senate, *Violations of Free Speech and Rights of Labor*, pp. 3824-3836.

33. *Louisville Courier-Journal*, November 11, 1934; *Pineville Sun*, November 15, 1934; *Middlesboro Daily News*, November 12, 1934.

34. Senate, *Violations of Free Speech and the Rights of Labor*, pp. 3864-3866; 3868-3875.

35. *Knoxville News-Sentinel*, December 4, 1934. This incident was not reported in the *Harlan Daily Enterprise*.

36. Senate, *Violations of Free Speech and Rights of Labor*, pp. 3878-3879; 3881; *Middlesboro Daily News*, December 10, 1934; *Louisville Courier-Journal*. December 9, 1934; *Harlan Daily Enterprise*, December 9, 1934.

37. Interview with Joe Bates, son of organizer Jim Bates at Lexington, Kentucky, May 20, 1967.

38. *Louisville Courier-Journal*, December 10, 1934; *Harlan Daily Enterprise*, December 10, 1934.

39. *Middlesboro Daily News*, December 15, 1934.

40. Harlan Circuit Court, Commonwealth Orders, No. 29, No. 30, January 5, 1934, No. 30; March 22, 1934, 538; May 5, 1934, 29.

41. *Middlesboro Daily News*, December 11, 1934.

42. *Louisville Courier-Journal*, December 10, 1934; *Middlesboro Daily News*. December 10, 1934.

43. *Louisville Courier-Journal*, December 11, 1934.

44. *Middlesboro Daily News*, December 17, 1934. The *Lexington Leader*, December 30, 1934, quoted Caddy: "The object of this meeting is to obtain the removal from office of Sheriff Middleton." Also the *Louisville Courier-Journal*, December 30, 1934.

45. *Knoxville News-Sentinel*, December 30, 1934; *Louisville Courier-Journal*, December 30, 1934.

46. According to the *Lexington Herald*, December 30, 1934, Sam Caddy had revealed on Saturday night, December 29, that almost $15,000 of the money had been turned in and that the remaining $10,000 had been pledged by 102 local unions in eastern Kentucky. *Louisville Courier-Journal*, December 30, 1934.

47. *Louisville Courier-Journal*, December 30, 1934.

48. Interview with Joe Bates, at Lexington, Kentucky, May 20, 1967. Bates said one gunman, whom the union employed, was an ex-convict from Tennessee.

NOTES TO CHAPTER 4

1. Senate, *Violations of Free Speech and Rights of Labor*, pp. 128-129.
2. *ibid.*, pp. 3925; 3929-3931; 3937.
3. Newspaper accounts varied regarding the number of organizers arrested. The *Knoxville News-Sentinel*, February 10, 1935 reported 22; the *Harlan Daily Enterprise*, February 14, 1935, placed the figure at 21, then on February 21, revised the number to 25. According to the Harlan County Court Commonwealth Order Book, No. 8, 1935, pp. 316-317, 25 organizers, including James Westmoreland, Frank Hall, John Stines, T.R. Clark, of District 30, and Tom White were arraigned on February 15.
4. *Middlesboro Daily News*, January 12, 14, 15, 1935; *Pineville Sun*, January 17, 1935.
5. See above, Chapter III, pp. 68-69, 71-72, 73-74.
6. *Middlesboro Daily News*, January 14, 1935. The *Pineville Sun*, January 17, 1935, reported Barnes as saying, "If there's a man in this house with a gun on him, I'm going to take it off of him. I'm old and not strong, but I repeat I'm going to take it off of him."
7. *Pineville Sun*, January 17, 1935. At the conclusion of this hearing, Turnblazer revealed that other cases had not been heard because the men feared losing their jobs if they testified. *Knoxville News-Sentinel*, January 15, 1935.
8. *Harlan Daily Enterprise*, January 14, 1935.
9. *Executive Journal*, February 12, 1935, II, p. 375. Other appointees to the Commission were Adolphus Gilliam, pastor of the Park Methodist Church, Lexington, and president of the Lexington Ministerial Association; C. Roy Steinfort, Covington realtor, who declined to serve; Oren Coin, of the Kentucky Relief Administration; and Hugh S. Gregory, Springfield farmer. Also the *Louisville Courier-Journal*, February 13, 1935. Hevener, *Which Side Are You On?*, 114.
10. *United Mine Workers Journal*, March 1, 1935, p. 1.
11. *Harlan Daily Enterprise*, February 13, 1935.
12. *Louisville Courier-Journal*, March 8, 1935. Marshall A. Musick stated that Turnblazer requested organizers never to carry weapons. Interview, January 4, 1967.
13. Accounts of the Denhardt hearings have been extracted from the *Louisville Courier-Journal*, March 8, 9, 10, 1935; the *Knoxville News-Sentinel*, March 9, 1935; the *Lexington Herald*, March 12, 1935.
14 *Louisville Courier-Journal*, March 10, 1935.

15. *United Mine Workers Journal*, September 15, 1935, pp. 18-19, 21. According to Brooks, the PMU agreed to pay $100 a month to George S. Ward, Ben Unthank, and Sheriff Middleton for protection.

16. *Lexington Herald*, March 12, 1935; *Louisville Courier-Journal*, March 9, 1935. Byrd filed with the commission copies of indictments, warrants, and material relating to the criminal records of Harlan deputy sheriffs.

17. *Pineville Sun*, March 28, 1935; *Louisville Courier-Journal*, March 26, 27, 28, 1935; *Harlan Daily Enterprise*, March 26, 1935; *Middlesboro Daily News*, March 27, 1935. Several officials reported that businessmen resented the organizers because business usually dropped off when they (the organizers) were in town.

18. *Louisville Courier-Journal*, March 29, 1935.

19. *ibid.*, May 7, 1935; *Middlesboro Daily News*, May 7, 1935.

20. *Louisville Courier-Journal*, May 24, 25, 26, 1935; *Pineville Sun*, May 30, 1935. Efforts to locate the original, or duplicate copies, of this report have been unsuccessful. A reproduction was submitted by Turnblazer in his testimony before the La Follette Committee.

21. *Harlan Daily Enterprise*, June 6, 1935.

22. Senate, *Violations of Free Speech and Rights of Labor*, pp. 137, 139.

23. *Harlan Daily Enterprise*, June 7, 1935.

24. *Middlesboro Daily News*, June 8, 1935. Editor of the *Daily News* at this time was Robert L. Kincaid, later president of Lincoln Memorial University and author of *The Wilderness Road*.

25. *Pineville Sun*, March 28, June 13, 1935.

26. *Knoxville News-Sentinel*, June 11, 1935.

27. *Louisville Courier-Journal*, June 7, *Harlan Daily Enterprise*, June 9, 1935.

NOTES TO CHAPTER 5

1. At the scene, seventeen sticks of unexploded dynamite and three "live" shotgun shells were found. *Harlan Daily Enterprise*, September 4, 1935. Middleton seemingly had a premonition about his death. See above Chapter III, pp. 71, 75.

2. *Harlan Daily Enterprise*, September 23, 24, 1935, January 13, 1936. The Hamptons and Noe were proprietors of slot machines, which the county attorney had fought since he took office.

3. *Harlan Daily Enterprise*, June 28, 1935; *Louisville Courier-Journal*, June 29, 1935. The names of the persons comprising this delegation were not disclosed by the *Daily Enterprise*. The *Courier-Journal* reported

that the group was composed of four Harlan labor leaders who requested that their names be withheld "because we might be beaten up if they knew we were here."

4. Commonwealth of Kentucky, Military Department, Special Orders, No. 89, June 1, 1935. The Special Orders did not make clear who alleged that Sheriff Middleton had withdrawn the deputies, and no other information was located regarding this point. The source of these reports, then, remains unclear, but they may have come from company officials. The Harlan County Order Book for 1935 has no record of the deputies Middleton reportedly released. Also *Louisville Courier-Journal*, June 3, 1935.

5. *Harlan Daily Enterprise*, June 28, 30, 1935; July 1, 1935. Middleton emphasized that as a result of this bargain, troops would be used to force the unionization of Harlan County.

6. *Louisville Courier-Journal*, June 2, 1935; July 2, 1935,

7. *Harlan Daily Enterprise*, July 2, 1935, July 3, 1935. Captain Noel S. Jones, commandant of the detachment of state policemen, said that the patrolmen would abide by the injunction except in their duties as highway patrolmen.

8. *Louisville Courier-Journal*, July 3, 1935.

9. *Executive Journal*, II, July 2, 1935, pp. 481-485; *Louisville Courier-Journal*, July 6, 1935.

10. *Harlan Daily Enterprise*, July 5, 7, 1935. The *Louisville Courier-Journal*, July 6, 1935, quoted the sheriff; "I have no comment to make," before departing for his Lee County, Virginia farm.

11. *Middlesboro Daily News*, July 7, 1935.

12. *Executive Journal*, II, July 30, 1935, p. 499.

13. *Ibid.*, August 30, 1935. According to the *Middlesboro Daily News*, August 31, 1935, Bill Clontz, Marshall A. Musick, and Robert Childers were among the first witnesses to testify. The *Pineville Sun*, September 5, 1935, stated that the testimony was similar to that related at the coal labor board hearing in Pineville during January, 1935. Governor Laffoon's *Executive Journal* revealed no information concerning the hearings.

14. Senate, *Violations of Free Speech and the Rights of Labor*, pp. 4181-4182. An entry, noting that the charges were dismissed, was made in Governor Chandler's *Executive Journal*, I, January 16, 1937, p. 160, but the full statement does not appear in the journal.

15. *Louisville Courier-Journal*, July 19, 1935; July 26, 1935.

16. *Louisville Courier-Journal*, July 26, 1935; *Harlan Daily Enterprise*, July 25, 31, 1935.

17. *Pineville Sun*, June 27, 1935; *Middlesboro Daily News*, July 27, 1935. The *Louisville Courier-Journal*, July 28, 1935, and the *Knoxville News-Sentinel*, July 28, 1935, indicated the crowd numbered about 1,500. The *Daily News* placed the crowd at from a few thousand to about 10,000 with 3,000 coming from Harlan.

18. See above, p. 105; *Louisville Courier-Journal*, July 28, 1935.

19. *Ibid.*, August 3, 1935; *Pineville Sun*, August 8, 1935.

20. *Louisville Courier-Journal*, August 3, 1935.

21. *Executive Journal*, II, August 5, 1935, pp. 501-502. Sheriff Middleton was also described as being "very partisan in his attitude." This order was probably the one on which the troops moved.

22. *Louisville Courier-Journal*, August 4, 1935. J. Howard Henderson wrote an on-the-scene report of the primary from Harlan; *Harlan Daily Enterprise*, August 4, 1935.

23. *Louisville Courier-Journal*, August 4, 1935.

24. *Harlan Daily Enterprise*, August 4, 1935, placed the number of troops at 1,300; Sheriff Middleton's statement used the figure 700; the petition for the injunction stated "more than 500."

25. *Louisville Courier-Journal*, August 4, 1935; the *Harlan Daily Enterprise*, August 4, 1935, quoted Denhardt: "Chandler would have gotten 15,000 votes had we not been here." *Harlan Daily Enterprise*, August 5, 6, 7, 1935. A few examples of mining camps which recorded top-heavy majorities for Chanler were: Verda No. 7 (252-50); Verda 7B (155-0); Verda 7C (180-4); High Splint (335-7); Lynch No. 21 (187-2); Tway (169-11); Yancey (550-3); and Three Point (443-28).

26. *Harlan Daily Enterprise*, August 9, 11, 1935.

27. *Ibid.*, August 20, 22, 31, 1935.

28. *Ibid.*, August 27, 28, 30, 1935; November 17, 24, 1935; *Executive Journal*, II, November 16, 1935, p. 560.

29. *Ibid,.* August 16, 1935.

30. Kentucky Court of Appeals, *Reports*, vol. 261, November 1, 1935, p. 84.

31. Harlan Circuit Court, Commonwealth Orders, No. 31, August 28, 1935, p. 84.

32. *Harlan Daily Enterprise*, August 23, 28, 29, 1935.

33. *Harlan Daily Enterprise*, July 23, 24, 1935. Affidavits, alleging these incidents, had been made by union members and forwarded to the governor.

34. *Harlan Daily Enterprise*, September 5, 1935; *Executive Journal*, II, September 5, 1935, p. 525; September 6, 1935, p. 530.

35. *Ibid.*, September 8, 1935; *ibid.*, September 6, 1935, p. 530. The

governor's executive order of September 6 referred to "conditions of unrest and lawlessness" and "a reign of terror" in Harlan County.

36. *Harlan Daily Enterprise*, September 10, 11, 1935. Chandler gained about 3,000 votes in the runoff in Harlan, Rhea gained about 900. The Mary Helen precinct, where no election was held on August 3, was the home of coal operator S.J. Dickenson, who was also a member of the county election commission.

37. John H. Fenton, *Politics in the Border States* (New Orleans: The Hausen Press, 1957), 24-25, 27-30, 33-34.

NOTES TO CHAPTER 6

1. United States Federal District Court for Eastern Kentucky, *United States of America vs. Mary Helen Coal Corporation*, et al., 1938, XVI, pp. 3807-3808; VI, p. 1762; 1753. Cited hereafter as *United States vs. Mary Helen Coal Corporation*.

2. The "second Battle of Evarts" has been reconstructed from testimony presented by both unionists and deputy sheriffs in the case *United States of America vs. Mary Helen Coal Corporation*, in London during the summer of 1938. The trial will be discussed fully in Chapter X. *United States of America vs. Mary Helen Coal Corporation*, XLIII, p. 10785. Apparently Lee was referring to the first "Battle of Evarts" of May 5, 1931, in which his son, Otto, was killed. See above, Chapter I, pp. 17-18. Lee reported that he had been threatened before assaulting the "fellow." *United States vs. Mary Helen Coal Corporation*, LXII, pp. 10785, 10788-10789; Hickey's testimony is found in Volume XXXIII, pp. 9449, 9452-9455; the testimony of Deputies Avery Hensley, Tom Trent, Jim Cornett, Lon Ball, Earl Jones, and Brutus Metcalf is found in Volume XLVIII, pp. 10641-10646; Volume XXXVIII, pp. 9370-9371; 9353-9354; Volume XVI, p. 3807; XXIV, pp. 5430-5433; Volume XXXV, pp. 8129-8142; 8245-8250; Merle Middleton denied being a deputy at this time but was owner of the V.T.C. bus line which operated on Clover Fork as well as in other parts of the county. The testimony of Merle is found in Volume XXIX, pp. 6544-6548; XII, pp. 4742-4750.

3. This law, popularly known as the Wagner Act, was sponsored in Congress by Senator Robert F. Wagner (D), New York. Hereafter the law will be referred to as the Wagner Act.

4. Samuel I. Rosenman, ed., *Public Papers and Addresses of Franklin D. Roosevelt* (13 vols., New York, 1938), IV, 294-295.

5. *U.S. Statutes at Large* XLIX, p. 449.

6. *United Mine Workers Journal*, December 1, 1934, p. 4; December 15, 1934, p. 4.

7. *Harlan Daily Enterprise*, December 23, 1934. The question placed before the Cornett-Lewis employees read: "I am working under the regulations of the Government code, or I am (for) (against) working without affiliation with an outside union organization." Lawson said the vote against the union was 269 to 5. Note the discrepancy in the vote tabulation, and the claimed secrecy, between the report published in the *Harlan Daily Enterprise* and that given by Lawson in Washington. Senate, *Violations of Free Speech and Rights of Labor*, p. 3856

8. *Knoxville News-Sentinel*, April 18, 1934. The three local union officials were President Charles Eads, Secretary E.J. Baumgardner, and Financial Secretary B.B. Bloomer. The eviction process was a key weapon in the hands of Harlan's operators because most employees lived in company-owned houses.

9. See above, Chapter II, p. 54, for further details of this contract.

10. *Knoxville News-Sentinel*, April 4, 5, 27, May 4, 1934; May 4, 5, 6, 12, 13, 20, 1934. Other members of the operator's delegation were R.C. Tway, Louisville, president of the R.C. Tway Company; Ben Reed, Louisville; and H.T. Graham, Cloversplint. The idled workers were employees at Black Mountain, Black Star, Insull, Creech, Cloversplint, High Splint, Cornett-Lewis; and seven or eight smaller mines. Also, Dubofsky and Van Tine, *John L. Lewis*, 199.

11. *Knoxville News-Sentinel*, March 22, April 2, 11, 15, 1935.

12. *Pineville Sun*, June 20, 1935.

13. *New York Times*, September 27, 1935. General Hugh S. Johnson, by administrative order, had set the wage rate at $5 for the entire bituminous industry. Harlan operators, however, had accepted the $4.60 wage rate in the contract covering that field and agreed to on May 20, 1934.

14. *Knoxville News-Sentinel*, October 15, November 1, 3, 1935.

15. *Ibid.*, September 29, 1935.

16. *United Mine Workers Journal*, May 15, 1935; *Knoxville News-Sentinel*, June 16, 1935. Hall denied knowledge of this incident which allegedly occurred following the rally.

17. *United Mine Workers Journal*, July 1, 1935; July 14, 1935.

18. Senate, *Violations of Free Speech and Rights of Labor*, pp. 4040-41; pp. 4045-4049; 4047; 4055. Williams did not know his captors at this time, but later identified two of them as Ben Unthank and George Lee.

19. *Louisville Courier-Journal*, September 29, 1935. General Denhardt reported receiving information of beatings, threats, and of several persons being ordered to leave Harlan County. *Executive Journal*, II, September 28, 1935, p. 539.

20. *Louisville Courier-Journal*, September 30, 1935; *Knoxville News-Sentinel*, September 29, 1935.
21. *Louisville Courier-Journal*, September 29, 1935.
22. Fuson had been appointed to succeed Elmon Middleton.
23. *Louisville Courier-Journal*, September 29, 1935. The *New York Times*, September 29, 1935, quoted County Attorney Fuson as saying, "We know of no disorders of any kind," and reported that County Judge Saylor had declared there was no trouble in the county.
24. Timko, president of Indiana's District 11, UMWA, had been ordered to report to Turnblazer on July 1, 1935, to assist in the reorganizational effort. Senate, *Violations of Free Speech and Rights of Labor*, pp. 4013-4014.
25. *Harlan Daily Enterprise*, October 1, 1935.
26. *Ibid.*
27. Senate, *Violations of Free Speech and Rights of Labor*, pp. 4042-46.
28. Harlan Circuit Court, Commonwealth Orders, No. 31, September 30, 1935, p. 153.
29. *Harlan Daily Enterprise*, July 7, 1936; Senate, *Violations of Free Speech and Rights of Labor*, p. 4046.
30. *Louisville Courier-Journal*, October 5, 1935.
31. *Ibid.*, October 8, 1935.
32. *United Mine Workers Journal*, November 1, 1935, p. 8. Lewis said that Chandler's victory would be a ringing endorsement of the policies of F.D.R.
33. *Harlan Daily Enterprise*, November 7, 24; December 1, 1935. Chandler won Three Point (621-18), Yancey (823-166); Mary Helen (425-144); Wallins (500-122); and two Benham precincts (426-215); and (398-106). Swope won Verda 7B (485-177); Verda 7C (399-161); High Splint (318-169) and Tway (675-47).
34. *Ibid.*, December 1, 1935. In an editorial, "Only 16 Days More," the *Daily Enterprise* looked forward to the end of the Laffoon administration. Ch. V, p. 112.
35. Hevener, *Which Side Are You On?*, 115-116.

NOTES TO CHAPTER 7

1. Senate, *Violations of Free Speech and Rights of Labor*, pp. 4013-14.
2. *Ibid.*, pp. 4014-4015; 4016-4017; 4017-4019; 4019-20. Timko said that he thought the men who had pulled up near his car at Wallins were some of the same deputies who had been at Cloversplint earlier. He stated that he later learned the man whom Pace called "Ben" was

Ben Unthank and that he had been "covered" on this occasion by the feared Frank White. UMWA organizers made their headquarters in Bell County at this time for reasons of safety. Bell County officials, especially Sheriff James W. Ridings and County Judge D.M. Bingham, were considered more favorable toward the union than their Harlan compatriots. Also see above, Chapter V, pp. 101-102; Chapter VI, pp. 129-130.

3. A cousin of Bryan W. Whitfield, Jr; Caudill, *Theirs Be The Power*, 111-12. The father of A.F. Whitfield, Jr. had started in the coal business in Alabama.

4. The attitudes toward the union of Lawson, Guthrie, Mahan and the Whitfields is found in *United States v. Mary Helen Coal Corporation*, XXIII, p. 5132; XXVI, p. 5710; XXIX, p. 6414; XXXI, pp. 7048-7050; XXXVI, pp. 8546-8549; 8558-8559. Also see above chaptcer I, pp. 15, 19.

5. Bennett, Creech and Ward expressed their views toward the union in *United States v. Mary Helen Coal Corporation*. XXXVII, pp. 8968-8969; XL, pp. 9784-9785; 9815; 9819; XIV, p. 5354. Ward's statement was made to Rev. Carl E. Vogel in September, 1935.

6. G.C. Jones, *Growing Up Hard in Harlan County* (Lexington, Kentucky, 1985), 130-134.

7. Operators Sienknecht, Burchfield, Hall, Bowling, Stras, and Gilbert stated their union positions in *United States v. Mary Helen Coal Corporation*, XIV, p. 5402; XXII, pp. 4916; 4960, 4969; XXVIII, pp. 9160-9162; pp. 7031-7032; XXXII, p. 7328. Also see Hevener, *Which Side Are You On?*, 107.

8. Thirteen of the suits were filed against Sheriff Middleton, only one against Judge Gilbert. James Westmoreland was one of the plaintiffs in one of the suits against Middleton. The only suit against Gilbert was filed by Howard Williams who had been unsuccessful in an earlier damage case. *Harlan Daily Enterprise*, December 29, 1935; *Louisville Courier-Journal*, December 29, 1935.

9. *Harlan Daily Enterprise*, December 29, 1935; *Pineville Sun*, January 2, 1936; *United Mine Workers Journal*, January 15, 1936, p. 11.

10. *Knoxville News-Sentinel*, December 4, 1936; *United Mine Workers Journal*, December 15, 1936, p. 3.

11. *New York Times*, April 16, 1936; Senate, *Violations of Free Speech and Rights of Labor*, pp. 128-131.

12. *Ibid.*, pp. 132; 134-135; *New York Times*, April 16, 1936.

13. *United Mine Workers Journal*, May 1, 1936, p. 4,

14. *Ibid.*, September 15, 1936, p. 7.

15. Senate, *Violations of Free Speech and Rights of Labor*, pp. 4177-

4178; *United Mine Workers Journal*, September 15, 1936, p. 7; October 1, 1936, pp. 12-13. *Louisville Courier-Journal*, September 1, 2, 3, 5, 1936.

16. Hevener, *Which Side Are You On?*, 107.

17. *Harlan Daily Enterprise*, September 1, 2, 1936; *Middlesboro Daily News*, September 2, 1936; *Louisville Courier-Journal*, September 3, 1936; Senate, *Violations of Free Speech and Rights of Labor*, p. 4178

18. Turnblazer wrote Chandler on December 28 requesting the protection. A copy of his letter is located in the Department of Military Affairs, War Records Division, Frankfort, Kentucky. Chandler to Turnblazer, December 31, 1936, Department of Military Affairs, War Records Division, Frankfort, Kentucky. This letter is an unsigned carbon copy. Chandler relayed the letter to Adjutant-General Lee McClain with the comment that the union could ask for protection when it became necessary.

19. *Knoxville News-Sentinel*, December 30, 31, 1936. Turnblazer told the *News-Sentinel* that he had sent a registered letter to Middleton "notifying him that we were coming and expected the same degree of protection as any other American citizen." George S. Ward refused to comment on the union's plans because he had been out of town for a week and had not consulted with the HCCOA.

20. *Harlan Daily-Enterprise*, December 31, 1936; *Middlesboro Daily News*, January 1, 1937.

21. *Knoxville News-Sentinel*, January 2, 1937. Dr. Cawood had signed the sheriff's bonds in 1934. See above. Chapter III, p. 65. Also, he had testified, during the court of inquiry that he had attended no persons beaten during the reign of terror. See above, Chapter VI, p. 129.

22. *Middlesboro Daily News*, January 4, 1937. Turnblazer told the miners that Middleton had returned, unopened, his registered letter requesting protection. "That is what Sheriff Middleton thinks of our organization," he declared. See also. Senate, *Violations of Free Speech and Rights of Labor*, pp. 4385-4387.

23. *Middlesboro Daily News*, January 4, 1937.

24. George J. Titler to Paul F. Taylor, November 26, 1972. Titler was later international vice-president of the UMWA under the administration of Tony Boyle, and led an organizing campaign in Harlan in 1938. Originally, he hailed from the West Virginia coal mining area.

25. *Middlesboro Daily News*, January 5, 1937; *Knoxville News-Sentinel*, January 4, 1937.

26. *Knoxville News-Sentinel*, January 5, 1937.

NOTES TO CHAPTER 8

1. Senate, *Violations of Free Speech and Rights of Labor*, p. 4185. Turnblazer said seven district and national representatives of the UMWA, headed by Arnett, had gone into Harlan on January 9. Apparently these were the same ones who had returned on January 11.

2. *Knoxville News-Sentinel*, January 6, 8, 10, 1937.

3. Senate, *Violations of Free Speech and Rights of Labor*, p. 4187. See above Chapter VII, p. 140.

4. See above, Chapter V, p. 105-106; Chapter VI, 131-132.

5. Senate, *Violations of Free Speech and Rights of Labor*, p. 4188; 4190-4191. The hotel "gassing" received very little coverage in the press. This account was derived from Arnett's testimony in Washington.

6. *Harlan Daily Enterprise*, January 24, 1937. The explosions which Arnett had heard at the time of the gas attack had been caused by the "bombing" of organizers' cars in the streets outside. Middleton did post a $200 reward for information leading to the arrest and conviction of persons responsible for the gassing of the hotel.

7. Senate, *Violations of Free Speech and Rights of Labor*, pp. 4385-86; Exhibit 1288-B, p. 4386; Exhibit 1287-B, p. 4385; Exhibit 1289-B, p. 4387.

8. Musick maintained that church services had been prohibited but that beer gardens and dance halls were wide open. Senate, *Violations of Free Speech and Rights of Labor*, pp. 4231-4232; 4243. The account of this attack did not appear in any of the newspapers consulted. This version was related by Musick before the La Follette Committee. James H. Brewer reported seeing the cars move down the road, but did not recognize the occupants because of the distance.

9. Senate, *Violations of Free Speech and Rights of Labor*, pp. 4242, 4245, 4247. This raid may have been a move designed to intimidate Brewer, who had been visited by Holmes on January 31.

10. Senate, *Violations of Free Speech and Rights of Labor*, p. 4193.

11. *Ibid.*, pp. 4194-4195.

12. *Ibid.*, pp. 4214-4215. Ferguson mentioned being accosted on January 20 in front of the New Harlan Hotel by a deputy who inquired the nature of his business. When he informed the deputy that he was in town on UMWA business, he was told, "You had better get the hell out of Harlan County and stay out of it." On January 22, Ferguson reported an encounter with Deputy-Sheriff L.E. Ball who stopped his car, allegedly on CCC property. He and his companions were told that they were on private property, and to "get on the hard road and get going

and keep going." On another occasion, four deputies, including Ball, encountered him and Musick at the High Splint post office, ordered them on, and would not permit them to remain five minutes until the post office opened so that they could mail a letter. *Ibid.*, p. 4217; 4194.

13. *Ibid.*, pp. 4234-4235. Still at home were four of the Musick's eight children.

14. *Knoxville News-Sentinel*, February 10, 11, 1937.

15. During a visit to the Musick home in Jellico, Tennessee, on January 4, 1967, the present writer saw a picture of Bennett.

16. Interview with Marshall and Mallie Musick at Jellico, Tennessee, on January 4, 1967.

17. *Pineville Sun*, February 11, 1937; *Harlan Daily Enterprise*, February 10, 11, 12, 1937.

18. Harlan Circuit Court, Commonwealth Orders, No.32, February 17, 1937, p. 121. One of the jurors, W.K. Kilbourn, when interviewed at his Cumberland, Kentucky home on December 30, 1966, could not remember being on the grand jury, remarking that this was "a long time ago."

19. *Harlan Daily Enterprise*, February 14, 1937. Why this statement should have been necessary is uncertain. That it was made seems to indicate that Harlan conditions were not tranquil.

20. Harlan Circuit Court, Commonwealth Orders, No. 22, February 17, 1937, p. 120-122. Also, see above, pp. 152, 153-154, 155-156.

21. See below, Chapter IX, pp. 170; 171-172.

22. *Knoxville News-Sentinel*, February 12, 15, 18, 1937.

23. *Pineville Sun*, March 4, 1937.

24. See above Chapter I, pp. 27-28. Also see, Paul F. Taylor, "London: Focal Point of Kentucky Turbulence," *Filson Club History Quarterly*, July 1975, pp. 252-261; Paul F. Taylor, "The Coal Mine War in Harlan County, Kentucky, 1931-32," Chapter VII, "Rendezvous of Radicals," pp. 135-193.

25. See above, Chapter IV, pp. 87-93.

NOTES TO CHAPTER 9

1. Clinch Calkins, *Spy Overhead: The Story of Industrial Espionage* (New York, 1937), 17-18. During the Harlan hearings, witnesses sat in the audience, while members of the press sat on either side of the rostrum.

2. Senate, *Violations of Free Speech and Rights of Labor*, pp. 3319, 3327-3328; 3229-3230; 3349; 3367; 3371; 3390-3391. Among the

companies furnishing records of munitions purchases were Wisconsin Steel Company, Harlan-Wallins Coal Corporation, Cloversplint Coal Company, Harlan Collieries Company, Harlan Fuel Company, and Green-Silvers Coal Corporation, of which Sheriff Middleton was president.

3. Titler, *Hell in Harlan*, 100, 104. Titler referred to Unthank as "chief thug" and as "generalissimo" of the anti-union forces; Ward called him "field man" for the HCCOA.

4. Senate, *Violations of Free Speech and Rights of Labor*, pp. 3232-33; 3506; 3510; 3521-3523; also see above, Chapter VIII, pp. 152-153, 154-155; 155-156.

5. Senate, *Violations of Free Speech and Rights of Labor*, pp. 4402-06; 3524-3525. Also Cf. above. Chapter I, p. 16. Chapter II, pp. 42-45; Chapter V, p. 109. This statement by Ward seems hardly plausible in view of the struggle for the county GOP chairmanship in 1931 and the primary elections of 1933 and 1935.

6. Senate, *Violations of Free Speech and Rights of Labor*, pp. 3526-3529. The record did not show when Middleton had served the six months term.

7. *Ibid.*, pp. 3533; 3538; 3548-3549; 3550; 3558; 3717-3718.

8. *Ibid.*, pp. 3558-3561. The drunken driving and detaining cases had been dismissed on August 9, 1935 because witnesses had left the county. The indictment for illegal voting had been quashed and referred to another grand jury on August 26, 1936. The two malicious shooting and wounding cases were later filed away with leave to reinstate. There are no records of trials in any of these cases.

9. *Ibid.*, pp. 3562, 3563-3570, 3733. Presented to the committee were documents from the Kentucky State Reformatory and the Federal Bureau of Investigation which showed the criminal records of Harlan deputy sheriffs.

10. *Ibid.*, pp. 3551-3552; 3553-3555; 3575; 4143-4146; 4147-4149. Middleton's financial transactions included: payment to James S. Greene, Sr., for 75 shares of stock, Green-Silvers Coal Corporation, $13,500; bought by himself and a Dr. Howard, 20 shares of stock in the Green-Silvers Coal Corporation, either for $9,000 or $12,000; paid for 160 shares of stock in Crummies Creek Company, $16,000; paid for 70 shares of stock in same company (1936), $17,000; paid for one-fifth interest in a La Follette, Tennessee coal firm, $15,000; paid for Pennington Gap, Va. farm, $18,000; paid for stock in Gold Seal Electric, Allegheny Corporation, Commonwealth Southern, Cities Service $1,428; paid for residence and lot $700. The sheriff stated that there

was still $8,000 outstanding on the farm and $16,000 outstanding on the Harlan store building. The committee assessed the total worth of Middleton's assets at this time as $102,728. *Ibid.*, pp. 4151-4155. The stock the Middletons owned in the Verda Supply Company netted them a return of 170% on their investment.

11. *Ibid.*, pp. 4155-4159; 4160-4161; 4162.

12. *Ibid.*, p. 4163.

13. *Ibid.*, pp. 4164; 4168-4170; 4171-4173. Testimony revealed that $10,700 of tax monies had been used to pay the brokerage firm and personal loans. Two notes for $1,000 and $1,800, had been paid from tax monies. By Middleton's admission, Harlan bank officials, some of whom were coal operators, assisted him in acquiring his personal fortune.

14. See above, Chapter VIII, pp. 152-153; 157-158. Senate, *Violations of Free Speech and the Rights of Labor*, pp. 4209-4210; 4346-4348.

15. *Ibid.*, pp. 4581-4587.

16. *Ibid.*, pp. 3571-3572; 3573-3574. Saylor admitted receiving dividends of about $200 a year, or a return of about ninety-six per cent on the Verda Supply Co. stock.

17. *Ibid.*, p. 4309; 4311-4312; 4322-4324; 4337-4338. Earlier Smith had served as defense counsel in several cases growing out of the "Battle of Evarts." But court records do not show the trials of many deputies during this period.

18. See above, Chapter VIII, p. 157.

19. Senate, *Violations of Free Speech and Rights of Labor*, pp. 4333-4334.

20. *Ibid.*, pp. 4332-4333; 4317.

21. *Ibid.*, pp. 3575-3581; 3591-3592; 4488-4489; 4491-4513; 4516-4519. Bassham confessed that all he knew about the Wagner Act was what he had "got out of the newspaper." He had attended thirty-four of thirty-seven board meetings from January, 1933 to March, 1937. On May 3, 1937 two Harlan-Wallins miners, brothers James and Garrett Fugate, divulged to the committee information regarding the raffle and testified that the men had been compelled to participate. Pearl Bassham, on May 4, added considerable detail of the operation of the system at Harlan-Wallins. Among the cars raffled was one belonging to Dr. P.O. Lewis, an Evarts mine doctor. Proceeds were used to support the Evarts football team.

22. *Ibid.*, pp. 3602-3603. Bassham defended Deputies Wash Irwin and C.C. Middleton before the La Follette Committee. Irwin had a criminal record but since the sheriff had appointed him, Bassham em-

ployed him as a mine guard.

23. *Ibid.*, pp. 4431-4436; 4457-4460; 4461-4465. See above Chapter VIII, pp. 154-156. Also James W. Booth, "Blood on Harlan," *Real Detective*, (October, 1937), p. 68. Booth was a special investigator for *Real Detective*. This issue was furnished by Mrs. Mallie Musick.

24. Booth, "Blood on Harlan," pp. 15, 67, 69. Also, Senate, *Violations of Free Speech and Rights of Labor*, pp. 4210-4211.

25. *Ibid.*, pp. 4259-4262; 4264; 4266-4270; 4272-4274; 4276-4279; 4289; 4353; 4357; 4360-4361, 4550-4556. Also Booth, "Blood on Harlan," p. 14, 68. Hugh Taylor testified that both White and Irwin had told him that there would be a $100 bonus if he accompanied them to the Musick home on the night of February 9. They intimated that the money would be obtained from Ben Unthank. Clarence Poer operated liquor stores, a tourist court, beer halls, and dance halls in Harlan County.

26. *Ibid.*, pp. 4564-4576; 4580-4584. Also James Sherburne, *Stand Like Men* (Boston: Houghton-Mifflin Company, 1973), 244, 267. Sherburne experienced the same reaction from many Harlan Countians as did the writer in the 1950's. Many residents either had "forgotten" about many events or they simply refused to talk about them. Notable exceptions were union coal miners.

27. *Ibid.*, pp. 3645-3646; 3987-3990. Also *New York Times*, June 22, 1937. *Harlan Daily Enterprise*, December 5, 1937. Also Booth, *Blood on Harlan*, p. 68; Creech was tried in Washington during November, 1937. Creech had alleged that Tackett had come to Washington, become intoxicated, and said things which he knew nothing about.

28. *Harlan Daily Enterprise*, April 25, 29, 1937; May 5, 1937.

29. *Ibid.*

30. Jerold S. Auerbach, *Labor and Liberty: The La Follette Committee and the New Deal* (Indianapolis, 1966), 128-129.

31. Hevener, *Which Side Are You On?*, 129.

32. See above. Chapter IV, pp. 93-94; Chapter I, p. 31.

33. U.S. Congress, Senate, *Private Police Systems*, Senate Report No. 6, part 2, 76th Congress, 1st Session, 1938, pp. 207-210. Also, Caudill, *Theirs Be The Power*, Ch. 7.

34. Affidavits, Dewey Barker to Special Agent J.M. O'Leary, Federal Bureau of Investigation, Department of Justice, at Harlan, Kentucky, July 2, 1937; Marion Smith to J.M. O'Leary, at Harlan, Kentucky, July 2, 1937; Walton Melton to Special Agent G.A. Stevens, Federal Bureau of Investigation, Department of Justice, at Harlan, Kentucky, July 2, 1937; Henry A. Rutherford to J.M. O'Leary, at Harlan, Kentucky, Sep-

tember 15, 1937; Robert L. Childers to Special Agents W.H. Heywood and James B. Porter, Federal Bureau of Investigation, Department of Justice, at Jellico, Tennessee, June 6, 1937; James Allen Bates to Special Agent P. Wyly, Federal Bureau of Investigation, Department of Justice, at Pineville, Kentucky, June 2, 1937. National Archives, Record Group 60, Box 3642, La Follette Committee Hearings, Miscellaneous notes folder #4.

35. United States District Court for Eastern Kentucky, *United States of America vs. Mary Helen Coal Corporation*, et al, Indictment No. 5990, September 27, 1937. A printed copy of this indictment was located in the United States District Clerk's Office, Lexington, by Mrs. Wavelyn Smith, Chief Deputy Clerk. Following is a list of the sixty-nine defendants: "Company defendants": Mary Helen Coal Corporation, Harlan Fuel Company, Bardo Coal Mining Company, Berger Coal Mining Company, Black Mountain Corporation, Blue Diamond Coal Corporation, Cloversplint Coal Company, Clover Fork Coal Company, Cornett-Lewis Coal Company, Crummies Creek Coal Company, Harlan-Wallins Coal Corporation, High Splint Coal Company, Kentucky Cardinal Coal Corporation, Mahan-Ellison Coal Corporation, Southern Mining Company, R.C. Tway Company, Three Point Coal Corporation, Creech Coal Company, Black Star Coal Corporation, Harlan Collieries Company, Harlan Central Coal Company, and Southern Harlan Coal Company; "Operator defendants": Silas J. Dickinson (sic), Charles S. Guthrie, George S. Ward, Kenes Bowling, Charles E. Ralston, Elbert J. Asbury, William H. Sienknecht, Armstrong R. Matthews, Denver B. Cornett, Robert E. Lawson, George Whitfield, Roscoe J. Petrie, Lewis P. Johnson, Pearl Bassham, John E. Taylor, James Campbell Stras, W. Arthur Ellison, Elijah F. Wright, Jr., Robert C. Tway, Elmer D. Hall, Robert W. Creech, Charles B. Burchfield, C. Vester Bennett, and Bryan W. Whitfield, Jr. : "Law-officer defendants": Th-eodore R, . Middleton, Ben Unthank, Brutus Metcalf, George Lee, John P. Hickey, Frank White, Mose Middleton, Sherman Howard, Lee E. Ball, Earl Jones, Charlie Elliott,'Merle Middleton, Ballard Irvin, Avery Hensley, Bob Eldridge, Hugh Taylor, Perry G. Noe, Lee Hubbard, Homer Turner alias "D.Y. Turner, Lee Fleenor, Bill Lewis, Allen Bowlin (sic), and Fayette Cox. ' -

36. *United States vs. Mary Helen Coal Corporation*, Indictment No. 5990, September 27, 1937, pp. 4-5, 8-10.

NOTES TO CHAPTER 10

1. *London Sentinel-Echo*, Diamond Jubilee Edition, Section F, August 12, 1934, p. 5. The Harlan defendants were accused of violating a federal statute, sec. 51 of the United States Code which was passed during Reconstruction to protect the rights of newly enfranchised freedmen. The Mary Helen conspiracy case marked the code's first use as an enforcement arm of the Wagner Act.

2. The material describing London, Kentucky, the trial town, and the preparations and arrangements for counsel, defendants, witnesses and visitors is taken from an article: Paul F. Taylor, "London: Focal Point of Kentucky Turbulence," *Filson Club History Quarterly* (July, 1975): 262-64.

3. *Harlan Daily Enterprise*, May 16, 1938. Assisting McMahon were special assistant attorney-generals Henry A. Schweinhaut, Welly K. Hopkins, Walter E. Gallagher, and Richard P. Shanahan. Joining this group were John T. Metcalf, United States District Attorney for the Eastern District of Kentucky, and his assistants, Claude S. Stephens and Charles R. Durrett. *U.S. vs. Mary Helen Coal Corporation*, p. 3; The *London Sentinel-Echo*, May 13, 1938 reported that McMahon and his staff took over an annex to the Hotel Laurel.

4. Assisting Dawson were Forney Johnston, a corporation and utilities lawyer from Birmingham; Cleon K. Calvert, Pineville corporation attorney; Judge William Lewis and Ray C. Lewis of London; H.C. Gillis, Williamsburg, Kentucky; C.C. Williams, Mt. Vernon, Kentucky; Arthur G. Dayton, Charleston, West Virginia; N.R. Patterson, Pineville, Kentucky; T.E. Mahan, Jr., Williamsburg, Kentucky; B.M. Lee, Harlan; J.J. Greenleaf, Richmond, Kentucky; Henry L. Bryant, Pineville; and John W. Carter, Harlan. The *Knoxville News-Sentinel*, May 16, 1938, reported that the defense took over the entire tourist camp, including the filling station. According to Lee Davis, a staff correspondent, because many of the defendants and witnesses lived within commuting distance of London, the town was deserted after court ended.

5. Interview with Mrs. Bessie Green, deputy clerk, at London, Kentucky, October 17, 1966. Mrs. Green showed the writer the small courtroom, commenting that it is much like it was in 1938. Hanging directly over the judge's bench was an oil portrait of Judge Ford, which his wife commissioned and had presented to the court.

6. *Knoxville News-Sentinel*, May 16, 19, 1938. The first violator of the "no smoking" rule was former Sheriff Middleton, "who had been in court more times, perhaps, than any of the other defendants. A deputy

marshal tapped Middleton on the shoulder and ordered him to douse the cigarette." The judge also told the defendants and union officials to take the same seats throughout the trial. *United States vs. Mary Helen Coal Corporation*, pp. 140-142; 144-146.

7. *New York Times*, May 17, 1938. Taylor was located at the home of his sister in Dominion, Va.

8. *Knoxville News-Sentinel*, May 17, 1938. When approached by Knoxville newspaperman Edward B. Smith on his arrival in London, Taylor drawled, "I'm not talking now. I've got a story that would take half the night to tell, but not to newspapermen."

9. *London Sentinel-Echo*, May 19, 1938.

10. This list of jurors was taken from the *New York Times*, May 21, 1938; the *Knoxville News-Sentinel*, May 20, 23, 1398; and from the trial record in *United States vs. Mary Helen Coal Corporation*. However, certain discrepancies may be noted. Juror Chestnut's name was spelled "Ellie" in the transcript, "Allie" in the *News-Sentinel*, and "Eli" in the *Times*. The present writer adopted the form used in the trial record. Juror W.B. Johnson was listed as "W.D." in the *News-Sentinel*. Juror Powell was "Aleck" in the *Times*. Juror Hibbard was "John" in both the *Times* and *News-Sentinel*. Juror Campbell was "Denten" in the *Times*. Juror L.F. Johnson was "L.J." in the *News-Sentinel*. The trial record listed W.H. Main and A.B. Sams as alternates, and both the *Times* and the *News-Sentinel* listed Hercules York as a juror but the trial record omitted him. Apparently he was not a juror. The *News-Sentinel* also listed the name Elijah Woodall, a Mt. Vernon WPA worker, as a juror, but none of the other sources did. Apparently Woodall was neither a juror nor an alternate.

11. *Knoxville News-Sentinel*, May 22, 1938; *United States vs. Mary Helen Coal Corporation*, pp. 1088-1089; 1091-1092; 1093-1099; 1100.

12. *Knoxville News-Sentinel*, May 24, 1938, *United States vs. Mary Helen Coal Corporation*, pp. 1107-1108; 1111-1112; 1120-1129; 1137, 1140. Dawson discussed the history of Harlan contracts during the years from 1933 to 1935, then closed with the quotation given.

13. See above, chapter IX, pp. 177-178.

14. *United States vs. Mary Helen Coal Corporation*, pp. 1159; 1311; 1395-99.

15. *Ibid.*, pp. 1307; 1314-1315; 1319. Jailer Clinton C. Ball was a Democrat who was elected in 1933, when Middleton was elected sheriff. In the 1937 primary, Ball was selected as Democratic nominee for sheriff, but lost in the general election to Herbert Cawood, the GOP nominee, who was Middleton's nephew. Cawood's election was con-

tested by Ball, but the Court of Appeals ordered Cawood to hold the office until a special election could be held in 1938. During the primary and general elections of 1937, Ball had denounced Middleton before meetings of local unions.

16. *United States vs. Mary Helen Coal Corporation*, pp. 1345; 1346; 1347-1348; 1350-1352; 1717-1715.

17. *Ibid.*, pp. 1198-1199; 1201; 1207; 1208-1208 1/2.

18. *Ibid.*, p. 1409.

19. *United States vs. Mary Helen Coal Corporation, Ibid.*, pp. 3721-3722; 3729-3734; 3744-3749; 3767.

20. *Ibid.*, 6625-6652; Hevener, *Which Side Are You On?*, pp. 139-140.

21. *Ibid.*, pp. 3801-3833; 3929-3940; 3980; 4018-4024; *New York Times*, June 11, 1938.

22. *New York Times*, June 23, 28, 1938. Operators who appeared were W.A. Ellison, Charles S. Guthrie, Kenes Bowling, Charles B. Burchfield, Elmer D. Hall, R.E. Lawson, William H. Sienknecht, Elbert J. Asbury, Armstrong R. Matthews, Bryan W. Whitfield, Jr., C.V. Bennett, F.E. Gilbert, T.E. Mahan, A.F. Whitfield, George Creech, and J.A. Dickinson. *United States vs. Mary Helen Coal Corporation*, p. 4969.

23. The testimony of miners, favorable to the operators and to the companies, is found in volumes XXII through XLIII of the trial record. Ten appeared for Cornett-Lewis; twenty-five for Harlan Fuel and Harlan-Wallins; thirteen for Harlan Collieries; Creech; and Mary Helen; twelve for Kentucky Cardinal and R.C. Tway; twenty-six for Clover Fork; seventeen for Harlan Central and Bardo; eleven for Crummies Creek; ten for High Splint; nine for Green-Silvers; four for Southern Mining; and three for Southern Harlan.

24. *Ibid.*, pp. 10226-10259.

25. *Knoxville News-Sentinel*, July 6-9, 1938.

26. Patterson had been convicted in 1932 in connection with the twin dynamitings of Lawrence Dwyer. See above, Chapter III, p. 61-62.

27. *Harlan Daily Enterprise*, July 6, 1938; *Knoxville News-Sentinel*, July 6, 1938. Reno had earlier killed Fleenor's father.

28. *Knoxville News-Sentinel*, July 10, 15, 16, 1938. What these FBI agents learned was not reported to the court nor in any of the sources consulted.

29. The lengthy testimony of peace officers, denying acts of intimidation and violence, is found in volumes XXII, XXIV, XXV, XXVIII, XIX, XXXV-XXXIX, and XLI-XLIII of the trial record. *Knoxville News-Sentinel*, July 14, 1938.

30. Included among the items reportedly picked up by Youngblood and his companions were two high-powered rifles, two shot-guns, and a basket containing "two and a half or three gallons of rifle cartridges." *Knoxville News-Sentinel*, July 6, 7, 1938; *United States vs . Mary Helen Coal Corporation*, pp. 11089-11293 1/2. Corroborating statements were offered by L.D. Keel, a Pineville barber; Continental Hotel clerk W.N. Witt; George Karloftis, proprietor of the Hub Restaurant; Deputy Constable Pincquard McCoy; Deputy Sheriff Chester Ridings; County Judge D.M. Bingham; and Pineville attorney James S. Golden, UMWA lawyer.

31. *Knoxville News-Sentinel*, July 21, 22, 1938.
32. *Knoxville News-Sentinel*, July 23, 1938.
33. *Knoxville News-Sentinel*, June 17, 21, 1938.
34. *Ibid.*. July 22, 25, 26, 1938; *United States vs. Mary Helen Coal Corporation*, pp. 7682-7752; 11369-11402. Volume XLVII of the trial record, containing the testimony of the Cawoods and of Spicer relative to the perjury mill, was not included in the transcript made available to the writer.
35. *Ibid.*, July 27, 28, 29, 30, 1938; *United States vs. Mary Helen Coal Corporation*, pp. 12080-12310; 12318-12408; 12409; 12480; 12482-12539; 12540-12595; 12690-12806; 12846; 12897. Dawson had portrayed Martha Howard "as a woman who flaunted her ill repute to the world and paraded before the jury with a story too fantastic to believe."
36. *United States vs. Mary Helen Coal Corporation*, pp. 12926-12970; 12998-13002.
37. *Knoxville News-Sentinel*, August 2, 1938.
38. *New York Times*, August 3, 1938.
39. *Knoxville News-Sentinel*, August 3, 1938.
40. Hevener, *Which Side Are You On?*, 148-150.

NOTES TO CHAPTER 11

1. *Louisville Courier-Journal*, May 15, 16, 1973. Although Chandler announced the end of the privately-paid deputy sheriff system in mid-May, 1937, the Kentucky General Assembly did not officially outlaw the system until January 21, 1938. See below, p. 215-216. Apparently state policemen sent by the governor in May, 1937 relieved Harlan's company-paid deputy sheriffs. *Knoxville News-Sentinel*, May 20, 1937.
2. *Harlan Daily Enterprise*, May 3, 10, 1937.
3. *Ibid.* Titler later authored the book *Hell in Harlan*, which described his Harlan County experiences. George J. Titler to Paul F. Taylor, No-

vember 26, 1972.

4. *Ibid.*, May 17, 1937. *The Louisville Courier-Journal*, May 17, 1937, reported that District 28 UMWA president John Saxton, not Caddy, delivered these remarks.

5. *Harlan Daily Enterprise*, May 17, 1937; *Knoxville News-Sentinel*, May 17, 1937.

6. *Louisville Courier-Journal*, May 21, June 22, 1937; *Harlan Daily Enterprise*, June 16, 22, 1937. According to Titler, the union at this point had thirty-three hundred men in seven mines under contract, including Black Mountain and Cloversplint.

7. See Chapter III, endnote 31 for an explanation of "check-off."

8. *Louisville Courier-Journal*, July 10, 1937. Two letters, George S. Ward to A.B. Chandler, July 12, 1937, and Chandler's response to Ward, July 16, 1937, refer to this conference. Ward denied Turnblazer's claim that the UMWA had made concessions on wages to the HCCOA. Chandler, expressing disappointment that the conference had failed to conclude an agreement, wrote that he hoped "the differences between the operators and the union can be ironed out." Albert B. Chandler Collection, First Gubernatorial Series, State Correspondence, 1937, Box 74. Special Collections, University Archives, University of Kentucky, Lexington, Kentucky. Hereafter referred to as the Albegt B. Chandler Collection.

9. *Harlan Daily Enterprise*, June 23, 1937.

10. *Ibid.*, June 23, 24, 27, 1937. This murder was apparently never solved. No record of indictments or trials were located.

11. *Ibid.*, June 24, 1937. Earlier, in spring, 1937, as an apparent outgrowth to the La Follette hearings, the county judge had issued warrants charging Frank White with murder in the death of Bennett Musick; and Ben Unthank, George Lee and White with "maliciously" shooting into Bill Clontz's home at Wallins. Saylor ordered Lee and White held to the grand jury, while Unthank executed an appearance bond for an examining trial. Records, however, do not show trials in any of these cases. Free on bond and later charged with threatening a High Splint man, the court placed White under a peace bond. Other charges against White included: carrying a concealed deadly weapon, breach of peace, reckless driving, and having no operator's license following an altercation with state policemen. Following dismissal of the most serious charges in county court, County Attorney pro tem George R. Pope resigned "because it's too easy to prosecute the little man and too hard to prosecute the big man in Harlan County." Transpiring in May, June, and July, 1937, the *Harlan Daily Enterprise* reported these events on

May 10, June 4, 25, and July 8, 11, 14, 1937.

12. *Harlan Daily Enterprise*, July 14, 1937.

13. *Knoxville News-Sentinel*, July 10, 1937; *Louisville Courier-Journal*, July 11, 1937.

14. National Labor Relations Board, *In the Matter of Clover Fork Coal Company and District 19, United Mine Workers of America*, Case No. C-213, November 27, 1937. Cited hereafter as Clover Fork Coal Company and District 19 UMWA. Pp. 107-108; 211-214. At the hearing, George Titler and James Bates testified that they had been threatened, cursed, and warned not to enter Harlan in January, 1937; sixty miners reported discharges; and that mine officials had said the union would not be tolerated. *Louisville Courier-Journal*, July 15, 1937.

15. *Harlan Daily Enterprise*, November 29, 1937.

16. *United States v. Mary Helen Coal Corporation*, p. 6467.

17. *Harlan Daily Enterprise*, October 13, 1937. Admitting that the company had sponsored the shows, Charles S. Guthrie, operator at Harlan Fuel, denied any attempt to distract from the union meetings. Defense counsel at London had mentioned the shows but Cleon K. Calvert maintained that the men also had sponsored some of them. Government attorney Henry A. Schweinhaut claimed that the company had sponsored them to counteract union sessions. *United States v. Mary Helen Coal Corporation*, XLIX, pp. 12430-12431; L, p. 12837. Also National Labor Relations Board, *In the Matter of Harlan Fuel Company and District 19, United Mine Workers of America*, Case No. C-489, July 5, 1938, p. 28.

18. *Harlan Daily Enterprise*, October 24, 1937.

19. *Ibid.*, December 7, 1937. Information derived from the various NLRB hearings suggest that, following the La Follette hearings, several company unions were formed, with the sanction of operators, to circumvent the Wagner Act. National Labor Relations Board, *In the Matter of Good Coal Company and District 19, United Mine Workers of America*, Case No. C-509, April 8, 1939, pp. 154-155.

20. *Knoxville News-Sentinel*, April 22, 1938. Records and reports of the Green-Silvers and Harlan Central hearings could not be located, but apparently the NLRB also found against these companies.

21. Kentucky General Assembly, *House Journal*, 1936, I, p. 242; II, p. 1412; III, pp. 2535, 2538; *Senate Journal*, 1936, II, p. 1676; *House Journal*, 1938, I, pp. 27, 132; III, p. 808. The vote was 80 to 3. *Senate Journal*, 1938, I, p. 669. Also *Louisville Courier-Journal*, January 25, 1938.

22. *House Journal*, 1938, I, pp. 136-137; III, p. 835; *Senate Journal*,

1938, I, p. 764; *Louisville Courier-Journal*, January 26, 1938.

23. *Louisville Courier-Journal*, May 31, 1938.

24. *Knoxville News-Sentinel*, August 3, 28, 1938. Representing the UMWA at the Cincinnati conference were William Turnblazer, George Titler, T.C. Townsend, UMWA counsel from Charleston, West Virginia, and Earl E. Hauck, head of the UMWA legal department in Washington and personal representative of John L. Lewis.

25. The *Knoxville News-Sentinel*, August 28, 39, 31, 1938, extensively covered all negotiations leading to the new contract as well as national, local and UMWA opinion of the agreement. *Harlan Daily Enterprise*, September 4, 1938.

26. *Knoxville News-Sentinel*, August 29, 1938.

27. *Harlan Daily Enterprise*, September 6, 1938; September 22, 1938; October 16, 1938. Formerly, Lynch workers had been affiliated with the Union of Lynch Employees, a company union. Later they had voted to join the American Federation of Labor with which the workers of the International Harvester subsidiary at Benham were connected.

28. *United Mine Workers Journal*, November 15, 1938,

29. *Harlan Daily Enterprise*, April 12, 13, 14, 28, 30, 1939. The man-trip was a motorized cable car used to lift the workers to the drift mouth of the mine.

30. *Ibid.*, April 17, 1939.

31. Harlan County Court, Commonwealth Orders, IX, 526.

32. *Harlan Daily Enterprise*, May 1, 1939.

33. *Ibid.*, May 3, 1939. Three Clover Fork employees wrote on May 8, 1939 that they desired to return to work but mass picketing prevented them from doing so. One hundred twenty-three men signed the letter. Albert B. Chandler Collection, Box 54.

34. *Harlan Daily Enterprise*, May 4, 1939; *Knoxville News-Sentinel*, May 3, 4, 1939.

35. *Ibid.*, May 8, 1939. On May 4, 1939, Turnblazer telegraphed Ward from New York where he was attending a joint union-operators conference, protesting the reopening of the mines. Albert B. Chandler Collection, Box 54.

36. C.E. Ball to A.B. Chandler, May 5, 1939. Albert B. Chandler Collection, Box 54.

37. William Turnblazer to A.B. Chandler, May 8, 1939. In a telegram the union chief referred to a tour of the county on May 7 in which he had found conditions stable. He scorned pressures by "double-crossing politicians" to get the militia into the county. Albert B. Chandler Collection, Box 54.

38. The Chandler Collection contains communications from Harlan businessmen, from miners at Molus, High Splint, Bardo, Lejunior, Benham, Tway, Kenvir, Louellen, Chevrolet, Brookside, Lynch, Creech, Mary Helen, all protesting the sending of troops. Several coal camp pastors wrote similar letters. Turnblazer, on May 11, wrote Chandler that the troops have "jeopardized my position on your behalf." Albert B. Chandler Collection, Box 54.

39. J.C. Stras to A.B. Chandler, May 4, 1939. Stras wrote that the governor had been misinformed about the seriousness of the Harlan situation and suggested that he select "impartial observers" to survey the county and recommend an appropriate course of action for the governor to take. Albert B. Chandler Collection, Box 54.

40. Commonwealth of Kentucky, Department of Military Affairs, Adjutant General's Office, Special Orders, No. 83 and No. 85, May 11, 15, 1939; Special Orders No. 87 and No. 88, May 17, 18, 1939. Subordinate officers included Colonel Roy W. Easley, Lieutenant-Colonel John Polin, Lieutenant-Colonel William S. Taylor, Major Oren Coin, Major Joseph M. Kelley, Lieutenant-Colonel George M. Cheschier, and Major Jesse S. Lindsey.

41. *Knoxville News-Sentinel*, May 15, 1939.

42. According to the special orders available in the Department of Military Affairs, War Records Office, Frankfort, the greatest number of troops in Harlan County during May, 1939, was 1,187.

43. In writing a fifteen-page report to Governor Chandler, General Carter said that Colonel Easley, assisted by 150 men, rounded up the pickets and "marched them two miles up the road toward Benham, with instructions to stay away." Report to Governor Chandler on Harlan County duty made by Brig. General Ellerbee W. Carter, Ky. N.G. July 22, 1939. Albert B. Chandler Collection, Box 54.

44. General Carter stated in his report to the governor that "disorders were scattered" after May 18 until the outbreak at Stanfill. Most incidents involved four or five pickets harassing a single miner. Albert B. Chandler Collection, Box 68.

45. According to General Carter's report, two to three thousand men, travelling eight to ten per vehicle and fifty to sixty in a ton and a half truck, paraded, jeered, threatened, abused and attacked miners who attempted to work and their families, both day and night during May, 1939. The Clover Fork area was a prime target of these roving bands of pickets. Albert B. Chandler Collection, Box 68.

46. *Knoxville News-Sentinel*, May 16, 17, 1939; *Harlan Daily Enterprise*, May 15, 16, 1939.

47. *Harlan Daily Enterprise*, May 19, 21, 22, 1939. The terms of United States Coal and Coke agreement were not revealed, except that it did not include a union shop.

48. Pearl Bassham to A.B. Chandler, May 22, 1939. Albert B. Chandler Collection, Box 54.

49. *Harlan Daily Enterprise*, May 14, 17, 18, 24, 25, 26, 31; June 1, 5, 1939 covered contract talks in New York and Harlan. It also reported the signing of individual companies to union contracts as well as the return of relative calmness to the county's mines.

50. *Knoxville News-Sentinel*, June 9, 15, 19, 1939; *Harlan Daily Enterprise*, June 11, 1939; June 19, 1939. The 5,000 miners were those working in mines operated by HCCOA members.

51. *Knoxville News-Sentinel*, June 21, 25, 1939. This figure is derived from the special orders available in the Department of Military Affairs, War Records Office, Frankfort.

52. A copy of Turnblazer's speech at the Lenarue rally is contained in the files of the Albert B. Chandler Collection Box 68. The excerpt quoted is taken from that copy of the speech. Also *Knoxville News-Sentinel*, July 10, 1939.

53. A document, "Report on Captain Hanberry's shooting at the Mahan-Ellison mine in Harlan County on July 12, 1939," is contained in the Chandler papers. In a three-page report signed by Major Frederick W. Staples, Captain Hanberry's name was spelled differently than in newspaper accounts. According to Major Staples' report, five hundred pickets were present at Stanfill. Pickets knocked down soldiers and then attempted to take their guns. When Captain Hanberry intervened, he was shot once in his left arm and once through the body. Hanberry then shot one man, who later died, in the chest. Albert B. Chandler Collection, Box 68. Also *Harlan Daily Enterprise*, July 13, 1939; *Knoxville News-Sentinel*, July 12, 1939. General Carter's report contains a detailed account of the "Battle of Stanfill."

54. *Harlan Daily Enterprise*, July 12, 13, 1939; *Knoxville News-Sentinel*, July 12, 13, 1939. The latter paper contains the most detailed accounts of Harlan events during the summer of 1939. General Carter's report, while stating that pickets were marched to the county seat, does not mention the riot in downtown Harlan, Also Commonwealth of Kentucky, Department of Military Affairs, Adjutant General's Office, Special Order No. 134, July 12, 1939.

55. *Knoxville News-Sentinel*, July 12, 1939. Governor Chandler declared that he would "request the Harlan grand jury indict Turnblazer for inciting riot and George Titler...should be kept in jail. Their meth-

ods are typical of those acts of violence advocated by John L. Lewis."

56. Harlan County Court, Commonwealth Orders, No. 9, July 17, 22, 26, 1939, pp. 555-556; Harlan Circuit Court, Commonwealth Orders, No. 33, July 14, 1939, p. 587; July 26, 1939, pp. 592-594; 600-601. A total of 145 others were indicted in connection with the "Battle of Stanfill" and defendants were released on bonds ranging from $7,500 to $20,000 except for George Titler, who declined bond and remained in jail. Also *Harlan Daily Enterprise*, July 17, 1939.

57. *Knoxville News-Sentinel*, July 13, 1939.

58. *Ibid.*, July 15, 19, 1939. George Titler was still in Harlan jail as the talks opened. The "house cases" were law suits initiated by the companies to remove striking miners from company houses. The penalty clause, a feature of the previous Appalachian agreement, provided for a $1 per day fine per man for unauthorized strikes, making "walkouts" impossible without violation of the contract. The union shop clause was a concession to the operators. Also *Harlan Daily Enterprise*, July 19, 1939.

59. *Knoxville News-Sentinel*, July 19, 1939.

60. *New York Times*, July 20, 1939.

61. *Knoxville News-Sentinel*, July 20, 23, 1939.

62. *Ibid.*, July 24, 28, 1939. The governor took this action after County Judge Cam E. Ball had wired his approval.

63. *Ibid.*, August 11, 1939.

64. *United Mine Workers Journal*, October 15, 1939, pp. 10-11. Records of the dismissals are found in Harlan Circuit Court, Commonwealth Orders, No. 34, September 29, 1939, pp. 114-116. The case in which the motion was made was that of Turnblazer and Titler.

NOTES TO EPILOGUE

1. See above, Chapter XI, p. 225-230.
2. Titler, *Hell in Harlan*, 113, 205.
3. *Ibid.*, p. 209.
4. *Ibid.*, pp. 207, 209.
5. Matthew 26: 52b.
6. The "switches" used by the Brookside women were actually sticks, clubs, broom handles.
7. Bryan Wooley and Ford Reid, *We Be Here When the Morning Comes* (Lexington, Kentucky, 1974), 7-8, 29-36, 78-79.
8. The writer and his Labor History students gained the recent opinions toward the UMWA in an oral history project conducted in Harlan County in May 1982, May 1984, October 1985, and October 1987.

bibliography

PRIVATE PAPERS

Albert Benjamin Chandler Papers, Special Collections Section, Margaret I. King Library, University of Kentucky.

PRIMARY MATERIALS

Bell County Court Records, 1934-1935

Order Books: Bell Quarterly Court, Commonwealth Docket, January, 1934; Bell Circuit Court, Commonwealth Orders, No. 21, February,1934; Bell Circuit Court, Commonwealth Orders, No. 22, May, 1935.

Harlan County Court Records, 1931-1939

Affadavits:

Joe Cawood vs. Leslie Ball, respondent, May 20, 1931.

Asa Cusick, Al Benson, W.B. Jones and Joe Cawood, request that Judge D.C. Jones vacate the bench during labor trials, May 19, 1931.

Indictments:

R.R. Smith and Chester McCrary, banding and confederating against Roy Hensley, Oscar Johnson and Laurance Right (Wright), May 7, 1931.

Bill Camp, W.L. Camp, Bill Masingale, George Masingale,

Spence Bray, Alford Dozier, Elza Davenport and Laz York, banding and confederating against Robert Blair, May 20, 1931.

Gill Green, D.F. Gibson and Ed Braden, banding and confederating against J.H. Blair, May 20, 1931.

Jack Griffith, Pascle Sweeten, Mose King, Lawrence Toney and Al Benson, robbery in connection with the theft of weapons from Darby Coal Co. Commissary, May 22, 1931.

Henry Eagle, Clyde Mulkey, James Maynard, Arthur Prollen (Medrogen or Metroglen), Ben Durkan, Tom Batthi, Johnson Murphy, Floyd Mills and J.H. Jones, banding and confederating against Charles Carpenter, August 19, 1931.

Simp Farley, Calvin Collins and Mrs. Simp Farley, storehouse breaking, August 20, 1931.

Harlie Mealer and Finley Powers, banding and confederating against W.A. Jackson, Mose Middleton and Merle Middleton, August 21, 1931.

Sam Reynolds, Fat Hibbard, John Lester, Lewis Layne, Tom Eppers (Epperson) , James Mahone and Cotton Lester, storehouse breaking (Evarts ASP), August 25, 1931.

Bill Gilbert, Hubert Gaines, Noah Colston, John Lester, Hugh Lester, Lige Vanover, Cass Vaughn, Andrew Vaughn and Jack Griffith, storehouse breaking (East Harlan Coal Co. Commissary), August 25, 1931.

Charley Pitman, Bill Lewis and Willie Lewis, banding and confederating against persons to the grand jury unknown, August 29, 1931.

Letters:

William Turnblazer to W.B. Jones, April 3, 1931.

Order Books: Harlan County Court, 1932, 1934, 1935, 1939; Harlan Circuit Court, No. 29, 1934; No. 30, 1934; No. 31, 1934; No. 32,

BIBLIOGRAPHY

1937; No. 33, 1939; Sheriff's Bond Book No. 4, 1933-1937.

Transcripts of Evidence:

Montgomery Circuit Court. Commonwealth, of Kentucky v. W.B. Jones. Vols. II, III, IV, V, U.S. National Archives, Record Group 60. Justice Department, General Records. Central Files. Classified Subject Files.

Montgomery Circuit Court. Commonwealth of, Kentucky v. William Hightower. Vols. IV, VIII. U.S. National Archives, Record Group 60. Justice Department, General Records. Central Files, Classified Subject Files.

GOVERNMENT DOCUMENTS

<u>Federal Publications</u>:

U.S. Congress, Senate, *Conditions in Coal Fields in Harlan and Bell Counties, Kentucky, Hearings*. before Subcommittee of Committee on Manufactures, U.S. Senate, 72d Cong., 1st Sess., on S. Res. 178, May 11, 12, 13, and 19, 1932. Government Printing Office, Washington, 1932.

U.S. Congress, Senate, *Violations of Free Speech and Rights of Labor, Hearings*, before Subcommittee of Committee on Commerce and Labor, U.S. Senate, 74th Cong., 2nd Sess., on S. Res. 266, 1936. Government Printing Office, Washington, 1936.

U.S. Congress, Senate, *Violations of Free Speech and Rights of Labor, Hearings*, before Subcommittee of Committee on Commerce and Labor, U.S. Senate, 75th Cong., 1st Sess., on S. Res. 266, 1937. Government Printing Office, Washington, 1937.

U.S. Congress, Senate, *Private Police Systems*. Senate Report No. 6, part 2, 76th Cong., 1st Sess., 1938. Government Printing Office, Washington, 1938.

U.S. National Archives. Record Group 9. National Recovery Administration, Bituminous Coal Labor Board, Division No. 1-South. *Case Files. Hearings and Decisions*.

National Labor Relations Board, *In the Matter of Clover Fork Coal Company and District 19. United Mine Workers of America.* Case No. C-213, November 27, 1937. Government Printing Office, Washington, 1937.

National Labor Relations Board, *In the Matter of Harlan Fuel Company and District 19, United Mine Workers of America.* Case No. C-489, July 5, 1938. Government Printing Office, Washington, 1938.

National Labor Relations Board, *In the Matter of Good Coal Company and District 19, United Mine Workers of America.* Case No. C-509, April 8, 1939. Government Printing Office, Washington, 1939.

United States Statutes at Large, Vol. XLIX, 1935. Government Printing Office, Washington, 1935.

FEDERAL COURT RECORDS

United States Federal District Court for Eastern Kentucky, *United States of America vs. Mary Helen Coal Corporation, et. al.* , Transcript of Evidence, 1938, 50 vols.

United States Federal District Court for Eastern Kentucky, *United States of America vs. Mary Helen Coal Corporation, et. al.*, Indictment No. 5990, September 27, 1937, 16 pp.

STATE PUBLICATIONS

Commonwealth of Kentucky, Department of Mines and Minerals, *Annual Report*, 1917. The State Journal Company, Frankfort, 1917.

Kentucky Court of Appeals, *Kentucky Reports*, Vol. 261, 1935. The State Journal Company, Frankfort, 1935.

Kentucky General Assembly, *House Journal*, Vols. I, III, 1936. The State Journal Company, Frankfort, 1936.

Kentucky General Assembly, *House Journal*, Vols. I, III, 1938. The State Journal Company, Frankfort, 1938.

BIBLIOGRAPHY

Kentucky General Assembly, *Senate Journal*, Vol. II, 1936. The State Journal Company, Frankfort, 1936.

Kentucky General Assembly, *Senate Journal*, Vol. I, 1938. The State Journal Company, Frankfort, 1938.

STATE RECORDS

Executive Journals:

Executive Journal, Governor Ruby Laffoon, I, II, 1935.

Executive Journal, Governor A.B. Chandler, I, 1937.

Letters:

William Turnblazer to A.B. Chandler, December 28, 1936, Department of Military Affairs, War Records Division, Frankfort, Kentucky.

A.B. Chandler to William Turnblazer, December 31, 1936, Department of Military Affairs, War Records Division, Frankfort, Kentucky.

Special Orders:

Commonwealth of Kentucky, Department of Military Affairs, Special Order No. 89, June 1, 1935. Commonwealth of Kentucky, Department of Military Affairs, Special Orders No. 83 and No. 85, May 11, 15, 1939; Special Orders No. 87 and No. 88, May 17, 18, 1939; Special Orders No. 124, July 12, 1939.

INTERVIEWS

Joe Bates, Lexington, Kentucky, May 20, 1967.

Al Benson, Kenvir, Kentucky, September 7, 1954.

William Clontz, London, Kentucky, October 17, 1966.

BLOODY HARLAN

Bessie Green, London, Kentucky, October 17, 1966.

G.W. Hall, District 19 representative, UMWA, Harlan, Kentucky, August 11, 1954.

Mrs. Ben Hughes, Harlan, Kentucky, August 16, 1954.

W.K. Kilbourn, Cumberland, Kentucky, December 30, 1966.

Marshall A. Musick, Jellico, Tennessee, January 4, 1967.

Mallie Musick, Jellico, Tennessee, January 4, 1967.

George Sweeten, Harlan, Kentucky, April 15, 1954.

Claude Taylor, Cumberland, Kentucky, December 30, 1966.

U,	Harlan, Kentucky, August 10,	1954.
V,	Harlan, Kentucky, August 10,	1954.
W,	Harlan, Kentucky, August 16,	1954.
X,	Evarts, Kentucky, August 16,	1954.
Y,	Harlan, Kentucky, August 23,	1954.
Z,	Harlan, Kentucky, August 24,	1954.

NEWSPAPERS

Harlan Daily Enterprise, 1931-1939.

Knoxville News-Sentinel, 1933-1939.

Lexington Herald, 1931-32; 1934, 1935.

Lexington Leader, 1934, 1935.

London Sentinel-Echo, 1938.

Louisville Courier-Journal, 1931-1939.

Middlesboro Daily News, 1931-1939.

New York Times, 1933-1939.

BIBLIOGRAPHY

Pineville Sun, 1931-1939.

United Mine Workers Journal, 1931-1939.

Washington Post, May, 1932.

Christian Science Monitor, May, 1932.

Cincinnati Enquirer, May, 1932.

PAMPHLETS AND BOOKS

Dreiser, Theodore, *Harlan Miners Speak*. Harcourt and Brace, New York, 1932.
Louisville and Nashville Railroad, *Coal Field Directory*. 1951.

PERIODICALS

"Essential Issues in Harlan County," *Christian Century*, XLVIII (November 18, 1931), p. 1444.
"Kentucky Editors Comment on Harlan Situation," *The Nation*. CXXXIV (May 18, 1932), pp. 571-573.

PRIVATE COLLECTIONS

Herndon J. Evans Collection, Pineville, Kentucky. This collection contains circulars distributed in the Bell-Harlan area by Communist-affiliated organizations, newspaper clippings, and other material pertinent to this conflict, especially the invasion by the radicals during late 1931 and early 1932.

PROCEEDINGS

American Federation of Labor, *Proceedings of 55th Annual Convention*. Atlantic City, New Jersey, 1935.

Kentucky State Federation of Labor, *Official Proceedings of 31st Annual Convention*, Frankfort, Kentucky, 1935.

United Mine Workers of America, *Proceedings of 33rd Constitutional*

Convention, Indianapolis, Indiana, 1934.

United Mine Workers of America, *Proceedings, of 34th Constitutional Convention*, Washington D.C., 1936.

United Mine Workers of America, *Proceedings of 35th Constitutional Convention*, Washington, D.C., 1938.

United Mine Workers of America, *Proceedings of 36th Constitutional Convention*, Columbus, Ohio, 1940.

United Mine Workers of America, *Proceedings, of 38th Constitutional Convention*, Cincinnati, Ohio, 1942.

MISCELLANEOUS

From the files, District 19 Headquarters, United Mine Workers of America, Middlesboro, Kentucky. List of appointments of deputy sheriffs made by Sheriff J.H. Blair, 1930-31.

SECONDARY MATERIALS

Books:

Ardery, Julia S., ed. *Welcome the Traveler Home: Jim Garland's Story of the Kentucky Mountains.* Lexington: The University Press of Kentucky, 1983.

Auerbach, Jerold S., *Labor and Liberty: The LaFollette Committee and the New Deal.* Indianapolis: Bobbs-Merrill Company, 1966.

Bellush, Bernard, *The Failure of the N.R.A.* New York: W.W. Norton and Company, 1975.

Bernstein, Irving, *The Lez Books*, Baltimore, 1966. Penguin Books, 1966.

Bernstein, Irving, *The New Deal Collective Bargaining Policy.* University of California Press, 1950.

Blakey, George T., *Hard Times and the New Deal of Kentucky, 1929-1939.* Lexington: The University Press of Kentucky, 1986.

Calkins, Clinch, *Spy Overhead: The Story of Industrial Espionage.* New York, 1937.

Carnes, Cecil, *John L. Lewis: Leader of Labor.* Robert Speller Publishing Corporation, New York, 1936.

Caudill, Harry M., *Night Comes to the Cumberlands : A Biography of a Depressed Area*. Little, Brown and Company, Boston, 1962.

Caudill, Harry M., *Theirs Be The Power: The Moguls of Eastern Kentucky*. Urbana and Chicago: University of Illinois Press, 1983.

Coleman, McAllister, *Men and Coal*. Farrar and Rinehart, Inc., New York, 1943.

Commager, Henry Steele, ed. *Documents of American History*. Appleton-Century-Crofts, New York, 1968.

Cronen, E. David, ed. *Labor and the New Deal*. Berkeley Series in American History, Rand McNally and Company, Chicago, 1963.

Day, John F., *Bloody Ground*. Lexington: University Press of Kentucky, 1981. (With a Foreword by Thorns D. Clark and an Afterword by Harry M. Caudill.)

Doan, Edward N., *The LaFollettes and the Wisconsin Idea*. Rinehart and Company, Inc., New York, 1947.

Dubofsky, Melvyn and Warren Van Tine. *John L. Lewis; A Biography*. New York: Quadrangle/New York Times Company, 1977.

Dulles, Foster Rhea, *Labor in America*. 4th ed. Harlan Davidson, Inc., Arlington Heights, Illinois, 1984.

Eavenson, Howard N., *The First Century and a Quarter of the American Coal Industry*. Waverly Press, Baltimore, 1942.

Fenton, John H. *Politics in the Border States*. New Orleans: Hauser Press, 1957.

Forester, William D., *Harlan County; The Turbulent Thirties*. n.p., 1986.

Fox, John, Jr., *The Trail of the Lonesome Pine*. New York: Grosset and Dunlap, 1908.

Grubbs, *Four Keys to Kentucky*. Louisville: Slater and Gilroy, 1949.

Hevener, John W., *Which Side Are You On? The Harlan County Coal Miners, 1931-39*. Urbana-Chicago: The University of Illinois Press, 1978.

Huberman, Leo. *The Labor Spy Racket*. Modern Age, New York, 1937.

Johnson, Robert T., *Robert M. LaFollette, Jr. and the Decline of the Progressive Party in Wisconsin*. The State Historical Society of Wisconsin, Madison, Wisconsin, 1964.

Jones, G.C., *Growing Up Hard in Harlan County*. Lexington: The University Press of Kentucky, 1985.

Josephson, Matthew, *Infidel in the Temple*. New York: Alfred A. Knopf, 1967.

Kahn, Kathy, *Hillybilly Women*. New York: Avon Books, 1973.

Kephart, Horace, *Our Southern Highlanders*. New York: The Macmillan Company, 1922.

Kincaid, Robert L. *The Wilderness Road*. Indianapolis: Bobbs-Merrills Company, 1947.

Marshall, F. Ray, *Labor in the South*. Harvard University Press, Cambridge, 1967.

Olmsted, Frederick Law, *Journay in the Back Country, 1853-56*. New York: Geo. P. Putnam's Sons, 1907.

Pearce, John Ed, *Divide and Dissent: Kentucky Politics, 1930-1963*. Lexington: The University Press of Kentucky, 1987.

Rayback, Joseph G., *A History of American Labor*. The Macmillan Company, New York, 1959.

Rosenman, Samuel I., ed. *The Public Papers and Addresses of Franklin D. Roosevelt*, Vol. IV. Random House, New York, 1938.

Ross, Malcolm, *Machine Age in the Hills*. The Macmillan Company, New York, 1933.

Schlesinger, Arthur M., *The Politics of Upheaval*. Houghton-Mifflin Company, Boston, 1960.

Shackelford, Laurel and Bill Weinberg, *Our Appalachia: An Oral History*. New York: Hill and Wang, 1977.

Sherburne, James, *Stand Like Men*. Boston: Houghton-Mifflin Company, 1973.

Swanberg, W.A., *Dreiser*. New York: Charles Scribner's Sons, 1965.

Tipton, J.C., *The Cumberland Coal Field and its Creators*. Pinnacle Printery, Middlesboro, Kentucky, 1905.

Titler, George J., *Hell in Harlan*. Beckley, West Virginia: BJW Printers, n.d.

Woolley, Bryan and Ford Reid, *We Be Here When the Morning Comes*. Lexington: The University Press of Kentucky, 1974.

Pamphlets:

Costello, E.J., *The Shame That Is Kentucky's*. (n.p., n.d.)

Kentucky Miners Defense, *Bloody Harlan*. Kentucky Miners Defense, New York, 1937.

Periodicals:

Auerbach, Jerold S., "The LaFollette Committee: Labor and Civil Liberties in the New Deal," *Journal of American History*, LI (December, 1964), pp. 435-459.

Barkley, Frederick R., "Bloody Harlan," *The Nation*. CXLIV (May 8, 1937), pp. 532-533.

Booth, James W., "Blood on Harlan," *Real Detective* XLI. No. 4 (October, 1937), 12-15, 67-9.

Brown, Francis, "LaFollette: Ten Years Senator," *Current History*, XLII (August, 1935), pp. 475-480.

Bubka, Tony, "The Harlan County Coal Strike of 1931," *Labor History*, XI (Winter, 1970), 41-57.

Cowley, Malcolm, "Kentucky Coal Town," *New Republic*. LXX (March 2, 1932), pp. 67-70.

Davenport, Walter, "Happy Couldn't Wait," *Colliers's*. CII, pt. 1 (July 16, 1938), pp. 12-13, 49-51.

Grauman, Lawrence, Jr., "That Little Dgly Running Sore," *Filson Club History Quarterly*, XXXVI (October, 1967), pp. 340-354.

Harsh, Joseph C., "Harlan on Trial," *New Republic*, LIXV (July 6, 1938), pp. 242-244.

Hays, Arthur Garfield, "The Right to Get Shot," *The Nation*, CXXXIV (June 1, 1932), p. 619.

Johnson, James P., "Drafting the NRA Code of Fair Competition for the Bituminous Coal Industry," *Journal of American History*, LII, No. 3 (December, 1966), pp. 522-537.

Stone, I.E., "It Happened in Harlan," *Current History*. XLIX (September 1938), pp. 29-31.

Taylor, Paul F., "London: Focal Point of Kentucky Turbulence," *The Filson Club History Quarterly*. 49, No. 3 (July, 1975), 256-265.

Villard, Oswald Garrison, "Issues and Men," *The Nation*. CXLV (August 14, 1937), p. 172.

Walker, Charles Rumford, "'Red' Blood in Kentucky," *Forum*. LXXXVII (January, 1932), pp. 18-23.

Addional Periodical Materials:

"A New Face for Harlan County," *New Republic*, LIXV (May 15, 1938), p. 59.

"Bloody Harlan Reforms," *The Nation*, CXLVII (August 6, 1938), p. 121.

"Bloody Harlan: U.S. Fight on Terrorism Hinges on Law of '70's," *Newsweek*, XI (May 30, 1938), pp. 11-12.

"Case of Mary-Helen," *Time*, XXXI, pt. 2 (May 30, 1938), p. 9.

"Coal and Kentucky," *The Commonwealth*, XXX (May 26, 1939), pp. 129-130.

"Dark and Bloody Harlan," *New Republic*, LIXIX (May 31, 1939).

"Death in Kentucky," *New Republic*, LIXV (July 20, 1938), p. 291.

"England Looks at Harlan," *Current History*, XLIX (October, 1938), p. 54.

"Harlan and Hague," *Life*, IV (May 30, 1938), p. 14.

"Harlan Comes to Terms," *New Republic*, C (August 9, 1939), pp. 2-3.

"Harlan's County's Reign of Terror Revealed," *The Christian Century*, LIV (May 19, 1937), p. 635..

"Harlan County Troubles," *The Nation*, CXLVIII (May 20, 1939), p. 573.

"Harlan Holiday: Mining Mountaineers Turn Trial into Carnival," *Newsweek*, XI, (June 6, 1938), p. 13.

"Harlan: LaFollette Finishes Spadework for Miners' Union," *Newsweek*. IX (May 15, 1937), p. 15.

"Kentucky Feudalism," *Time*, XXIX (May 3, 1937), pp. 13-14.

"Mistrial in Harlan," *New Republic*, XCVI (August 10, 1938), p. 2.

"Peace in Harlan County," *Time*, XXXVIII, pt. 2 (October 27, 1941), pp. 21-22.

"Reign of Terror Still Grips Harlan," *The Christian Century*. LII (August 28, 1935), p. 1093.

"The Repatriation of Harlan County," *New Republic*, C (October 11, 1939), p. 155.

"The Shape of Things," *The Nation*, CXLVI (June 11, 1938), p. 658.

"The Week," *New Republic*, XC (May 5, 1937), pp. 370-371.

"The Week," *New Republic*, XCI (May 12, 1937), pp. 2-3.

"The Week," *New Republic*, XCI (June 2, 1937), p. 86.

Unpublished Theses and Dissertations:

Chapman, Mary Lucile, "The Influence of Coal in the Big Sandy Valley," Doctoral Dissertation, University of Kentucky, 1945.

Frisch, Isadore, "The Twentieth Century Development of the Coal Industry in Eastern Kentucky, " University of Kentucky, 1938.

Hinrichs, A.F. "The United Mine Workers of America and the Non-Union Coal Fields". Ph.D. dissertation, Columbia University, 1923.

Pearce, Albert, "The Growth and Overdevelopment of the Kentucky Coal Industry," University of Kentucky, 1930.

Taylor, Paul F. "The Coal Mine War in Harlan County, Kentucky, 1931-32." M.A. thesis, University of Kentucky, 1955.

Taylor, Paul F., "Coal and Conflict: The UMWA in Harlan County, Kentucky." Ph.D. dissertation. University of Kentucky, 1969.

Index

A

Abt, John 141
Acuff. J.C. 87
Albert, E.V. 87, 170
Allen, Benjamin 138
Allen, Jim 119
Alverson, J. M. 68
Arnett, L. T. "Tick" 129, 131, 132, 133, 134, 135, 138, 171, 232

B

Bablitz, A. A. 42, 43, 45, 74, 155
Baker, Larkin 62, 86
Baldwin, Arch 163
Baldwin, Elizabeth 43
Ball, Cam E. 190
Ball, Clinton C. 165
Ball, L.E. 88, 134
Barnes, Charles B. 58, 82, 88, 96
Bassham, Bill 144
Bassham, Pearl 67, 110, 138, 144, 147, 149, 150, 151, 155, 165, 180
Bates, Ernest Sutherland 40
Bates, Jim 85
Battle of Evarts 33, 42
Battle of Stanfill 195, 196, 197, 199
Battle of Tway 55
Bell, Edwin 163
Bennett, Harry 157
Bennett, Hens 148
Bennett, Vester C. 110, 121, 149, 184
Benson, Al 29, 32, 35, 209
Berger Coal Mining Company 27, 193
Bingham, D.M. 64
Bittner, Van A. 58, 75, 82, 83
Bituminous Coal Labor Board 82
Black, James D. 31
Black Mountain 16, 18, 22, 24, 27, 28, 29, 31, 32, 33, 34, 47, 48, 54, 56, 94, 95, 104, 110, 119, 129, 148, 165, 166, 193
Black Mountain Coal Corporation 31, 110
Black Star Coal Corporation 17, 113, 122, 148, 192
Blair, John Henry 13, 25, 38, 48, 54, 62
Blizzard, William 129
Bolin, Henry 169
Bowlin, Allen 51, 132, 165, 181, 202
Bowling, C.C. 116
Bowling, Kenes 122
Brewer, James H. 134
Brock, Bill 76
Brock, H.M. 145
Brock, Will A. 26, 38, 48, 69
Brookside Strike 203
Brooks, J.M. 13, 40
Brooks, J.W. 86
Brown, John Y. 124, 125, 126, 127, 138
Bunch, Matt 135

Index

Burchfield, C.B. 122, 176
Burke, Jack B. 147
Burnett, Bill 27, 29, 31, 35
Burrows, William C. 190
Burton, George C. 125
Byrd, A. Floyd 87

C

Caddy, Sam 75, 79, 89, 117, 124, 128, 180
Caldwell, Dock 195
Callahan, P.H. 125
Calvert, Cleon K. 65, 98, 146, 172
Campbell, Denton 163
Campbell, Peter 29, 129
Carpenter, Charles 27, 31
Carrell, Daniel M. 29, 88
Carroll. T.C. 125
Carter, Ellerbee W. 75, 99, 190
Carter, J.B. 68
Carter, Matt 149
Cawood, Bruce 171
Cawood, Herbert 168
Cawood, Jim 55
Cawood, Joe 29, 35
Cawood, W.P. 68, 116
Chandler, A.B. "Happy" 97, 98, 99, 102, 105, 106, 117, 118, 124, 127, 128, 129, 131, 132, 133, 179, 180, 181, 185, 189, 190, 193, 194, 196, 197, 198, 199, 210
Checkweighman 58, 82, 84, 111
Chestnut, Ellie 163, 170
Childers, E.B. 24
Childers, Robert 51, 157
Clontz, William 54, 73, 74, 83, 96, 111, 115, 116, 181
Clouse, John 150
Clouse, Markham 150
Clover Fork 15, 16, 17, 18, 23, 26, 27, 28, 51, 54, 67, 121, 182, 183, 184, 188, 189, 190, 192, 203, 205
Cloversplint Coal Company 94
Cochran, A.M.J. 40, 42, 44
Conner, John 193, 197
Conway, Roy 124, 125, 184
Cornett, A.B. 148
Cornett, D.B. 167
Cornett-Lewis Coal Company 66, 74, 110, 120, 148, 167, 188
Cox, Estes 28
Cox, Fayette 134
Cox, Palmer 78
Creech Coal Company 17, 73, 77, 82, 121, 188, 194
Creech, R.W. 77, 115, 153
Creech, Ted 115, 116, 153
Crummies Creek 16, 145, 146, 165, 201, 202
Cunningham, W.J. 197
Cusick, Asa 29, 35

D

Daniell, F. Raymond 161
Daniels, Jim 27, 28, 32, 34
Davisworth, Lonnie 48
Dawson, Charles I. 162, 186, 199
Denhardt, Henry H. 54, 61, 75, 76, 77, 78, 83, 84, 87, 88, 89, 90, 91, 92, 94, 95, 98, 99, 100, 101, 102, 103, 104, 113, 115, 118, 124, 127, 139, 155
Detroit Edison 16
Dickenson, Silas J. 26, 67, 100, 142
Dietzman, Richard Priest 98
Dotson, Clifford 154
Dreiser Committee 39
Dreiser, Theodore 38
Duke Power Company 203
Dunbar, Ernest 147
Durrett, Emmett 193
Dwyer, Lawrence "Peggy" 22, 23,

24, 49, 50, 51, 53, 54, 58,
61, 62, 63, 64, 65, 66, 67,
75, 78, 85, 133, 182, 188

E

Easley, Roy W. 105
Eastover Mining Company 203
Edmunds, George 21
Eggers, Avery 170
Eldridge, Bob 133, 134
Elliott, Frank 51
Ellis Knob Coal Company 27
Ellison, W. Arthur 58, 111, 187
Erwin, Julian 87
Evans, Charles 163, 173
Evarts, KY 16, 18, 22, 24, 25, 26,
27, 28, 29, 32, 33, 34, 35,
36, 38, 42, 52, 54, 85, 87,
88, 89, 95, 107, 108, 109,
114, 116, 128, 129, 131,
133, 135, 136, 143, 164,
167, 169, 170, 171, 189,
190, 202, 209

F

Fagan, Patrick 24
Farley, Bill 47
Farmer, Bob 93, 94
Ferguson, Thomas 135
Fleenor, Everett 170
Fleenor, Lee 40, 43, 67, 69, 134,
144, 168, 170, 181, 182,
202
Ford, H. Church 117, 159
Forester, Edgar 48
Forester, Jim 47
Forester, J.S. 69
Fox, Kelly 151, 167
Frank, Waldo 13, 39
Frank White 202
Fuson, Harvey H. 65

G

Gann, Thomas N. 22

Garland, Jim 24, 36, 43
Gibson, T.M. 55
Gilbert, Ben 149
Gilbert, Bob 55
Gilbert, James 56
Golden, Ben B. 31, 35, 64
Golden, James S. 50, 64, 182,
187, 189, 199
Goodlin, Oscar 202
Greene, James S. 68
Gross, Bige 69
Gross, John B. 54, 56
Gunter, L.C. 112
Guthrie, Charles S. 121, 165, 167,
183, 197, 203

H

Hall, Elmer D. 68, 122, 165, 167
Hall, Frank 85, 88
Hall, Rob 39, 43, 92
Hall, Talton 82, 113
Hall, Wash 196
Hall, W.F. 26
Hamilton, W.C. 31
Hampton, Ernest 94
Hampton, Joe 94
Hampton, Virgil 202
Hanberry, John 195, 199
Harlan Central Coal Company
17, 110, 121, 149, 157
Harlan Collieries 17, 67, 121,
156, 183, 188, 203
Harlan County Coal Operators
Association 26, 35, 44, 62,
87, 95, 96, 113, 122, 127,
131, 142, 148, 149, 150,
155, 157, 158, 163, 164,
166, 167, 172, 175, 176,
182, 186, 187, 193, 194,
197, 198, 199, 201, 203
Harlan Daily Enterprise 52, 66,
68, 69, 84, 90, 104, 116,
117, 123, 127, 154, 187
Harlan Fuel Company 17, 50,

Index

121, 167, 183
Harlan-Wallins Coal Coporation 17, 67, 82, 84, 110, 144, 145, 146, 148, 149, 170, 180, 193
Harsh, Joseph C. 161
Hays, Arthur Garfield 40, 92
Hays, Smith 42
Hensley, Babe 64
Hevener, John W. 10, 154
Hibbard, J.M. 163, 173, 175
Hickey, John 28
Highbaugh, Homer 138, 148
High Splint 117, 121, 152, 192, 193, 203, 205, 206, 207
Hightower, W.M. 29, 30, 34, 35
Hodge, Robert 197
Hofferbert, Louis 192
Holmes, Tom 101, 133, 134, 138
Hopkins, Welly K. 167, 171, 197, 199, 200, 201
Hopper, Richard 163, 173
Hoskins, Albert 170
Howard, Bert O. 137
Howard, E.L. 166
Howard, E.M. 54, 68
Howard, Hamp 166
Howard, H.C. 89
Howard, H.H. 29, 49
Howard, Lawrence 151, 153
Howard, Martha 151, 152, 166, 172

I

Industrial Workers of the World 36
International Harvester 16, 82
Irwin, Wash 134, 151, 152, 165, 166, 181, 182, 202

J

Jackson, "Aunt Molly" 36
Johnson, Arnold 43
Johnson, H.C. 86
Johnson, Hugh S. 57, 111
Johnson, Keen 199
Johnson, L.F. 172, 173
Johnson, L.P. 165
Johnson, W.B. 163
Johnson, William C. 152
Johnston, Forney 174
Jones, A.C. 87, 116
Jones, Clyde 133
Jones, Davy Crockett (Baby) 13
Jones, Earl 202
Jones, Fred M. 31, 47, 48, 69
Jones, Howard 29
Jones, Lawrence Dean 205
Jones, W.B. 26, 29, 31, 36, 85

K

Kelly, Joseph 196
Kennedy, Thomas 22, 113
Kentenia Corporation 17
Kentucky Federation of Labor 29, 62, 95, 129
Knoxville News-Sentinel 49, 52, 53, 55, 63, 70, 91, 121, 126, 128, 131, 134, 137, 150, 151, 174, 175, 179, 187, 192, 195, 210

L

Laffoon, Ruby 39, 48, 51
La Follette Civil Liberties Committee 130, 138, 141
La Follette, Robert M., Jr. 141
Lane, Belle 108
Lawson, R.E. 74, 87, 116, 120, 138, 197
Layne, J.I. (Ike) 36
Lay, W.R. 64, 69
Lee, George 29, 53, 67, 74, 76, 81, 86, 107, 108, 115, 116, 119, 131, 151, 181, 182, 202
Lee, Joe 55
Lee, Otto 29
Lee, W.R. 64

Leonard, Bill 93, 94
Lester brothers (Fred, Hugh, John) 33
Lewallen, Ben 75
Lewallen Hotel 76, 77, 85, 86
Lewis, Bill 78, 150, 201, 202
Lewis, Henry M. 165
Lewis, John L. 21, 70, 75, 117, 180, 186, 189, 197
Lewis, P.O. 24
Lewis, W.W. 68, 144, 147, 148, 172
Logan, M.M. 43
London, Kentucky 114, 158
Lyons, Hugh 129

M

Mahan, E.G. 58, 82
Mahan, T.E. 121
Malone, Dudley Field 40
Martin's Fork 15, 16, 17
Mary Helen Coal Corporation 17, 26, 67, 148, 159, 177
Matthews, Armstrong R. 94
May, A.J. 78
McCann, Irving 182
McClain, Lee 133
McMahon, Brien 160, 169, 171, 172, 173, 199
McNew, R.E. 87
Menefee, Joseph R. 71
Metcalf, Henry 181
Metcalf, John T. 162
Middlesboro Daily News 90, 97
Middleton, Ben 87
Middleton, Charlie 78
Middleton, Clarence 67, 165
Middleton, Elmon 54, 55, 56, 68, 73, 82, 93, 101, 104, 105, 115, 120
Middleton, Logan 78
Middleton, Merle 67, 74, 78, 101, 108, 151, 169
Middleton, Milt 78

Middleton, T.R. 53, 79, 90, 91, 163
Mitchell, Broadus 40
Mitch, William 128, 129
Moore, Ben 199
Moses, B.H. 51, 54
Moses, Harry M. 88
Munholland, William 107, 108
Murray, Philip 20, 24
Musick, Bennett 136, 138, 140, 142, 151, 152, 153, 166, 167, 169, 172, 205, 206
Musick, Jennings 196
Musick, Mallie 136, 138, 166
Musick, Marshall A. 54, 70, 73, 83, 85, 96, 107, 133, 140, 209

N

National Industrial Recovery Act 156
National Labor Relations Act 106
National Miners Union 36, 38, 43, 44
National Student League 39, 43
New Harlan Hotel 75, 131, 134, 138, 142, 147
Noe, Harmon 166
Noe, Otis 93, 94
Noe, Perry G. 181, 202
Norman, Carl G. 189

P

Pace, A.T. 75, 80, 83, 85, 113, 119, 182
Pace, Jesse 27, 29
Parks, Doris 13, 37
Patterson, Chris 62, 64, 66, 168, 202
Patterson, N.R. 64
Perkins, Diamond E. 76, 77, 102, 115
Perkins, Frances 197
Perry, Wesley Vick 98

INDEX

Petrie, Roscoe 24
Phillips Elzie 35
Phillips, Phillip G. 187
Pineville Sun 38, 39, 91, 123, 209
Poer, Clarence 152
Polin, John A. 99, 105
Polk, W. G. 112
Poore, Chester 35
Poor Fork 15, 16, 17, 110
Pope, George R. 181
Pope, R.L. 31, 34, 64, 69
Powell, Alex 163
Prewitt, Henry R. 30
Puckett's Creek 15
Purciful, Shepherd 28

R

Reece, Florence 11, 36
Reed, Gloster 51
Reed, Paul H. 189
Reynolds, Jim 30, 35
Rhea, Tom 95, 97, 99, 100, 102, 106, 113
Rice, J. Ray 68, 87
Richmond, Carl 28, 29
Ridings, Chester 133, 136
Riley, W.E. 68
Roark, Arthur 47
Roark, Robert 47
Roberts, T.N. 163
Robsion, John M. 30, 31, 34, 35
Roosevelt, Franklin D. 17, 48, 114
Root, J.G. 87
Ruth, Charles 202

S

Sampson, Flem D. 29, 40, 42, 43
Sams, A.B. 163
Sargent boys 166, 169
Saxton, John 75
Saylor, Andy 68
Saylor, Grant 68, 149
Saylor, Morris 52, 53, 54, 55, 56, 68, 116, 144, 148, 155, 181
Schweinhaut, Henry A. 197
Shipman, Luther 21
Sienknecht, William H. 122, 187
Sizemore, Walter 163
Smith, C.L. 87
Smith, Daniel Boone 52, 53, 55, 56, 59, 64, 148, 155, 201
Smith, Herb 106
Smith, L.O. 48, 87, 166, 187
Smith, Walter B. 13, 64, 189
Snyder, J. B. 31, 85
Southern Appalachian Coal Operators 112
Southern Labor Union 203
Spicer, C.B. 170
Stapleton, Dale 113
Steelman, John R. 197
Stepp, Henry C. 78
Stevens, George A. 164
Stines, John 88
Stites, James W. 104
Stras, J.C. 66
Surgener, Chester 64
Swope, King 117

T

Tackett, Joseph P. 124
Tackett, Richard C. 62, 153
Taub, Allan 13
Taylor, Hugh 134, 152, 162, 182
Taylor, Jay H. 64
Timko, Joseph J. 116, 119, 120, 124
Timmins, Geneva 86
Titler, George Joy 10, 180, 183, 186, 187, 190, 193, 194, 195, 196, 199, 202
Townsend, T.C. 115, 122, 123, 129, 137, 138, 197, 199
Trent, Tom 78
Turnblazer, William 21, 22, 25, 29, 33, 34, 48, 49, 50, 57, 58, 63, 64, 67, 73, 74, 75,

76, 77, 78, 79, 80, 85, 86,
89, 95, 96, 99, 109, 111,
112, 113, 116, 120, 123,
124, 127, 128, 130, 131,
132, 133, 137, 138, 179,
180, 182, 183, 185, 186,
187, 188, 189, 190, 192,
193, 194, 196, 199
Tway, R.C. & R.C. Tway Coal
Company 17, 68, 148, 149
Tye, Ed 202

U

United Mine Workers of America
10, 21, 22, 23, 24, 25, 32,
35, 36, 42, 44, 45, 48, 50,
51, 57, 58, 59, 61, 62, 63,
70, 71, 73, 75, 76, 77, 79,
81, 82, 83, 84, 86, 87, 88,
89, 96, 97, 104, 112, 113,
114, 115, 117, 120, 121,
122, 123, 124, 125, 126,
127, 128, 129, 130, 131,
132, 133, 134, 135, 137,
138, 140, 141, 142, 146,
148, 156, 157, 158, 165,
167, 168, 169, 170, 171,
174, 176, 179, 181, 182,
183, 184, 185, 186, 188,
189, 193, 195, 196, 197,
199, 201, 202, 203, 204,
205, 206, 207
United States Coal and Coke
Company 16, 88
United States Steel Corporation
16, 156
Unthank, Ben 51, 53, 62, 64, 65,
66, 67, 74, 75, 76, 86, 87,
115, 116, 120, 124, 135,
142, 148, 149, 152, 155,
157, 163, 165, 167, 171,
176, 182, 202

V

Vogel, Carl E. 72, 165

W

Wallins Creek 15, 16, 17, 54, 73,
184, 189, 190
Ward, George S. 26, 43, 73, 91,
113, 122, 132, 142, 149,
158, 164, 166, 167, 184,
187, 197
Ward, W.L. 133
Westmoreland, James 73, 74, 85,
86, 123, 130, 196
White, Frank 27, 35, 51, 53, 67,
74, 76, 81, 86, 108, 134,
135, 150, 151, 152, 165,
167, 170, 202
White, Tom 81, 85
White, W. Bridges 31
Whitfield, A.F., Jr. 67, 121
Whitfield, Bryan W., Jr. 67, 121,
139, 183, 203
Whitfield, George 183
Williams, Billy G. 206
Williams, Carl 75, 76, 96
Williams, Howard 114, 115, 116,
117, 123
Williams, Lutishea 114
Wohlforth, Robert 141
Wright, M.L. 149

Y

Yarborough, Norman 203
Youngblood, Belton 169, 170,
181

www.ingramcontent.com/pod-product-compliance
Lightning Source LLC
Chambersburg PA
CBHW030433010526
44118CB00011B/612